Punchdrunk on the Classics

Emma Cole

Punchdrunk on the Classics

Experiencing Immersion in *The Burnt City* and Beyond

Emma Cole
School of Communication and Arts
University of Queensland
Brisbane, QLD, Australia

ISBN 978-3-031-43066-4   ISBN 978-3-031-43067-1 (eBook)
https://doi.org/10.1007/978-3-031-43067-1

© The Editor(s) (if applicable) and The Author(s), under exclusive license to Springer Nature Switzerland AG 2024

This work is subject to copyright. All rights are solely and exclusively licensed by the Publisher, whether the whole or part of the material is concerned, specifically the rights of translation, reprinting, reuse of illustrations, recitation, broadcasting, reproduction on microfilms or in any other physical way, and transmission or information storage and retrieval, electronic adaptation, computer software, or by similar or dissimilar methodology now known or hereafter developed.
The use of general descriptive names, registered names, trademarks, service marks, etc. in this publication does not imply, even in the absence of a specific statement, that such names are exempt from the relevant protective laws and regulations and therefore free for general use.
The publisher, the authors, and the editors are safe to assume that the advice and information in this book are believed to be true and accurate at the date of publication. Neither the publisher nor the authors or the editors give a warranty, expressed or implied, with respect to the material contained herein or for any errors or omissions that may have been made. The publisher remains neutral with regard to jurisdictional claims in published maps and institutional affiliations.

Cover illustration: Miranda Mac Letten and members of *The Burnt City* company © Julian Abrams

This Palgrave Macmillan imprint is published by the registered company Springer Nature Switzerland AG
The registered company address is: Gewerbestrasse 11, 6330 Cham, Switzerland

Paper in this product is recyclable.

For Adelaide and Otto

Acknowledgements

The idea for this book originated in 2017, when I first learnt of Punchdrunk's plans to create a large-scale masked performance based upon Aeschylus' *Agamemnon* and Euripides' *Hecuba* and became interested in exploring the company's process of transforming Greek literature into immersive experience. I am indebted to the Arts and Humanities Research Council of UKRI, and particularly to the AHRC members of the Peer Review College who assessed my application, for awarding me an AHRC Leadership Fellowship/UKRI Innovation Fellowship to conduct the research underpinning this book. The fellowship enabled me to go on secondment to Punchdrunk during the R&D phase and rehearsal period for *The Burnt City*; it is no exaggeration to say that without this opportunity *Punchdrunk on the Classics* would not exist. Thank you to Sam Lambshead from the University of Bristol's Research, Enterprise, and Development team for his guidance during the drafting of my application, and to Pantelis Michelakis who acted as mentor during the grant. Thanks also to the Faculty of Arts at the University of Bristol, who supported my research through a term of research leave and provided me with funding to do a writing retreat at Gladstone's Library. I am enormously grateful to the staff at Punchdrunk, all of whom supported my eagerness to develop our collaboration on *Kabeiroi* into a two-way partnership for *The Burnt City*, and who were project partners on my grant. Thank you to Felix Barrett, for being receptive of my pitch to collaborate and for engineering my involvement, and to both Felix and Maxine Doyle for inviting me into their creative process not just as an academic advisor but as a contributor. I so appreciate your generosity and spirit of collaboration. Thank you also to Lucy Whitby and Lauren Storr, who supported the practicalities of my secondment and who granted me permission to use the images of *The Burnt City* within this monograph, and to Kath Duggan and the original performing company of *The Burnt City*, all of whom were welcoming and supportive of my hybrid role as dramaturg and researcher.

I am grateful for the support I have received from friends, family, and colleagues following my secondments with Punchdrunk and during the process of writing this book. In the time between submitting my grant proposal and *The Burnt City* opening, I went from having no children to having two, and I also (like us all) lived through a pandemic. Completing a research project and writing a book during such seismic life changes would have been impossible without their support. My husband Ben was steadfast in his commitment to ensuring I could complete my research and fulfil my career ambitions, moving to London with me for the Punchdrunk rehearsals and taking shared parental leave to enable me to go back to work to complete my secondment. My parents and extended family were supportive and encouraging throughout; special thanks to my father-in-law Garry, who always asked about my book and who has gone above and beyond on various occasions to support our family. Rosa Andújar, David Bullen, Kate Cook, Ben Folit-Weinberg, Chris Hay, Lucy Jackson, and Pantelis Michelakis provided generous feedback on drafts, and my colleagues and friends Paul Clarke, Lyndsay Coo, Bob Fowler, Miriam Leonard, Ellie Mackin Roberts, Fiona Macintosh, Jess McCormack, Ellen O'Gorman, Ellie Rycroft, Kirsty Sedgman, and Vanda Zajko were always valuable sounding boards and encouraging presences. Thank you to Laura Maclean and Lee Rowsell in the School of Humanities at the University of Bristol for their assistance with administrative components of the grant, and to Esther Eidinow and Patrick Finglass for the help they gave in their capacities as Heads of Department during my research fellowship. As I commenced the final draft of this monograph, I moved from the discipline of classics to drama, and from the University of Bristol to the University of Queensland; thank you to my new colleagues in drama, Stephen Carleton and Bernadette Cochrane, to Alastair Blanshard in classics, and to my Head of School Bronwyn Lea, for their support during this transition as I completed my manuscript.

I received helpful feedback on this research at the Immersivity and Antiquity conference, the Knowledge Exchange and the Creative Industries seminar series, the Cambridge Greek Literature research seminar, the University of Durham Classics research seminar, the University of Bristol Classics and Ancient History research seminar, the 2022 TaPRA (Audience, Experience, and Popular Culture Working Group) conference, and the 2023 ADSA conference. All remaining errors are my own.

Contents

1	**Introducing *The Burnt City* and Beyond**	1
	Introducing The Burnt City's *Ancient Sources*	4
	Introducing The Burnt City	9
	The Structure of this Book	16
	Methodology	18
	Works Cited	28
2	**Punchdrunk on the Classics: A History**	33
	Works Cited	51
3	***The Burnt City* in Development: Rehearsal as Mythopoiesis**	55
	Origins of The Burnt City	58
	The Burnt City *in Development*	62
	The Pandemic	68
	Hide and Seek	71
	On-site Rehearsals	74
	Full Run	82
	1:1	84
	Finale	89
	Works Cited	98

4	*The Burnt City* in Development: Abstracting Ancient Literature	101
	Approaching Agamemnon *and* Hecuba	105
	Abstracting Narrative	107
	Abstracting Emotion and Psychology	119
	Abstracting Language	129
	Works Cited	140
5	*The Burnt City* in Performance: Place, Space, and Experience	143
	Place	146
	Space	152
	Experience	168
	Works Cited	179
6	*The Burnt City*'s Legacy: Immersivity, Mimesis, and Enargeia	183
	Immersivity	185
	Mimesis	193
	Enargeia	204
	Works Cited	217
7	Conclusion	223
	Works Cited	228
Index		229

About the Author

Dr Emma Cole is Senior Lecturer in Drama at the University of Queensland and Fellow of the Royal Historical Society; previously, she was Senior Lecturer in Liberal Arts and Classics at the University of Bristol (2015–2023), and an UKRI Innovation Fellow (2019–2022). She is a classicist and a theatre historian and is an expert on Greek tragedy in contemporary theatre. She is currently editing the volume *Experiencing Immersion in Antiquity and Modernity: From Narrative to Virtual Reality* for Bloomsbury, as well as the Student Edition of *Women of Troy* for Methuen Drama. Her prior publications include *Postdramatic Tragedies* (Oxford University Press, 2019) and *Adapting Translation for the Stage* (co-edited with Geraldine Brodie, Routledge, 2017). Alongside her research, she works as a dramaturg and academic consultant on new writing and classical adaptation projects.

List of Figures

Fig. 2.1	A two-page spread advertising *The House of Oedipus* from an early promotional booklet for Punchdrunk (then called Punchdrunk Theatrical Experiences). The booklet is undated but references productions from the period of work the company classifies as 'Act 1' (2000–2008). Image credit: Punchdrunk Enrichment	37
Fig. 2.2	Punchdrunk's *Kabeiroi* (2017). Image credit: Stephen Dobbie	44
Fig. 2.3	Martha Graham Dance Company in *Deo*. Choreography by Maxine Doyle and Bobbi Jene Smith. Image credit: Brian Pollock. Courtesy of the Martha Graham Resources	50
Fig. 3.1	Stefanie Noll and Omagbitse Omagbemi as Iphigenia and Clytemnestra in Scene Two, ('Bear Dance') of *The Burnt City*. Image Credit: Julian Abrams. Courtesy of Punchdrunk	67
Fig. 3.2	Jordan Ajadi as Askalaphos in Punchdrunk's *The Burnt City*. Image credit: Julian Abrams. Courtesy of Punchdrunk	86
Fig. 4.1	The Greek army enters Troy in Scene Five ('Fall of Troy') of *The Burnt City*. Image credit: Julian Abrams. Courtesy of Punchdrunk	118
Fig. 4.2	Andrea Carrucciu and Dafni Krazoudi as Aegisthus and Iphigenia in Scene Three ('Wedding Breakfast') of *The Burnt City*. Image credit: Julian Abrams. Courtesy of Punchdrunk	122

Fig. 4.3	Omagbitse Omagbemi as Clytemnestra in the final image of the 'Greece' finale in *The Burnt City*. Image credit: Julian Abrams. Courtesy of Punchdrunk	132
Fig. 5.1	Pin Chieh Chen as Kampe in Punchdrunk's *The Burnt City*, pictured in a corridor within Troy. Image credit: Julian Abrams. Courtesy of Punchdrunk	163
Fig. 5.2	Sam Booth as Hades in Punchdrunk's *The Burnt City*, pictured in The White Cyprus sake bar in Troy. Image credit: Julian Abrams. Courtesy of Punchdrunk	166
Fig. 6.1	Morgan Bobrow-Williams as Apollo in Punchdrunk's *The Burnt City*. Image credit: Julian Abrams. Courtesy of Punchdrunk	200

CHAPTER 1

Introducing *The Burnt City* and Beyond

The September 2021 announcement that British theatre company Punchdrunk would soon be opening *The Burnt City*, an epic, immersive performance based upon the Trojan War in London's Royal Arsenal, generated enormous press buzz. Punchdrunk, established in 2000, are regarded as one of the founders of immersive theatre and boast a slew of hyperbolic quotations attesting to their field-leading status on their website, heralding themselves 'pioneers of the "immersive theatre" phenomenon' (*The Telegraph*) and 'hands down the best immersive theatre company in the world' (*Time Out*).[1] At the time of the announcement, the company's continuously-running productions of their *Macbeth*-inspired *Sleep No More* had been playing simultaneously in New York City and Shanghai since 2011 and 2016 respectively. However, despite being London based, Punchdrunk had not opened a major production for British audiences since their *Woyzeck*-inspired *The Drowned Man* in 2013–14. *The Burnt City* announcement came at a time when British audiences were not just starved of Punchdrunk's form of theatre, but had had little chance to see *any* indoor performance for the best part of eighteen months due to the coronavirus pandemic. Following Punchdrunk's announcement, Lyn Gardner wrote that 'the company's return to London is likely to remind why they are still the leaders of the pack with work whose complexity,

---

[1] See Punchdrunk (2022).

© The Author(s), under exclusive license to Springer Nature Switzerland AG 2024
E. Cole, *Punchdrunk on the Classics*,
https://doi.org/10.1007/978-3-031-43067-1_1

scale and attention to detail remains unparalleled', while Chris Wiegand in *The Guardian* whetted his readers' appetites by noting that this 'future noir' retelling of the fall of Troy would be the company's 'costliest and most ambitious project to date'.[2] As the 21 April 2022 opening night approached, a second round of press built additional excitement and drip-fed readers clues about the complexity of the performance. Charlotte Higgins revealed, for example, that 'the level of detail is again almost bewildering', observing in her behind-the-scenes tour during rehearsals 'hints of 1920s Art Deco in a slightly sci-fi mode' along with a 'layering-in of the realm of Hades in yet another palimpsest of what promises to be a dense and rich story'.[3] Following opening night, five-star reviews in *The Observer* and *The Stage*, and four star reviews in the *Evening Standard*, the *Financial Times*, *The Independent*, and *Time Out* confirmed Punchdrunk's long-awaited return as a production of substantial cultural significance.[4]

Punchdrunk are global leaders within the creative industries and are pioneers of the participatory form of performance known as immersive theatre, where audiences are incorporated into the world of the performance and positioned as roaming participants whose own actions (where they go and which performers they follow) and tactile engagement with the set (which rooms they enter, drawers they open, props they touch) dictate their version of the production's narrative and its meaning.[5] Punchdrunk's work responds to a tradition of live art and installation-based practice and is now widely imitated internationally. Although the company express discomfort over the labelling of their work as immersive, with Barrett noting in 2022 that the company do not use the term about themselves and that 'we've always said we're site-sympathetic', within journalism the company's work is synonymous

---

[2] Gardner (2021) and Wiegand (2021). For other press reactions, see, for example, Hemley (2021) and Dex (2021).

[3] Higgins (2022).

[4] The press coverage was almost uniformly positive; the only two star reviews (the lowest rating the production received) in the mainstream press were in *The Times* and *The Daily Mail*.

[5] The company's status as global leaders is reflected in the amount of scholarship they have generated, including multiple book-length studies such as Biggin (2017) and Westling (2020).

with immersive theatre.[6] Within scholarship, too, the theorisation of how Punchdrunk's performances foster immersivity has shed light upon the form, function, and meaning of Punchdrunk's work.[7] The company's immersive practice weaves across a variety of formats, from digital gaming (including *Silverpoint* and a collaboration with Silicon Valley software developers Niantic), television (*The Third Day*), education (via Punchdrunk Enrichment, now a charity independent of Punchdrunk), commercial partnerships (including Alexander McQueen, Absolut., and Louis Vuitton), and intimate performances for one or two audience members at a time (*The Borough*, *Kabeiroi*). However, it is their large-scale responses to canonical texts which have become the example *par excellence* of twenty-first-century immersive theatre and for which Punchdrunk are best known. Here, masked audiences of up to 600 individuals investigate experiential reinterpretations of canonical texts, which are fragmented across up to 200 rooms and reimagined by a cast of up to fifty performers.[8] *The Burnt City* is the seventh large-scale masked Punchdrunk performance co-directed by Felix Barrett (Punchdrunk's founder and Artistic Director) and Maxine Doyle (Punchdrunk's associate director and choreographer).[9]

Punchdrunk on the Classics: Experiencing Immersion in The Burnt City *and Beyond* draws attention to Punchdrunk's recurring focus upon ancient Greek literature as a source of inspiration for their artistic outputs. It documents and analyses the effects of combining ancient literature with immersive practice during both Punchdrunk's creative development windows, including the research and development (R&D) and rehearsal periods, and Punchdrunk's final staged productions. *The Burnt City* is my

---

[6] Saville (2022). See also Biggin (2017: 177).

[7] See, for example, Biggin (2017: 177), who argues that Punchdrunk's work fosters immersion and notes that 'the use and manipulation of performance space is one of the clearest indicators that a piece of theatre might define itself (or end up being defined by others, whatever the artist's own preferences) as *immersive*'.

[8] Josefina Komporaly terms the type of textual fragmentation contained within Punchdrunk's masked productions such as *The Drowned Man* a form of 'radical adaptation'. See Komporaly (2017, esp. pp. 93–126).

[9] Barrett and Doyle's prior masked performances include *Sleep No More* (2003), *The Firebird Ball* (2005), *Faust* (2006), *The Masque of the Red Death* (2008), *The Duchess of Malfi* (2010), and *The Drowned Man* (2013). The company have revived *Sleep No More* on multiple occasions, including the still-running versions in New York City and Shanghai.

predominant focus; not only is the production the company's most recent masked performance and their largest-scale response to Greek literature, making it a defining part of the twenty-twenties British cultural industries and a key piece of the company's history, but it is also a production on which I worked as dramaturg and thus can write about with a level of authority inaccessible through archival research and performance analysis alone.

Punchdrunk on the Classics has two primary aims. Firstly, it seeks to unpack how practitioners draw upon and transform ancient Greek literature for the realisation of immersive experience, and secondly, it seeks to analyse how ancient literature shapes engagement within an immersive experience. I write with a broad range of readers in mind, from scholars of the classics, through to theatre studies, and even those outside of the academy who are invested in Punchdrunk's practice. This introduction provides essential background information about the Greek literature that underpinned *The Burnt City*, alongside core information about Punchdrunk's production, the methodology underpinning my research, and the structure of this book. Due to the interdisciplinary fusing of classics and theatre studies within the volume, I offer what may appear to be rudimentary background information about both Greek tragedy and Punchdrunk's unique theatrical practice, bearing in mind that readers coming to this volume from different disciplinary standpoints will have different blind spots.

INTRODUCING *THE BURNT CITY*'S ANCIENT SOURCES

The Burnt City primarily drew upon Aeschylus' *Agamemnon* (specifically Ted Hughes' translation) and Euripides' *Hecuba* (no specific translation). These two Greek tragedies premièred at the annual City Dionysia theatre festival in fifth-century BCE Athens and are both set in the immediate aftermath of the Trojan War. *Agamemnon* depicts the action taking place in Greek Mycenae as Agamemnon returns to his Palace and his wife Clytemnestra after a ten-year absence, while *Hecuba* is set just prior to the events in *Agamemnon*, midway through the Greeks' voyage home from Troy where the army has paused with their captured Trojan woman just north of Troy in Thrace. Each tragedy was originally presented as part of a tetralogy (three tragedies and a satyr play) authored by their respective playwrights, which was entered into the dramatic competition at the Dionysia; *Agamemnon*, the first tragedy in our only extant trilogy, the *Oresteia* (458 BCE), was an immediate classic, winning Aeschylus first prize during the competition. It remains regularly performed to this day. *Hecuba*'s (c. 424–3 BCE) initial reception, in contrast, is less assured.[10] The precise year of the première production (and hence *Hecuba*'s ranking) is unknown. The play was highly renowned in antiquity and was later part of the Byzantine triad of Euripidean plays included in education curricula. However, modernity has not looked favourably upon *Hecuba* and it has received far fewer modern-day productions than *Agamemnon*.[11] Comparing *Hecuba* with Euripides' *Trojan Women*, which similarly focuses upon Hecuba's fate immediately after Troy's defeat, is indicative of the tragedy's fortune; while *Trojan Women*, as Helene P. Foley notes, has been performed in response to every major war in virtually every Western country during the twentieth and twenty-first centuries, *Hecuba* was largely absent from mainstage European and US theatres until the 1980s.[12]

The dramatic tension in *Agamemnon* centres around the relationship between Clytemnestra and Agamemnon, who are reunited in the tragedy for the first time since Agamemnon sacrificed their daughter Iphigenia at the beginning of the Trojan War. The narrative of Agamemnon's homecoming was well established in Greek literature prior to Aeschylus' *Oresteia*. Agamemnon's death is described in, for example, Homer's *Odyssey* and Stesichorus' (now fragmentary) lyric *Oresteia*. Aeschylus takes

---

[10] *Hecuba* is usually dated to around 424 or 423 BCE. However, this dating is based upon a pattern of increasing metrical resolutions in Euripides' lyrics, rising from 1.45% in the 431 BCE *Medea* to 8.74% in the c. 405 BCE *Bacchae* and *Iphigenia at Aulis*. The metrical resolutions are used as a temporal indicator of stylistic shifts within Euripides' playwriting. Slotting the undated plays into where they fit within this chronology is appealing but is based upon the presumption that a writer's stylistic evolution is linear, and that they always premièred their plays in the order in which they were written. I have reservations about both presumptions. On metrical resolutions in Euripides, see Cropp and Fick (1985).

[11] *Hecuba* was a popular text between antiquity and the renaissance and had an important reception history in the early modern era (on which see Kenward 2016: 180–191). However, it has not proved particularly popular in modernity; the Archive of Performances of Greek and Roman Drama (APGRD), for example, records a total of 165 productions of *Hecuba* internationally, in comparison with 904 productions of *Agamemnon*. The APGRD database is a work-in-progress and is incomplete, but nevertheless the ratio between the two tragedies is a good gauge of their relative popularity.

[12] Foley (2015: 3). Euripides' *Trojan Women* is set just prior to *Hecuba* and similarly depicts the Trojan women at the conclusion of the war. The APGRD records 455 productions of *Trojan Women* in modernity, more than double the rate of *Hecuba*.

this well-trodden narrative and further develops the characterisation of the main House of Atreus figures, with his innovations likely including deepening Clytemnestra's characterisation, who is here not only the architect and executioner of Agamemnon's murder but is also a fiercely intelligent, authoritative ruler as well.[13]

Agamemnon is set directly outside the Mycenaean Royal Palace and commences with a solitary watchman delivering a prologue, during which he sees the fire beacon that signals the Greeks' victory in the Trojan War and their imminent homecoming. The chorus' *parodos* (first song) includes a flashback to Iphigenia's sacrifice, carried out on her father Agamemnon's command to obtain favourable winds to sail to Troy. Despite the horrific circumstances surrounding Agamemnon's last interaction with his wife Clytemnestra, when he arrives home, accompanied by the enslaved Trojan princess and prophetess Cassandra as a war bride, Clytemnestra welcomes him with open arms. Yet appearances are deceiving; Clytemnestra immediately outmanoeuvres Agamemnon and persuades him to enter the Palace by treading upon and thus soiling ornate tapestries. Clytemnestra's triumph over Agamemnon during the carpet negotiations is representative of her continuing, socially problematic position as head of the household even after Agamemnon's return. Her continued authority and her real intentions towards Agamemnon are cemented during the fourth episode of the play, when the chorus of old men hear and describe the offstage Clytemnestra murdering Agamemnon and Cassandra. At the tragedy's conclusion, Clytemnestra appears to the audience triumphant over the two murdered corpses, before later appearing with her lover and co-conspirator Aegisthus, Agamemnon's cousin, during the play's *exodos*. The tragedy is, to this day, a tightly focused *tour-de-force* filled with arresting characters who have what appear to be decidedly contemporary psychological profiles. The resonances of the characters' actions go back to the past, where the lives of Agamemnon's forefathers are similarly defined by acts of violence and vengeance, and forwards into the future, where Clytemnestra and Agamemnon's children avenge Agamemnon's death and ultimately bring the cycle of revenge to a conclusion.

---

[13] Clytemnestra's murder of Agamemnon is also referenced in Pindar's *Pythian 11*, although the relative dating of this poem to the 458 BCE *Oresteia* is uncertain.

In contrast to the unity of *Agamemnon*, *Hecuba* is famous for being a diptych.[14] It is also renowned for its high degree of original myth-making, with much of the tragedy's narrative likely to be Euripidean innovation.[15] The tragedy is set outside of Agamemnon's tent in the Greek encampment on the Thracian coast and opens with the ghost of the Trojan prince Polydorus explaining how his family's Thracian guest-friend Polymestor murdered him for his gold at the conclusion of the Trojan War. Polydorus then informs the audience of the play's upcoming narrative, describing how a second ghost, the ghost of Achilles, has appeared and demanded the Trojan princess Polyxena be sacrificed at his tomb before the Greeks depart. The first half of the tragedy stages the Greeks communicating this demand to the Trojan queen Hecuba, and then to Polyxena herself, with Polyxena's death—framed as a willing and noble death and described in a highly erotic manner—detailed in a messenger speech during the second episode [518–582]. As Hecuba prepares to conduct burial rites for Polyxena, a servant arrives and announces the discovery of Polydorus' corpse. Having lost two children in quick succession (not to mention her city, her freedom, her husband, and many of her other children during the war) and indignant at Polymestor's violation of the laws of *xenia* (guest friendship), Hecuba becomes set on vengeance and, in the third episode, obtains Agamemnon's agreement that although he himself will not punish Polymestor, he will not intervene in Hecuba punishing him. In the exodos, Hecuba, pretending not to know of Polydorus' death, tricks Polymestor and his sons into entering Agamemnon's tent on the ruse of entrusting him with Trojan treasure, where she and her fellow Trojan captives proceed to blind him and murder his children; like Agamemnon's murder in *Agamemnon*, the action here takes place offstage, only to later be fully detailed for the audience in an *agon* (debate) between Hecuba and Polymestor, where Agamemnon acquits Hecuba. The narrative thus swings like a pendulum, from the vanquished Trojans suffering further indignity and loss as the Greeks demand the death of Polyxena, to the women, under Hecuba's leadership, avenging some of the injustices they have faced in an act of exceptional brutality and

---

[14] On the question of so-called Aristotelian unities in *Hecuba*, see Foley (2015: 29–34).

[15] The narratives surrounding the Thracian Polymestor murdering Polydorus, and Hecuba subsequently blinding Polymestor and murdering his children are, unless they are local Thracian stories, likely to be a Euripidean invention. On Euripides' innovations in *Hecuba*, see Foley (2015: 14).

gore.[16] Although Hecuba's rich characterisation and rhetorical prowess are well established throughout the play, the way the drama manoeuvres between her interactions with Polyxena, Agamemnon, and Polymestor means that Euripides prioritises examining broader circumstance over a deep dive into the dramaturgy of Hecuba's relationships. *Hecuba* is thus complex—and complicated—in ways distinct from *Agamemnon*.

Despite the distinct reception histories and dramaturgical profiles of *Agamemnon* and *Hecuba*, the plays share more in common than simply their post-Trojan War temporalities. The structure of both tragedies is that of a revenge tragedy, where the action is motivated by a protagonist's desire for revenge and ends in a climactic—albeit offstage—bloodbath. Within this overarching structure, there are three key parallels across the two tragedies, between Clytemnestra and Hecuba, between Iphigenia and Polyxena, and between Agamemnon and Polymestor. Clytemnestra and Hecuba are twinned in their positioning as architects of revenge and in, as Grace Zanotti details, the thematic centring of their violence around ideas of justice and kinship.[17] Their revenge is motivated specifically by their victim's violation of the mother/child bond and their need to obtain justice for their unavenged children. In the case of Hecuba, who has no living male relatives, one can argue that such an act is motivated not simply by personal fury but is her socio-cultural duty as well.[18]

Agamemnon and Polymestor are paralleled in their function as the victims of the two queens' acts of violence. Euripides plays upon the audience's uncertainty regarding how close this parallel will go, with Polymestor making the exact same cry of 'Ahh! And again!' [1037] as Hecuba takes out his second eye as Agamemnon does when Clytemnestra lands her second fatal blow [1345]. The audience, as Battezzato notes, do not know that Polymestor will remain alive, meaning Euripides leaves open the possibility for several lines that there will be a strict similarity between the denouement of *Agamemnon* and *Hecuba*.[19]

---

[16] Society's changing acceptance of Hecuba's violence is in part responsible for the tragedy's modulating popularity. For a recent take upon Hecuba's revenge, arguing it is not savage but justified, see Zanotti (2019).

[17] Zanotti (2019: 5).

[18] See Foley (2015: 32) and Mossman (1995: 180 n. 35), who note how unavenged victims could pollute entire cities, as Laius does in *Oedipus the King*, and could expect family members to obtain retribution for their injustices.

[19] Battezzato (2018: 203).

Iphigenia and Polyxena, as the two young royals murdered at the behest of the Greeks, are also twinned in their function as virgin sacrifices and markers of the horrors that war inflicts upon women's bodies. Euripides takes their kinship further through close intertextual references to the language of Aeschylus' analeptic choral ode. Although Punchdrunk are unusual in their coupling of the two texts, they are following Euripides' lead in connecting the two plays. They are also following a tradition within late twentieth- and early twenty-first-century theatre of expanding the *Oresteia* narrative, which is usually undertaken by compounding Aeschylus' trilogy with Euripides' *Iphigenia at Aulis* to substantiate the psychological justification for Clytemnestra's act of vengeance.[20] By twinning *Agamemnon* and *Hecuba*, Punchdrunk did not dive deeper into Clytemnestra's psychology but rather zoomed out to make a wider statement about the impact of war on women and the lengths to which women in Greek mythology go to avenge their families.

Introducing *The Burnt City*

Although *Agamemnon* and *Hecuba* provide the core narrative scaffold for *The Burnt City*, a familiarity with these two plays is insufficient for comprehending the full style and scale of Punchdrunk's production. *The Burnt City* is emblematic of Punchdrunk's large-scale performance style, which utilises a looping structure involving eleven or twelve five-minute scenes repeating three times per performance. Barrett originally developed the loop structure for his final undergraduate production of *Woyzeck* at Exeter University in 2000. Such performances begin with what the company term a 'cross-fade' to facilitate the audience-participants crossing, as Punchdrunk claim, 'physically and imaginatively, from the everyday world into the world of the event'.[21] For *The Burnt City*, the cross-fade took the form of a mock museum exhibition of artefacts unearthed from the site of historic Troy, in Hisarlık, Turkey. The audience were funnelled into the exhibition in staggered groups over the first loop, where they were given their bone-white full-face Punchdrunk mask, which they had to wear for the performance (in contrast to the

---

[20] For examples of productions that stage *Iphigenia at Aulis* as a prequel to the *Oresteia*, see, for example, Ariane Mnouchkine's 1990 *Les Atrides* (Le Théâtre du Soleil) and Robert Icke's 2015 *Oresteia* (Almeida Theatre).

[21] Machon and Punchdrunk (2019: 69–70).

unmasked performers) and which have become something of a signifier for Punchdrunk themselves.

The Burnt City consisted of eleven five-minute scenes which played on a loop, from Scenes One to Eleven, three times, before a concluding finale brought the audience together and facilitated their exit from the space. During the three loops, the free-flow promenade audience could explore the performance venue, which was two former munitions factories housed in Woolwich's Royal Arsenal, at their leisure. Within the warehouses lay exceptionally detailed labyrinthine worlds filled with touch-real sets. The first warehouse, Building 17 of the Arsenal, represented Greek Mycenae and was a vast open space with the central part of the original warehouse shell still visible. The ground floor represented a No Man's Land and was the base for the Greek soldiers, while the mezzanine represented the Mycenaean Royal Palace and was the focus of Clytemnestra's narrative and the location of Agamemnon's murder. The part of the ground floor that lay underneath the mezzanine hosted an installation referencing the Greek army camp, and in rooms off to the side of No Man's Land were a shrine to Artemis and a barracks. The second warehouse, Building 19, represented Troy and was a bustling metropolis with a design installation inspired in part by Fritz Lang's 1927 film *Metropolis*. The cosmopolitan Troy had a more 'lived-in' feel and represented a city under siege. It featured a bistro called Ciacco's, an opera house called the Palladium, the department store Alighieri's, a souk, and a red-light district modelled on *Metropolis*' Yoshiwara. There was also a layering-in of locations drawn from the Underworld of Greek mythology, including Hades' House, a tenement structure designed as the home of the residents in the Underworld's Tartarus, as well as a florist called Hesperides which belonged to Askalaphos, the mythological guardian of Hades' orchid. Punchdrunk's concept for the production was to meld the two Greek tragedies with a range of dystopic science-fiction intertexts as 'collision' sources and to set the purgatorial looping re-enactment of the Trojan War within the frame of the Underworld, where Hades was replaying history again and again. The characters of Hades and Persephone were the only two characters (not only in *The Burnt City* but in any Punchdrunk masked show) to sit outside of the loop structure; their narrative trajectory lasted for the entirety of the second and third loop and involved Persephone re-emerging into the Underworld and rediscovering her role as dread queen, having lost her memories due to re-entering the Underworld via the river Lethe.[22]

The narrative of *Agamemnon* and *Hecuba* was performed through a largely non-verbal, dance-based language. As part of the immersive world the company created, audiences were invited to observe characters from a 360-degree perspective. The characters thus rarely went 'offstage' but rather had their narratives fleshed out so that spectators could continue to follow the characters and witness Punchdrunk's creative imaginings regarding the characters' interactions and behaviours in between the moments documented in the source texts. As such, the company added numerous other intertexts to *Agamemnon* and *Hecuba*, including for example fusing the description of Iphigenia's sacrifice in *Agamemnon* with narrative content about her arrival at Aulis and the aftermath of her sacrifice from Euripides' *Iphigenia at Aulis* and *Iphigenia among the Taurians* respectively.

The characters found within *The Burnt City* were split between what Punchdrunk term travelling and resident characters. Travelling characters were physically demanding dance-based roles drawn primarily from the two tragedies. They consisted of Agamemnon, Aegisthus, Clytemnestra, Cassandra, Hecuba, Iphigenia, Polydorus, Polymestor, and Polyxena, alongside two Greek soldiers, Neoptolemus and Patroclus, and four gods, Hades, Persephone, Apollo, and Artemis. The residents were additional characters that Punchdrunk included to add depth to *The Burnt City*'s universe; Barrett referred to the roles in rehearsals as 'the heartbeats of the space'. In *The Burnt City*, there were thirteen resident roles, including a cluster of Trojan citizens named Macaria, Askalaphos, Luba, Zagreus, Kronos, Kampe, and Laocoön, one Greek soldier, known as The Watchman, a Mycenaean Oracle, and three residents of the in-house bar, Peep.[23] The narrative arc of each resident character intersected with the

---

[22] For the first loop Hades and Persephone performed outside the central performance space, as part of the cross-fade which facilitated the audience's entry.

[23] The programme positions Kampe as part of Peep Cabaret; however, Kampe spent more than two-thirds of their loop in Troy and only appeared in Peep for two songs, whereas the other three residents (two bar hosts and the singer Orpheus) spent almost the entirety of their loops inside Peep. As such, I have positioned Kampe as a citizen of Troy rather than a resident of Peep. Most of the residents were named after mythological figures from the ancient Greek Underworld: Macaria is a daughter of Hades, Askalaphos is guardian of Hades' orchid, Zagreus is a son of Hades, Kronos is a Titan found in Tartarus, and Kampe is a monster who guards Tartarus. The other two characters are

source tragedies but was often fleshed out through other sources and via new material devised by the performing company.

The Burnt City thus involved twenty-eight performers spread throughout 100,000 square feet of performance space. Each of the up to 600 spectators per performance was empowered to chart their own pathway through the performance and have entirely unique experiences. Many audience members would follow one performer for a period of time to gain access to their narrative arc. The looping structure enabled two different characters' loops to be experienced (almost) in their entirety, although spending a portion of the performance exploring the space and transitioning between observing different characters was also a popular mode of engaging with the production.[24] However one chose to experience *The Burnt City*, the individuality and partiality of each spectator's experience was intrinsic to the ecology of the work. It would take countless visits to experience the performance, in terms of both its space and its characters, in its entirety, and the presence of one-on-one experiences meant that one could never be guaranteed access to a character's entire loop even if one chose to follow them consistently.

One-on-one experiences are another trademark of Punchdrunk's large-scale work and involve a performer taking a single audience member into a private space for a scene, where the audience member becomes not a masked observer but an unmasked participant.[25] Over half-a-dozen one-on-one scenes, involving both travelling and resident characters, were embedded within *The Burnt City*. Which audience member would get to experience a character's one-on-one was unpredictable, which furthered the difficulty of experiencing a Punchdrunk performance, even through repeat attendance, in its entirety and helped ensure the uniqueness of

---

exceptions: Laocoön is a Trojan priest whose story is documented in Virgil's *Aeneid* and is famously represented in the Laocoön sculpture group, while Luba's name references the character Luba Luft from the 1968 novel *Do Android's Dream of Electric Sheep* and its 1982 film adaptation *Blade Runner;* her name is a nod to the dystopic science-fiction collision sources.

[24] It was impossible to experience three full loops as the first audience members entered *The Burnt City* performance space from the cross-fade part-way into Loop One.

[25] There are exceptions to the one-on-one experiences being between a solo audience member and performer. In *The Burnt City*, for example, there was a one-on-two experience, involving a single audience member and two performers (Apollo and Zagreus), and a three-on-one experience, involving three (and, later in the run, five) audience members and Persephone.

each spectator's experience. The scenes were often gifted to audience members who were cautiously curious or particularly invested in a character's journey and were highly sought after by Punchdrunk's dedicated fan base of so-called superfans.[26]

My introduction to *The Burnt City* showcases the discrepancies surrounding how any two audience members might have experienced the production in terms of what they witnessed and with whom they engaged. Recent scholarship has showcased how these different experiences of the show's content are matched by contrasting scholarly understandings of the audience's conceptual experience of Punchdrunk's immersive and interactive worlds, too. It is commonplace within scholarship on Punchdrunk's masked theatre to use Jacques Rancière's *The Emancipated Spectator* as an interpretative lens through which to consider the agency that Punchdrunk offer to audiences.[27] In *The Emancipated Spectator*, Rancière argues that when artists try to emancipate audiences from being passive consumers of art, and instead create theatre where the spectator is 'removed from the position of observer calmly examining the spectacle offered to her', then the outcome involves a principle of inequality and a process of stultification.[28] Instead, one must recognise the activity present in looking or spectating, and change their understanding of theatre, rather than the form of theatre, to affirm the intellectual equality of all involved. Punchdrunk's masked performances transform spectators into performers; the masked audience members became a part of the performance's scenography, and their behaviour during the show becomes integral to (their perception of) the performance's narrative and wider meaning. The application of Rancière's ideas to Punchdrunk's masked performances has resulted in two dominant perspectives upon the form of spectatorship offered in performances such as *The Burnt City*.

The first trend in understanding spectatorship in Punchdrunk's masked performances consists of a straightforward application of Rancière's *Emancipated Spectator*.[29] Punchdrunk are here positioned as the latest instalment in a long line of practitioners, which for Rancière originates

[26] On Punchdrunk's one-on-one experiences, see Machon and Punchdrunk (2019: 203–208).
[27] Rancière (2009).
[28] Rancière (2009: 4).
[29] See Rancière (2009).

with Brecht and Artaud, who experiment with theatrical form to resist a perceived dichotomy between passive spectators and active performers, but whose interventions ultimately reinforce a principle of inequality and fail to give audiences real agency. Proponents of this perspective focus upon the contingency of the agency granted to spectators within the world of Punchdrunk's performances. Holly Maples, for example, notes that despite a rhetoric that encourages audience participation, the reality of Punchdrunk's work is that 'the spectator is often pushed aside, refused access, or violently removed from the performance space'.[30] Mary Luckhurst confirms the sense that there are barriers to exercising one's agency, noting that in her experience of *The Drowned Man* she 'was pulled out of spaces three times by Punchdrunk minders [black-masked stewards] because a stage routine was about to ensue, [and] the choreography was apparently so rigid that invisible proscenium arches had been constructed in order to avoid unwanted audience interaction'.[31] Other scholars position the audience's masks as a kind of mobile forth wall; W. B. Worthen, for example, sees the mask as performing 'the work of the darkened auditorium and the theatre seat, separating, individualizing, and interiorizing us as a group of spectators'.[32] For these scholars, the liberation of the spectator from the confines of their chair grants only a limited, and sometimes problematic, form of emancipation and is precisely the type of theatrical innovation that Rancière cautions against.

The second interpretation of Punchdrunk's masked work consists of reading Rancière against the grain and demonstrating how participation empowers. In some ways, this reading makes a straw man of Rancière, as he does not deny that active audience experiences, such as can be found in immersive theatre, can lead to intellectual emancipation, but simply demonstrates that physical emancipation is not necessary for intellectual emancipation and can even work against it. Indeed, Gareth White draws attention to how participatory and immersive performance can emancipate through reference to Rancière's wider corpus, demonstrating how a body-based intersubjectivity does not have to be stultifying but can allow the audience to be both in the work and a spectator of it, where one

---

[30] Maples (2016: 120).
[31] Luckhurst (2017: 13).
[32] Worthen (2012: 94–95).

can exercise their will and experience subjectivation.[33] Justifications of audience agency in Punchdrunk's masked work look for evidence firstly within the performances themselves. Carina Westling, for example, makes a case for both actors and audience members to be considered as, in a sense, performers, by suggesting that audience anonymity flattens the hierarchies of agency and sees 'actors perform "behind" their character, just like audiences participate "behind" their masks, positioning them on a shared plane'.[34] White, writing specifically about Punchdrunk's large-scale works, turns to Punchdrunk's strategy of masking the audience as evidence of emancipation. In contrast to those arguments that see the mask as a type of fourth wall, White suggests that the mask empowers audiences 'to become participants in the action as well as part of the scenery of the show'.[35] And it is not just the activities of audiences within Punchdrunk's work that are used as evidence of audience emancipation, but spectators' behaviour outside of the confines of the theatrical space, too. Westling, for example, argues that Punchdrunk superfans co-create 'an extended narrative played out through their repeat participation in live performance, and in their remediation of live experience online', which gives audiences so much agency that they generate narratives which 'to company members directly involved with the design and build of the production, neither exist nor were intended to exist'.[36]

Now that both viewpoints have become relatively standard touchstones in the discourse surrounding Punchdrunk's work, there is a temptation to reduce the dynamics of spectatorship down to this binary opposition. The two perspectives become mutually exclusive and provide a scholarly justification for an aesthetic judgement on the relative merits of Punchdrunk's productions. I outline them here to showcase how scholarship has frequently met productions akin to *The Burnt City* in the past, and to demonstrate how not only are there many ways of participating in Punchdrunk's masked performances, but there are also different ways of

---

[33] White (2016: 29–31).
[34] Westling (2020: 146).
[35] White (2009: 224).
[36] Westling (2020: 31–32).

theorising how to comprehend and interpret these modes of participation as well.³⁷

The Structure of this Book

Punchdrunk on the Classics aims to contribute to the study of the interrelationship between the classics and immersivity through a focused analysis upon Punchdrunk's *The Burnt City*. My next chapter introduces Punchdrunk's work with Greek literature beyond *The Burnt City*, encompassing *The House of Oedipus* (2000) and *Kabeiroi* (2017) as well as their Enrichment project *The Oracles* (2017). Maxine Doyle's *Deo* (2019) for the Martha Graham Dance Company is also discussed, due to Doyle's role as long-time Punchdrunk choreographer and associate director, and as choreographer and co-director of *The Burnt City*.³⁸ These productions occurred at key moments within Punchdrunk's history, including during the formation of their signature style of performance and during their experimentation with geo-locative forms of immersion. I document the role of the ancient text within each immersive experience and the formative role that each production played during the company's history. My next three chapters are devoted to *The Burnt City*. *The Burnt City* was Punchdrunk's first new masked show since their 2013–14 *The Drowned Man* and was the company's largest-ever endeavour in terms of financial outlay (described as the company's 'costliest and most ambitious' work), design (requiring full construction within a warehouse shell), and development (a decade in the making as a concept, over two years in formal development, and four months in rehearsal).³⁹ I worked as an embedded researcher and dramaturg on the production in a knowledge exchange

---

³⁷ There are, of course, some scholars who reject a binary view of audience agency and instead suggest a blended, or graded, form of spectator emancipation. For such approaches, see Lavender (2016: 181), Alston (2013), and Biggin (2017: 83). Julia M. Ritter's argument that the audience in immersive performance is operationally restricted by choreography, which leaves little room for individual agency but offers space for agentive decision-making through improvisational scores, similarly takes a middle ground when discussing audience agency; see Ritter (2020, esp. p. 85).

³⁸ Although *Deo* is not a Punchdrunk work, it is relevant to the discussion as Doyle based the performance upon the Demeter and Persephone myth. The research conducted for this production informed Doyle's work on *The Burnt City*.

³⁹ See Wiegand (2021). *Sleep No More* Shanghai opened between *The Drowned Man* and *The Burnt City* but was a new production of a pre-existing Punchdrunk work.

arrangement, meaning I facilitated access to and a depth of understanding surrounding the classical material for the cast and creatives, and in turn participated in the production's research and development (R&D) and rehearsal periods as a form of fieldwork. My final substantive chapter puts Punchdrunk's practice into dialogue with ideas of immersion in antiquity, to showcase how studying immersive antiquities can not only tell us about modern-day creative practice but can also cast fresh light upon the ancient world as well.

Chapters 3–6 fall into two halves. Chapters 3 and 4 focus on process and consist of a rehearsal study of the creation of *The Burnt City*. In Chapter 3, I take a survey approach and move chronologically through the R&D, rehearsal, and preview periods. I tack back and forth between big-picture information regarding when and how antiquity was turned to and reconceptualised within the creation of *The Burnt City*, and close-up illustrative examples showcasing how the artists made their own meaning from individual pieces of source material. The chapter builds the argument that Punchdrunk created *The Burnt City* via a form of mythopoiesis, involving the company braiding together a variety of materials into their own unique text ready to be experienced as what Sarah Iles Johnston terms a coherent and credible storyworld. In Chapter 4, I zoom in and turn to the company's handling of the two tragic source texts in rehearsal. I examine how Punchdrunk reinvented the narrative, emotion, psychology, and language of the Greek tragedies. I put forward the argument that the company's process of reconceptualising *Agamemnon* and *Hecuba* equated to a form of intermedial translation, involving reinterpreting the Greek texts through choreographic language and finding new meanings within the texts ripe for communication through the body. The chapters work in partnership; in Chapter 3, I take a big-picture approach to documenting the development of *The Burnt City* and attempt to give a sense of the full range of working practices involved in creating a work of the scale and complexity of *The Burnt City*, while in Chapter 4 I take a narrower focus to showcase how Punchdrunk handled the dramaturgy of ancient literature and abstracted Greek tragedy into immersive experience.

Chapters 5 and 6 then focus on the production and its legacy and involve an analysis of the final performance and an analysis of the performance in dialogue with ideas about immersion from antiquity, respectively. The two chapters again work in partnership. In Chapter 5, I consider how the classical content reinforced the possible immersivity of *The Burnt City*, while in Chapter 6 I consider how *The Burnt City* can help one to understand the concept of immersivity in antiquity. I define an immersive experience as one that holds four qualities, namely that it: (1) displaces one from their present reality; (2) engulfs one's senses; (3) encourages one to feel differently; and (4) encourages one to think differently. In Chapter 5, I explore Punchdrunk's engagement with, and representation of, architectural and geographic place and dramaturgical and designed space in *The Burnt City*, and consider how the audience's experience was encoded in relation to both. I argue that the specific layering of place and space in *The Burnt City* helped encourage the audience to experience the first quality of an immersive experience. Crucially, I highlight how audience experiences in all Punchdrunk's masked shows are often theorised in a way, by both scholars and Punchdrunk themselves, that is linked to classical antiquity. A distinctive synergy thus exists between the narrative universe, the representation of space, and the audience experience in *The Burnt City* due to the production's status as a classical reception. Chapter 6 then explores the ideas of *mimesis* and *enargeia*, meaning representation and vividness respectively, as concepts linked to immersivity in antiquity which can be illuminated when put into conversation with contemporary immersive experiences. Just as the classics helped reinforce the possible immersivity of *The Burnt City*, so too can *The Burnt City* help us understand immersivity in antiquity. I highlight how putting *The Burnt City* in dialogue with mimesis and enargeia foregrounds often overlooked dimensions in both concepts, including the relevance of ideas of theatricality and the embodied materiality of performance. I suggest that studying a poetics of immersion that stretches back to the earliest examples of ancient Greek textuality and forwards to twenty-first-century immersive performance encourages new understandings of immersion in antiquity, and a reconceptualisation of the current preoccupation with immersive antiquities in modernity. The four chapters collectively work to provide a broad sense of the benefits to be found, for both artists and audiences, in immersive experiences that are connected to antiquity.

Methodology

Punchdrunk on the Classics is primarily based upon fieldwork conducted during secondments to Punchdrunk between 2019 and 2022, as well as archival research and performance analysis. My four central chapters employ the autoethnographic research methodology known as Spectator-Participation-as-Research to bring my positionally to the forefront and to provide a methodological bridge between the rehearsal study contained in Chapters 3 and 4, and the performance analysis contained in Chapters 5 and 6. In Chapters 3 and 4, Spectator-Participation-as-Research is combined with the principle of a rehearsal ethnography.

The rehearsal room is ideally a safe space for artists to engage in the trial and error required to create performance. It is almost always a space closed to outside observers, whose watchful gaze may be perceived as judging and inhibit a performer's capacity for play and experimentation. Sensitive production and company information circulates throughout the R&D and rehearsal periods, including matters of intellectual property, budgetary considerations, and sponsorship negotiations, disclosure of which to outsiders is often inappropriate and can be expressly prohibited. As such, accounts of theatrical creative development are commonly authored by artists who are personally involved in the production in question and include diarised accounts and photographic records such as Anthony Sher's *The Year of the King* and Complicite's *rehearsal notes* [sic].[40] When outside observers do gain access to the rehearsal room, their accounts often fall into two categories. Accounts of rehearsal which, as Kate Rossmanith describes, 'focus on chronology – "what happened" – rather than analysis' represent the first of these categories and include David Selbourne's *The Making of a Midsummer Night's Dream*, Jim Hiley's *Theatre at Work*, and Susan Letzler Cole's *Directors in Rehearsal* and *Playwrights in Rehearsal*.[41] Such accounts are often based upon partial access to rehearsals, which can range from sitting in on just one day of research and development through to witnessing several weeks of rehearsals in the lead up to a performance; Robert Marsden even draws attention to 'outsider-outsider accounts', where 'a journalist or researcher does not even enter the rehearsal room' and instead describes rehearsal narratives based upon interviews.[42] Granted, and as Gay McAuley notes, it is difficult to define the boundaries of rehearsals as many creative decisions, such as casting and set design, are

---

[40] Sher (1985) and Ainslie et al. (2010).
[41] Rossmanith (2009), and see Selbourne (1982), Hiley (1981), and Cole (1992, 2001).
[42] Marsden (2022: 13).

often made prior to the official rehearsal period commencing. Nevertheless, accounts such as Cole's are often based upon only partial access to what we might term the rehearsal period proper, or the point from which freelance performers are contractually employed for rehearsals.[43] Such accounts are often not methodologically-driven; Cole notes that her research techniques were 'not very technologically advanced, were mainly those of listening—and writing down everything I heard and saw'.[44] More recently, a more methodologically-rigorous form of rehearsal study has developed. Rossmanith notes that these analyses 'are more than simply an account of things said and done [...] they attempt to make sense of the way that practitioners made sense of the work in which they were engaged', citing studies that have explored the creative decisions that led to the final performance, and the differences between a conscious discourse about a practice and a less-conscious discourse within a practice.[45] Within classics, both Oliver Taplin and Lucy Jackson have authored such accounts based upon their involvement in rehearsals as academic consultants.[46] The Discipline of Theatre and Performance Studies at the University of Sydney, with which McAuley and Rossmanith have both been associated and of which I am a graduate, is responsible for a high percentage of accounts due to their pioneering of an ethnographic-inspired approach to the study of rehearsals.

McAuley first noted that ethnographic practice has much to teach us about the complex and subtle issues of power and presence governing the relationship between observer and observed in 1998, and since then several publications, including numerous articles, one special issue of an

---

[43] McAuley (1998: 79). Cole (2001) does not specify the percentage of each rehearsal period attended in her eight examples. However, Cole's first chapter begins with her arriving on the fourth day of a rehearsal period, indicating partial access.

[44] Cole (1992: xiii).

[45] Rossmanith (2009). Rossmanith also details the experimental rehearsal studies completed within the 1970s and 1980s through transactional analysis. Although there has been a resurgence of interest in cognitive approaches to the humanities in the twenty-first century, the limitations of transactional analysis in capturing the dynamics of rehearsal and facilitating nuanced interpretation remain in place and have meant that this particular approach remains unpopular.

[46] See Taplin (2001) and Jackson (2017).

academic journal, and McAuley's own monograph have featured ethnographic studies of rehearsal.[47] The anthropological practice of participant-observation, where an outsider immerses themselves into another culture while continuously writing 'scratch notes' or 'field notes' for later expansion, has offered scholars a methodology for the practice of being an observer in a foreign cultural environment. Ethnography provides an additional framework for writing up research via Clifford Geertz's notion of 'thick description', which encourages a moving back and forth between the everyday minutiae and the wider structures that give it meaning.[48] Although true ethnography involves the researcher being fully immersed within the culture being studied, the 'Sydney school' encourages a level of scholarly detachment in its rehearsal studies and suggests that scholars do not hold an active role in the creative development of the production in question. McAuley justifies this approach by arguing that observation is a full-time role, proposing that there are methodological limitations when one is part of a creative team and simultaneously studying rehearsals.[49] McAuley's approach is increasingly being adopted for international rehearsal studies, with Gary Cassidy, for example, noting that McAuley's work is 'the single most significant point of scholarly reference' in his rehearsal study of Anthony Neilson's 2013 *Narrative* at the Royal Court.[50] Cassidy borrows from McAuley's methodology (although Cassidy had only partial access to rehearsals, from the third week of rehearsals until press night) and combines it with insider insights drawn from his relevant professional experience as an actor; his research also includes the publication of documentary footage from rehearsals to showcase the dynamics of rehearsal further.

The impossibility of a sole researcher completing an ethnographic-style rehearsal study of Punchdrunk's theatre was apparent from my first day in rehearsals for *The Burnt City*. Although it is implicit in her writing,

---

[47] McAuley (1998: 77). The 2006 volume of *About Performance* features several contributions from then-University of Sydney academics, including Ginters (2006), Rossmanith (2006), and McAuley (2006). See McAuley (2012) for her monograph-length study of Michael Gow's *Toy Symphony*.

[48] Geertz (1973: 3–30).

[49] McAuley (1998: 81). See also McAuley (2012: 9), where she reiterates this line of argument and states that the ethnographic work will be 'at risk' if one also has responsibility for part of the creative process.

[50] Cassidy (2021: 5).

McAuley's model is developed for studio-based rehearsals, where a team works collaboratively in one space and it is possible for an academic (theoretically) to sit on the side-lines and survey and notate the entirety of the action. In contrast, Punchdrunk's large-scale immersive theatre is rehearsed on-site, which for *The Burnt City* meant across the two Woolwich warehouses. Each day, the entire cast of performers were called to different parts of the set to devise, simultaneously, all the action that would take place across the set during a specified scene. During Scene One of *The Burnt City*, for example, there were sixteen separate locations of the set featuring performed action. Were I able to observe rehearsals on a day when Punchdrunk were rehearsing Scene One (as opposed to being called to a specific area of the set to provide dramaturgical guidance on the classical source material), then I could only witness one sixteenth of the action taking place. Not only was a McAuley-style ethnographic study impossible from a practical perspective, but it was also unfeasible due to my role within the creative team, too. Complete objectivity is arguably always impossible when writing about rehearsals, and in my case, I became so closely involved in the project's development that critical distance was especially challenging to maintain. I commenced my work on *The Burnt City* (and thus this book) having a prior relationship with Punchdrunk, having worked on their 2017 production *Kabeiroi*, and would have always developed a heightened investment in the success of *The Burnt City* following my contributions during the R&D and rehearsal phases. However, the way the project unfolded meant I became further invested in the production. Firstly, delays due to the coronavirus pandemic facilitated my being involved over a much longer timespan than anticipated. In total, I spent around six months, on and off, with the company between 2019 and 2022. Secondly, my contributions exceeded what I had anticipated and saw me work across the communications team, the creative team, and the design team. I was directly involved in rehearsals, giving information about the myth cycles surrounding the show's source texts, as well as about ancient cult and ritual activities. It is worthwhile clarifying, however, that although I was a member of *The Burnt City* creative team, I worked with Punchdrunk via a secondment from my academic position and was never an employee of Punchdrunk. The arguments put forward in this book are the result of my research and analysis and should not be taken as representative of company views. My adoption of a Spectator-Participation-as-Research methodology is, in part, an attempt to put my positionality at the forefront of my analysis, to account for the insider form of spectatorship through which I experienced *The Burnt City*.

An ethnographic approach to Punchdrunk's performance preparation remains relevant, despite my active role, for two reasons. The first is due to Julia M. Ritter's use of ethnography for analysing the role of audiences in immersive theatre. Ritter argues that there is mileage in considering audiences as incidental and intentional ethnographers doing fieldwork both during the performance and during the 'extended audiencing' that follows within fan communities.[51] Ritter's positioning of spectators as accidental ethnographers does not involve their status being limited due to their note-taking inability or partial perspective, but is illuminating as to how even an unacknowledged ethnographic stance can lead to the articulation of embodied experience. Her essay demonstrates the value of a participant-observation framework for the study of immersive theatre. The second reason why the approach remains relevant is because my more active role, rather than purely compromising my academic stance, facilitated access to a longer duration of creative development than is standard for rehearsal studies. The duration of my involvement goes some way to addressing McAuley's comments about the difficulties of defining the boundaries of rehearsals and accessing the origins of various creative decisions. Punchdrunk's immersive response to the extant Trojan War tragedies was in development for over a decade and was floated for performance on several occasions, only for venue negotiations to collapse and for the project to be postponed. I was first made aware of the concept in 2017, when working as an academic consultant on Punchdrunk's *Kabeiroi*, and became formally involved in July 2019 at the commencement of an AHRC Leadership Fellowship/UKRI Innovation Fellowship, on which Punchdrunk were a project partner. Throughout the second half of 2019, I was involved in creative development discussions both in-person and via videoconferencing on half-a-dozen occasions with, among others, director Felix Barrett, producers Lucy Whitby and Lauren Storr, and designers Livi Vaughan and Beatrice Minns. During 2020, I participated in six weeks of creative development led by Barrett and co-director/choreographer Maxine Doyle. I then participated in two further creative development periods, via weekly videoconferencing meetings with Barrett and Doyle in June 2021 and in-person, this time with the cast as well, in

---

[51] Ritter (2017).

September 2021. I was then present from the beginning of rehearsals until the third week of previews, at which point the cast were performing seven shows per week and only called for minimal rehearsal hours due to equity limits. I returned for press week in April 2022 and maintained access to rehearsal reports, show reports, and performer notes throughout. I did not participate in or witness all conversations and creative development periods prior to rehearsals commencing; for example, I was not present for the build of the set and the design installation. Nevertheless, my participation was more encompassing than is found in other academic-authored rehearsal studies, and I was exposed to, for example, processual elements such as the protracted negotiations with the venue, the evolving budget and the way it affected casting and design, the impact of the coronavirus pandemic upon fundraising and the production launch, and the way that personal circumstances such as maternity leave (including my own!) can affect creative process. This broader access enriches my ethnography and counteracts what McAuley perceives as the methodological problem of compromised observation.

In my rehearsal study, I consequently retain the principle of rehearsal ethnography and utilise a thick-description approach to enable a tacking back and forth between broad brushstroke, big-picture information about how *The Burnt City* was created, and close-up, illustrative examples of individual moments of rehearsal to showcase Punchdrunk's specific approach to transforming and supplementing ancient Greek literature. I adapt this methodology by combining it with the autoethnographic form of audience research known as Spectator-Participation-as-Research, or SPaR. One of the original contributions of this monograph is my development of a new methodology for rehearsal studies, which develops the Spectator-Participation-as-Research approach into an autoethnographic methodology for studying rehearsals of immersive, participatory, and one-on-one theatre. The augmenting of a rehearsal ethnography with an autoethnographic methodology also partially addresses the colonising mentality of ethnography, by acknowledging and accommodating different subjectivities, and by foregrounding my participation in and influence on the research.

Deidre Heddon, Helen Iball, and Rachel Zerihan developed SPaR in 2012 to theorise their individual, experiential processes of reception during the one-on-one performance *i confess...* [sic].[52] The authors relate SPaR to the more-established notion of Practice-as-Research, but tailor it to the participatory role of the audience in immersive and one-on-one performance rather than the practitioner's role as creator and researcher. The methodology combines first-person, phenomenological-based accounts with more traditional scholarly analysis to replicate the author's 'multifarious role within, and in relation to, the performance – as participants inside the work, spectators to their own experience, and analysts reflecting on it in the "aftermath" of participation'.[53] There are two key distinctions between how Heddon, Iball, and Zerihan use SPaR, and how I use it. Firstly, Heddon and her co-authors employ the methodology specifically for one-on-one performance, where the individual researcher represents the entirety of the audience in any singular performance. Secondly, they use SPaR collaboratively, in a comparative study involving the three authors putting their separate uses of SPaR for *i confess...* into dialogue. As I was the sole researcher in *The Burnt City* rehearsals, my analysis will only represent my singular and partial experience, but I will not be the first to adopt SPaR for theatrical experiences outside of the one-on-one experience, or to utilise SPaR within a sole-authored piece of analysis.

The suite of books and articles that followed Heddon, Iball, and Zerihan's work on SPaR include, first and foremost, Rose Biggin's 2017 monograph *Immersive Theatre and Audience Experience: Space, Game, and Story in the work of Punchdrunk*. Biggin's examination of Punchdrunk's work includes details from a period of embedded research with the company (2010–14), and the monograph consequently, she argues, 'sits in the tradition of SPaR' as it combines Biggin's own first-person accounts as an audience member of Punchdrunk's work with more theoretical analysis.[54] A 2016 special issue of the *Journal of Contemporary Drama in English* also featured several sole-authored contributions that analysed first-person spectatorial experiences of immersive performance

---

[52] Heddon et al. (2012).

[53] Aragay and Monforte (2016: 7). For another examples of SPaR analysis, see Quigley (2016).

[54] Biggin (2017: 3).

through SPaR, and the issue's editorial even referred to SPaR as a 'rapidly developing emerging methodology'.[55] My work remains distinct from these prior publications, however, in its development of SPaR into a rehearsal methodology, and in its use of the approach in a monograph-length study of a single production. Although Biggin attended some Punchdrunk rehearsals, her research does not explicitly reference individual moments of rehearsal and contains a more sweeping coverage of Punchdrunk's practice rather than a deep dive into one artistic output. SPaR is ideal for a rehearsal study as it does not aspire to analyse a full process but allows for partiality. Although Punchdrunk's way of working means my simultaneously all-encompassing yet partial exposure to their rehearsals is extreme, all rehearsal studies are based upon, to an extent, partial access to the creative process. Furthermore, SPaR values, due to its grounding in participatory forms of performance, the dual position of someone who is simultaneously an observer and a co-creator within an artistic environment. The methodology thus embraces what McAuley cautions against and is a viable alternative to a traditional ethnographic methodology for rehearsal studies.

I utilise SPaR not only in my rehearsal study, however, but also in my performance analysis, as a methodological bridge connecting the two halves of this book. I do this to build unity across my chapters, and because it puts my positionality at the forefront of my performance analysis. In her 2019 intervention for *Contemporary Theatre Review*, Kirsty Sedgman critiques the false binary arising between theatre scholars who do qualitative, empirical audience research, and so-called theorised or critical studies of spectatorship which often refer to an idealised spectator, rather than actual audience experience.[56] Due to the uniqueness of each individual visit to Punchdrunk's masked performances, scholarship on the audience experience of Punchdrunk's work tends to be divided along such lines. The former group often use the ample material that Punchdrunk's superfans generate to document their experiences of

---

[55] Aragay and Monforte (2016: 6–7). It is worth noting that the journal's labelling of the methodology as rapidly developing was somewhat premature; Ritter (2020) is one of the only publications to employ a SPaR approach for the analysis of immersive and/or participatory performance since, although there are examples of scholars using a reflexive autoethnographic approach to analyse non-participatory forms of performance (see, for example, Lynch 2022).

[56] Sedgman (2019).

performances on social networking platforms such as Facebook, Tumblr, and Discord, while the latter offer a type of reader-response or reception theory-inflected form of critical performance analysis. When it comes to analysing performances of classical receptions from within the discipline of classics, the latter approach is the default almost without exception (including in my own earlier scholarship), with expert analysis placing a performance within a social, cultural, and temporal landscape and arguing for a particular interpretation of its material. Biggin notes that analysing immersive performance from the perspective of an idealised spectator can result in reductive readings, 'resulting in either an uncritically celebratory reading of the form and its potentials or an equally uncritical damnation of its perceived limitations or flaws'.[57] There are ethical issues, too, surrounding having a singular, expert voice define the meaning of a cultural output in a particular time and place. Utilising SPaR, which allows one to analyse first-person experience within, for example, rehearsal and immersive performance whilst highlighting the singularity of that perspective and putting subjectivity at the forefront of the analysis, is one way of combatting these ethical issues. The following chapters thus seek to give an account of how ancient material shapes process and experience within Punchdrunk's immersive theatre, and within *The Burnt City* in particular, using a methodology that allows me to reflect upon how embedded research shapes academic process and experience as well.

---

[57] Biggin (2017: 20).

Works Cited

Ainslie, Sarah, Russell Warren-Fischer, and Complicite. 2010. *Complicite: Rehearsal Notes*. London: Complicite.

Alston, Adam. 2013. Audience Participation and Neoliberal Value: Risk, Agency and Responsibility in Immersive Theatre. *Performance Research: A Journal of the Performing Arts* 18: 2: 128–138. https://doi.org/10.1080/13528165.2013.807177

Aragay, Mireia, and Enric Monforte. 2016. Introduction: Theatre and Spectatorship—Meditations on Participation, Agency and Trust. *Journal of Contemporary Drama in English* 4: 1: 3–20. https://doi.org/10.1515/jcde-2016-0002.

Battezzato, Luigi. Ed. 2018. *Euripides: Hecuba*. Cambridge: Cambridge University Press.

Biggin, Rose. 2017. *Immersive Theatre and Audience Experience: Space, Game and Story in the Work of Punchdrunk*. Cham: Palgrave Macmillan.

Cassidy, Gary. 2021. *Contemporary Rehearsal Practice: Anthony Neilson and the Devised Text*. Oxon and New York: Routledge.

Cole, Susan Letzler. 1992. *Directors in Rehearsal: A Hidden World*. London and New York: Routledge.

———. 2001. *Playwrights in Rehearsal: The Seduction of Company*. London and New York: Routledge.

Cropp, Martin, and Gordon Fick. 1985. *Resolutions and Chronology in Euripides: The Fragmentary Tragedies* (BICS, Supplement 43). London: Institute of Classical Studies.

Dex, Robert. 2021. Immersive Theatre Punchdrunk Brings the Siege of Troy to London in New Show. *London Evening Standard*, September 6.

Foley, Helene P. 2015. *Euripides: Hecuba*. London: Bloomsbury.

Gardner, Lyn. 2021. Punchdrunk's The Burnt City. *Stagedoor*, September 5. https://stagedoorapp.com/lyn-gardner/punchdrunks-the-burnt-city?ia=1011. Accessed 16 September 2022.

Geertz, Clifford. 1973. *The Interpretation of Culture*. New York: Basic Books.

Ginters, Laura. 2006. "And There We May Rehearse Most Obscenely and Courageously": Pushing Limits in Rehearsal. *About Performance* 6: 55–74.

Heddon, Deirdre, Helen Iball, and Rachel Zerihan. 2012. Come Closer: Confessions of Intimate Spectators in One to One Performance. *Contemporary Theatre Review* 22: 1: 120–133. https://doi.org/10.1080/10486801.2011.645233.

Hemley, Matthew. 2021. Punchdrunk Sets Up London Home and Announces Largest Live Show to Date. *The Stage*, September 6. https://www.thestage.co.uk/news/punchdrunk-sets-up-london-home-and-announces-largest-live-show-to-date. Accessed 25 July 2023.

Higgins, Charlotte. 2022. "Adrenaline-Fuelled": Punchdrunk Return with the Horrifically Timely Siege of Troy. *The Guardian*, March 21. https://www.theguardian.com/stage/2022/mar/21/adrenaline-fuelled-punchdrunk-horrifically-timely-siege-troy. Accessed 26 September 2022.

Hiley, Jim. 1981. *Theatre at Work: The Story of the National Theatre's Introduction of Brecht's Galileo*. London: Routledge & Kegan Paul Ltd.

Jackson, Lucy. 2017. Forces at Work: Euripides' *Medea* at the National Theatre 2014. In *Adapting Translation for the Stage*, eds. Geraldine Brodie and Emma Cole, 104–117. London and New York: Routledge.

Kenward, Claire. 2016. The Reception of Greek Drama in Early Modern England. In *A Handbook to the Reception of Greek Drama*, ed. Betine van Zyl Smit, 173–198. Chichester: Wiley Blackwell.

Komporaly, Jozefina. 2017. *Radical Revival as Adaptation: Theatre, Politics, Society*. Cham: Palgrave Macmillan.

Lavender, Andy. 2016. *Performance in the Twenty-First Century: Theatres of Engagement*. Oxon: Routledge.

Luckhurst, Mary. 2017. Punchdrunk, the Immersive and Gothic Tourism. *About Performance* 14–15: 7–18.

Lynch, Signey. 2022. The Gaze Turned Inward: A Reflexive Autoethnographic Approach to Theatre Research. In *Impacting Theatre Audiences: Methods for Studying Change*, eds. Dani Snyder-Young and Matt Omasta, 88–99. Oxon and New York: Routledge.

Machon, Josephine, and Punchdrunk. 2019. *The Punchdrunk Encyclopaedia*. London and New York: Routledge.

Maples, Holly. 2016. The Erotic Voyeur: Sensorial Spectatorship in Punchdrunk's *The Drowned Man*. *Journal of Contemporary Drama in English* 4: 1: 119–133. https://doi.org/10.1515/jcde-2016-0010.

Marsden, Robert. 2022. *Inside the Rehearsal Room: Process, Collaboration and Decision-Making*. London: Methuen Drama.

McAuley, Gay. 1998. Towards an Ethnography of Rehearsal. *New Theatre Quarterly* 38: 183–194. https://doi.org/10.1017/S026646X00011751.

———. 2006. Introduction. *About Performance* 6: 7–13.

———. 2012. *Not Magic But Work: An Ethnographic Account of a Rehearsal Process*. Manchester and New York: Manchester University Press.

Mossman, Judith. 1995. *Wild Justice: A Study of Euripides' Hecuba*. Oxford: Clarendon Press.

Punchdrunk. 2022. *Punchdrunk*. https://www.punchdrunk.com/. Accessed 16 September 2022.

Quigley, Karen. 2016. Letting the Truth Get in the Way of a 'Good' Story: Spectating Solo and Blast Theory's *Rider Spoke*. *Journal of Contemporary Drama in English* 4: 1: 90–103. https://doi.org/10.1515/jcde-2016-0008.

Rancière, Jacques. 2009. *The Emancipated Spectator*. Trans. Gregory Elliot. London and New York: Verso.

Ritter, Julia M. 2017. Fandom and Punchdrunk's *Sleep No More*: Audience Ethnography of Immersive Dance. *TDR: The Drama Review* 61: 4: 59–77.

———. 2020. *Tandem Dances: Choreographing Immersive Performance*. Oxford: Oxford University Press.

Rossmanith, Kate. 2006. Feeling the Right Impulse: "Professionalism" and the Affective Dimension of Rehearsal Practice. *About Performance* 6: 75–92.

———. 2009. Making Theatre-Making: Fieldwork, Rehearsal and Performance-Preparation. *Reconstruction: Studies in Contemporary Culture* 9: 1.

Saville, Alice. 2022. Punchdrunk Is Back! Behind the Scenes at New Show The Burnt City. *Evening Standard*. https://www.standard.co.uk/culture/theatre/punchdrunk-the-burnt-city-behind-the-scenes-woolwich-b989141.html. Accessed 16 September 2022.

Sedgman, Kirsty. 2019. We Need to Talk About (How We Talk About) Audiences. *Contemporary Theatre Review* 29: 3. https://www.contemporarytheatrereview.org/2019/we-need-to-talk-about-how-we-talk-about-audiences/. Accessed 26 September 2022.

Selbourne, David. 1982. *The Making of 'A Midsummer Night's Dream'*. London: Methuen.

Sher, Anthony. 1985. *Year of the King*. London: Chatto and Windus.

Taplin, Oliver. 2001. The Experience of an Academic in the Rehearsal Room. *Didaskalia* 5: 1. https://www.didaskalia.net/issues/vol5no1/taplin.html. Accessed 10 December 2019.

Westling, Carina E. I. 2020. *Immersion and Participation in Punchdrunk's Theatrical Worlds*. London and New York: Methuen Drama.

White, Gareth. 2009. Odd Anonymized Needs: Punchdrunk's Masked Spectator. In *Modes of Spectating*, eds. Alison Oddly and Christine White, 219–229. Bristol and Chicago: Intellect Books.

———. 2016. Theatre in the "Forest of Things and Signs". *Journal of Contemporary Drama in English* 4: 1: 29–31. https://doi.org/10.1515/jcde-2016-0003.

Wiegand, Chris. 2021. Punchdrunk to Stage Epic "Future Noir" Drama in Old London Arms Factory. *The Guardian*, September 6. https://www.theguardian.com/stage/2021/sep/06/punchdrunk-stage-the-burnt-city-Royal-arsenal-london-arms-factory-immersive-trojan-war. Accessed 16 September 2022.

Worthen, W. B. 2012. "The Written Troubles of the Brain": *Sleep No More* and the Space of Character. *Theatre Journal* 64: 1: 94–95. https://doi.org/10.1017/CBO9781107295544.003.

Zanotti, Grace. 2019. κυνὸς σῆμα: Euripides' *Hecuba* and the Uses of Revenge. *Arethusa* 52: 1: 1–19. https://doi.org/10.1353/are.2019.0004.

CHAPTER 2

Punchdrunk on the Classics: A History

Ancient tragedy is a repeated presence in many British theatre companies' back catalogues. Punchdrunk are no exception to this trend. The company's three engagements with Greek tragedy are not, however, simply a statistical note, but are symptomatic of Artistic Director Felix Barrett's personal interest in the genre.[1] Greek tragedy played a crucial role in Barrett's conceptualisation of his trademark style of immersive theatre, and his company turned to the genre at decisive moments within their history. *The Burnt City*, as Punchdrunk's most recent classical reception, is representative of an established trend whereby Punchdrunk use Greek tragedy as a vehicle for innovation. Analysing Punchdrunk's past engagements with Greek tragedy (as well as with Greek literature and mythology more broadly) is revelatory as to how the company developed,

[1] Due to Barrett's role as Artistic Director of Punchdrunk from the company's founding, and the fact that many now-trademark Punchdrunk techniques originated in Barrett's final-year undergraduate productions, Barrett's œuvre and the company history of Punchdrunk are somewhat inseparable. The device of a masked audience and a looping narrative, for example, originated in Barrett's final undergraduate project, which was a production of *Woyzeck* in a found space; this production is also listed as the first Punchdrunk performance in the company's encyclopaedia. As such, I write as if Barrett's directorial history and Punchdrunk's organisational history are one and the same in the early parts of the company history, prior to when the company split into two separate organisations (the incorporated company Punchdrunk Global and the charitable organisation Punchdrunk Enrichment).

© The Author(s), under exclusive license to Springer Nature Switzerland AG 2024
E. Cole, *Punchdrunk on the Classics*,
https://doi.org/10.1007/978-3-031-43067-1_2

what value they place upon the tragic genre, and why classical antiquity has proved appealing as the lynchpin for their work at the start of the twenty-twenties.

Punchdrunk's first three shows, staged in the year 2000 and all directed by Barrett, each revolved around a central source, namely Chekhov's *The Cherry Orchard*, Barry Pain's *The Moon-slave*, and Sophocles' *Oedipus the King* and *Antigone*.[2] Each production played a role in shaping the overall direction of Punchdrunk's practice and it would be a mistake to privilege any one as a watershed. However, it is noteworthy that ancient tragedy was significant to the company's formative year, and that it was the performance of the two Sophoclean tragedies, which were played in tandem in a production titled *The House of Oedipus*, that provided one of the 'eureka' moments of Barrett's career.[3]

The House of Oedipus (Fig. 2.1) was a one-off durational and promenade production of Sophocles' *Oedipus the King* and *Antigone*. The thirteen-acre wild Victorian gardens of Devon's derelict Poltimore House served as the venue for the production. Poltimore House is a grade-two Tudor property and one-time hospital, which was constructed in 1550 and had been in disrepair since a 1987 arson attack. The ivy-covered house acted as an English echo of a Greek ruin and provided the backdrop for the performance, which took place on a Saturday afternoon in the late summer of 2000. For the six-hour production, Barrett preserved the structure of a looping narrative with which he had first experimented in his finalist production of *Woyzeck*. Whereas in *Woyzeck* Barrett directed twenty minutes of content per performer, which was repeated three times across three hours, in *The House of Oedipus* the loop was much longer and involved staging the two plays on repeat.[4] Small cuts to the text were made, including the removal of the choral odes, but the tragedies were otherwise produced in full, which in a departure from Punchdrunk's current practice meant that most of the plays' dialogue was staged. There were no collision texts as can be found in later productions such as *Sleep No More* (with Hitchcock's *Rebecca*) or *The Drowned Man*

---

[2] Machon and Punchdrunk (2019: 3).

[3] See Machon and Punchdrunk (2019: 4 and 140).

[4] On the loop structure in *Woyzeck*, see Machon and Punchdrunk (2019: 109). The twelve-part loop structure (although *The Burnt City* had an eleven-part loop structure, due to the length of the finale) that is characteristic of Punchdrunk's masked performances today was not honed until a later stage. See Machon and Punchdrunk (2019: 173).

(with Nathanael West's *The Day of the Locust*); rather, the collision lay in the engagement between installation and dialogue. Although the piece was visually astounding, with the audience invited to roam freely and to follow actors, cut between different stories, and interact with installations erected in secret groves of the garden, the primary personal value that Barrett found in the work lay in what he perceived as the production's two failings. The production's first failing was its use of dialogue, which Barrett argued 'destroyed the effect' of the production.[5] Its second failing lay in the presence of daylight, which meant the audience could see upcoming installations in the distance and thus never experienced a sense of mystery and the 'reveal' of subsequent discoveries.[6] Two key lessons consequently emerged from *The House of Oedipus*, namely the need to find a more gestural language that complemented rather than fought with the scenography, and the necessity of being able to control the environment by removing natural light and instead customising light to encourage curiosity and manipulate the 'reveal'. Both realisations formed part of Barrett's 'eureka' moment and indelibly shaped Punchdrunk's future work.[7]

The House of Oedipus is also noteworthy due to the role it played in helping Barrett hone the function of the Punchdrunk mask. Barrett's decision to mask his audience to differentiate them from the actors and to embolden them to engage with the performance, which he identifies as his other 'eureka' moment, originated in his undergraduate production of *Woyzeck*.[8] In contrast to the neutral white mime mask that Barrett used for *Woyzeck*, for *The House of Oedipus* Barrett vacuformed a new, oversized design with a fabric back which was based upon a Greek chorus mould; Gareth White described it as 'a kind of melancholic Greek chorus mask'.[9] In the first decade of Punchdrunk's work, Barrett was interested in creating different masks uniquely suited to the form and theme of each show; however, in *The House of Oedipus* the

---

[5] Barrett, quoted in Machon and Punchdrunk (2019: 94).

[6] Machon and Punchdrunk (2019: 4).

[7] See Machon and Punchdrunk (2019: 4, 140).

[8] On the first eureka moment, see Machon and Punchdrunk (2019: 140).

[9] White (2009: 225). On the history of Punchdrunk's mask up to the present, see Machon and Punchdrunk (2019: 178–180).

bespoke mask proved a 'disaster' as the choric form obstructed the audience's voyeuristic role by creating the illusion that one had to contribute actively to the scenography.[10] Barrett noted, for example, that 'the Greek chorus form gave the mask a personality, it gave the audience too much authority, it didn't remove their presence but accentuated the fact that they were in the space'.[11] The choric-style mask was also found lacking from a usability perspective, as its size resulted in the mask flopping forward.[12] The lessons from the mask design in *The House of Oedipus* were consequently integral to Punchdrunk's later, more neutral mask design, which prioritised comfort and breathability over performance customisation.[13]

Not only is the mask one of Punchdrunk's more iconic innovations, but it is also one of its more controversial. The mask is central to discussions about how active a role the audience plays in Punchdrunk's work. Those arguing in favour of an active audience, see the mask as integral to enabling the audience's emancipation from not only their chairs, but also from a passive form of spectatorship, while those arguing against such a position see the mask as merely a mobile fourth wall which makes the rules governing theatrical engagement more rigid than ever. Punchdrunk themselves, for example, see the mask as a 'critical mechanism for participation' which removes audiences from their more traditional 'passive, hidden' role.[14] In contrast, David Shearing sees the mask as creating the 'theatrical distance of end-on proscenium theatre', and similarly Colette Gordon argues it is a 'fetish of the fourth wall'.[15] The reality, like is the case with many binary arguments, is somewhere between the two perspectives, with the anonymisation provided by the mask disinhibiting

---

[10] On the mask as a 'disaster' see Barrett, quoted in Machon and Punchdrunk (2019: 178), and on bespoke masks for each performance see Machon and Punchdrunk (2019: 180).

[11] Punchdrunk and Machon (2019: 178).

[12] See, for example, White (2009), esp. 225–226.

[13] Despite the mask in *The House of Oedipus* being deemed a 'disaster', Punchdrunk nevertheless still experimented with a new design based upon a Greek helmet model for *The Burnt City* during the production's R&D phase. Again, however, the design was deemed too specific and the model was never deployed in production.

[14] Machon and Punchdrunk (2019: 178).

[15] Shearing (2015: 82) and Gordon (2012: 6). For an overview of these perspectives, see Biggin (2017: 24–25).

Fig. 2.1 A two-page spread advertising *The House of Oedipus* from an early promotional booklet for Punchdrunk (then called Punchdrunk Theatrical Experiences). The booklet is undated but references productions from the period of work the company classifies as 'Act 1' (2000–2008). Image credit: Punchdrunk Enrichment

audiences and empowering them to exercise agency within the performance, while simultaneously visually demarcating audiences as standing outside of the narrative and acting as a constant reminder that their agency in regard to narrative intervention is limited. The contradictions embodied in Punchdrunk's mask are further heightened by the fact that the mask inverts the traditional opposition between masked performers and unmasked audience members. As such, the mask designates to the wearer that they are fulfilling a performative function, while simultaneously having the visual effect of casting the audience as part of the scenography that frames the action rather than performs it. The semiotic power of the mask is clearly broader than questions of agency and can be unpacked in more detail through recourse to theatrical masks in ancient Greek theatre.

Theatrical masks in ancient Greece were helmet-like and were constructed from linen rags which were moulded and stiffened with glue.[16] The word used for mask, *prosōpon*, was the same as the word for face. As David Wiles notes, prosōpon translates literally to something along the lines of 'before the gaze', with the gaze in question equally able to belong to the seer or to the seen.[17] Françoise Frontisi-Ducroux provides further information about ancient understandings of the mask, noting that in antiquity masks were not considered to hide the face but rather abolished the performer's face and the individuality that lay underneath the mask.[18] The mask replaced one's identity with the incarnated theatrical character. A shift occurs, as Wiles identifies, from a negative act of concealment to a positive act of becoming.[19] The duality embodied in the ancient mask, which affected both the seer and the seen, is a useful frame for reconceptualising Punchdrunk's mask, as it allows us to see the opposing pulls towards performativity and passivity as a continuum rather than as competing interpretations. It also provides a historical link to discussions about how audience engagement in Punchdrunk's masked performances differs to that in other immersive experiences. In her much-cited *Contemporary Theatre Review* intervention, Sophie Nield draws attention to the problems surrounding the 'rise

---

[16] Wyles (2011: 14).
[17] Wiles (2007: 1).
[18] Frontisi-Ducroux (1995: 40).
[19] Wiles (2007: 1).

of the Character named Spectator' in immersive theatre, where the audience might be addressed by actors. She notes how the schism between, for example, the performers' period dress and the audience's everyday clothing can lead to audience discomfort and uncertainty surrounding their role within the fictive world of the performance.[20] The positive psychological effects of the ancient mask that Frontisi-Ducroux and Wiles identify, which transforms the psyche or consciousness of its wearer, allows one to conceptualise the mask as a device which works towards negating embarrassment by neutralising discrepancies between the identity of the wearer and the socio-cultural world of the performance.[21] The ancient lens builds upon anecdotal evidence about Punchdrunk's mask emboldening audiences to exercise navigational and haptic agency. Wiles further notes that masks in ancient Greece may have imposed a degree of sensory deprivation and led to 'experiential immersion'; applying this argument to Punchdrunk's masks, which cover the mouth and nose and shape the gaze, gives the argument that Punchdrunk's masks encourage a deeper form of immersion than is necessarily available in other immersive experiences a historical connection.[22] It is not my intention to claim that Punchdrunk's masks ensure that the audience experience is categorically distinct in Punchdrunk masked shows as opposed to other forms of participatory performance, or to argue that they guarantee a particular depth of audience immersion. Rather, my point is that just as scholarship sees the mask in ancient Greece as working, in theory, to remove and replace one's identity and encourage experiential immersion, so too do masks in Punchdrunk's work hold this potential. The questions surrounding the function of masks are shared across theatrical practice from ancient Greece through to Punchdrunk's performances. The synergy between debates about masks in both contexts contextualises Punchdrunk's practice and reveals another connection between their work and antiquity.

The House of Oedipus is also significant for the decisive role it played in helping Barrett conceptualise his audience as a tragic chorus. There are obvious parallels between Punchdrunk's audience and the Greek tragic chorus, with both collectives being a masked mass who are spectators to the main narrative but usually unable to intervene within it, although

---

[20] Nield (2008).
[21] Wiles (2007: 285, 289).
[22] Wiles (2007: 289).

there are nevertheless distinct differences including the fact that the tragic chorus is a singing and dancing collective that injects its own narrative into the performance through the content detailed in their choral odes. Barrett's envisioning of the audience, clad in their choric-style masks, as chorus in *The House of Oedipus* enabled him to remove the chorus from the source texts. Barrett's decision informed his understanding of the audience's role in all future masked performances; in a 2013 post-show question and answer session for *The Drowned Man*, Barrett argued that his audience is always 'sort of like a modern-day Greek chorus. They're judging, they're the Furies, they're watching, they're casting their vote'.[23] Barrett's invocation of the Furies, which I take to refer specifically to the chorus in Aeschylus' *Eumenides*, is slightly confused, as although the Furies are present at Orestes' trial, it is Athena and a group of Athenians, and not the Furies, who vote for his fate. Barrett's conflation of the pursuing Furies and the jury of Athenians is, however, useful for clarifying the audience's role in Punchdrunk's theatre, as spectators must seek out performers just as the Furies search for Orestes, while simultaneously weighing up their options and deciding whether to stay with and invest in one character, or to abandon pursuit of a character in favour of exploring another dimension of the performance.

The audience's pursuing function has led Barrett to conceptualise the entity in a further separate manner, which is equally as illuminating as to the centrality of ancient tragedy in Barrett's thinking. This second entity is drawn from the dramatis personae of *Oedipus at Colonus*, and specifically refers to Oedipus' communication to the Athenian King Theseus of his final resting place. Oedipus tells Theseus, in a quotation that Barrett cited in the critical commentary to his final undergraduate project, that 'These things are mysteries, not to be explained; but you will understand when you get there, alone' [1526–7].[24] Punchdrunk went on to use the quotation as their company slogan during their first period of work, and again as a portal to their website from 2015 to 2020.[25] Barrett noted that Oedipus' story 'underscores the awe and wonder that is at the centre of Punchdrunk's mission', with Theseus's self-discovery of Oedipus' secret

---

[23] Price (2014).
[24] Machon and Punchdrunk (2019: 292).
[25] See Beard (2011: 21) and Machon and Punchdrunk (2019: 292).

tomb mirroring the audience's self-discovery of the secrets of a Punchdrunk performance.[26] Barrett's two attempts at theorising the role of the audience in Punchdrunk's masked work have therefore been conducted with reference to the two primary entities in Greek tragedy, namely the chorus and the protagonist. Clearly, just as *The House of Oedipus* was a formative production in the development of Punchdrunk's signature style, so too was Greek tragedy in general central to Barrett's thinking.

It was not until 2017 that Punchdrunk returned to Greek literature as a source text for a public-facing production. In the time between *The House of Oedipus* and 2017 the company took steps towards professionalising. They then spent a major period (2008–2015), termed 'Act Two' in their encyclopaedia, improving and perfecting their formula for performance. Other authors, notably Shakespeare, provided more recurrent source material during this 'bedding in' period. However, there is more to the company's history that their record of productions implies, and the company came close to mounting a production that again drew upon Greek tragedy in 2010 at the old Central St Martins campus in Southampton Row, Holborn, titled *The Fates and the Furies*. Like *The Burnt City*, *The Fates and the Furies* would have told the story of the fall of Troy across two buildings, albeit with different characters and collision sources than would ultimately be drawn upon for their 2022 production.[27] Although the tragic source texts were the same as in *The Burnt City*, the production was envisaged very differently, with a planned fifty characters performing across three hundred rooms as well as a stronger science fiction collision dimension. The company went as far as moving into the site and commencing work for the production and were mere weeks away from publicly launching the show before negotiations with the building collapsed and the production was aborted. If *The Fates and the Furies* had gone ahead, then the history of classical literature within Punchdrunk's œuvre would deviate from a history of experimentation and innovation to one which permeated all stages of the company's history, including their period of professionalising and their growth in international reputation. As it stands, however, Greek literature

---

[26] Barrett, quoted in Machon and Punchdrunk (2019: 292).

[27] For more information on *The Fates and the Furies*, see Anna James' and Tom Waite's interviews with Barrett and Doyle, in James (2022) and Waite (2022) respectively.

next featured when the company returned to an objective of innovation and experimentation post-2015.

In 2017, the company turned to ancient Greece on two separate occasions, namely for their immersive reimagining of Aeschylus' lost Greek tragedy *Kabeiroi*, and for their enrichment project for Key Stage 2 school children based upon Hercules' labours, titled *The Oracles*.[28] *Kabeiroi* was Punchdrunk's first UK production for adults since their major masked show *The Drowned Man* (2013–2014) and was, like *The Burnt City*, a production with which I had some involvement, in this case as academic advisor. It represented a change of direction for the company, whereby instead of making performances in intricately designed, labyrinthine spaces for audiences numbering into their hundreds, Punchdrunk instead developed a geo-locative four-to-six-hour durational experience that took place on the streets of London for just two (unmasked) audience members at a time. Although the company experimented with promenade, participatory performances for small audience numbers on other occasions, such as *The Borough* (2013), *Kabeiroi* was a different beast in scale and objective. The production ran from 26 September to 5 November 2017. Several pairs of audience members experienced the production each day, running to a total of 864 spectators across the course of the run. Demand for tickets far surpassed capacity, and tickets could only be bought through a lottery system due to exponential demand. In a departure from Punchdrunk's usual decision to orient their work around a recognisable source text, where a percentage of their audience might be assumed to have some basic knowledge of the plot of the text around which to scaffold their experience, here Punchdrunk chose Aeschylus' rather obscure fragmentary tragedy *Kabeiroi*.

Very little is known about Aeschylus' *Kabeiroi*, including when it was staged, the plot of the tragedy, and the companion plays which accompanied *Kabeiroi* as part of Aeschylus' entry to the annual City Dionysia. Athenaeus records that the play featured Jason and the Argonauts, and that Aeschylus' depiction of them included the first instance of drunkenness on the tragic stage [10.428f], while a scholion to *Pythian 4* notes that the drama contained a full catalogue of the Argonauts.[29] The

---

[28] I use the Latinised spelling Hercules in keeping with Punchdrunk's publicity for the production. See, for example, *The Oracles* Final Report in Punchdrunk Enrichment (2018).

[29] See $\sum$ Pindar, *Pythian* 4.303b.

Kabeiroi deities featured as the play's chorus, who on the basis of wider mythology we can assume at some point initiated Jason and the Argonauts into their mystery religion.[30] Outside of this anecdotal information, three fragments of the play survive.[31] The first involves a protagonist stating 'but I do not make you an omen of my journey' [TrGF 3 F95]. The second involves the chorus promising 'that there shall never be a dearth of jars, neither of wine nor water, in this wealthy home' [TrGF 3 F96], while the final fragment sees the chorus, according to Plutarch, 'playfully threatening' to make the house run short of vinegar [TrGF 3 F97].[32] The rhetoric surrounding Punchdrunk's marketing of the production implied that they would be remounting a lost play, but in reality the company did not even remount what is known of the tragedy but rather capitalised upon the ambiguity inherent in the lost text to blur the boundaries between the fictive and the real in an entirely original immersive experience.

Punchdrunk's *Kabeiroi* (Fig. 2.2) did not seek to reconstruct Aeschylus' lost tragedy but rather was a new and innovative performance which preserved the sense of lacunae contained in the surviving material. The company only engaged with one of the three surviving fragments explicitly; furthermore, their engagement with the line in question ('but I do not treat you as an omen of my journey') occurred in the publicity for the performance rather than in the show's content.[33] The production's form, however, had a tripartite structure which paralleled the number of surviving fragments. These three sections took the form of a smartphone-led audio tour, a scavenger-hunt-style adventure done as a pair, and then one done as an individual. The experience saw audiences navigate from Bloomsbury to Tottenham Hale, on foot and via the London underground, and complete task-based activities at the British Museum, a YMCA, a storage facility, and the Grange Langham hotel. A final scene at Punchdrunk's then headquarters in Tottenham Hale saw the audience members, who had been cast as Jason throughout, ultimately reach safety and become initiated into the mysterious Kabeiroi cult.

---

[30] The Argonauts are initiated into the Cult of the Kabeiroi in both Apollonius of Rhodes [1.915–21] and Valerius Flaccus [2.432–42].

[31] See Cole (2021) for an outline of what we know about Aeschylus' *Kabeiroi*.

[32] Sommerstein (2009: 109).

[33] Punchdrunk Enrichment (2023a).

Fig. 2.2 Punchdrunk's *Kabeiroi* (2017). Image credit: Stephen Dobbie

Punchdrunk took a different approach to Greek tragedy in *Kabeiroi* from *The House of Oedipus*. In *Kabeiroi*, none of the (admittedly limited) text was staged, barely any actors were present, there was next to no installation to engage with, no masks were worn, and the freedom for the audience to explore whatever part of the performance they wished, at whatever pace they liked, was replaced with a task-based experience. The audience was required to make a specific journey, from and to fixed locations, in a timeframe that was simultaneously elastic but also pressured, from a narrative perspective due to the sense of needing to escape pursuing forces and from a practical perspective due to the company's need for each audience pair to complete the experience in the same order in which they began. Each individual was no longer a voyeuristic observer but rather was the protagonist of the experience. The function of the ancient text was not as a semantic scaffold for the audience to pin their experience upon but rather as something that bestowed a sense of mystery upon the production, both in terms of the form of the fragments and in their content regarding initiation into an ancient mystery religion. These differences were precisely what makes *Kabeiroi* so noteworthy; just as *The House of Oedipus* played a decisive role in shaping the mask style, loop format, and gestural language of Punchdrunk's first two decades of work, so too did *Kabeiroi* prove crucial in shaping the modes of performance towards which Punchdrunk would increasingly venture. Barrett commented, for example, upon his growing interest in using technology to augment immersive experience is a 2023 interview, where he discussed his desire to have a second, smaller, more technology-based show in London run parallel to *The Burnt City*.[34] Meanwhile, Punchdrunk's continued interest in geo-locative modes of experience was reflected in their 2020 announcement of a partnership with Silicon Valley software developers Niantic to create immersive Augmented Reality theatre experiences.[35] Future Punchdrunk work that incorporates geo-locative technology can be thought of as a continuation of the experimentation conducted through *Kabeiroi*.

Kabeiroi's significance lies in its attempt to experiment with a different form of audience agency. The limitations seen in Punchdrunk's large-scale works, where some argue that the mask functions as a mobile fourth wall, were removed in *Kabeiroi*. Instead, the audience as protagonist was central to the narrative, and the place-based, game-infused interactive experience veered towards the practice of other company's such as Coney, with Punchdrunk's continued employment of a classic (albeit fragmentary) source text their differentiating feature. The blurring of the world of the performance with everyday reality fostered what Punchdrunk term a 'deeper' form of immersion, where it was difficult to tell who was a planted performer and who was a bystander, and which witnessed events were choreographed versus natural occurrences.[36] The deepening of immersion had the potential to heighten the phenomenological impact of the performance, and to increase audience adrenaline. At the same time, however, the audience's path through the world of the performance was broadly set: there were right and wrong navigational turns that could be made, and incorrect choices could necessitate Punchdrunk intervening into the audience experience to reorient audience-participants.[37] Similarly, the narrative arc that each audience member experienced was

---

[34] Parker (2023).

[35] Statt (2020).

[36] Machon and Punchdrunk (2019: 12).

[37] It is possible to argue that any re-routing of audience in *Kabeiroi* extended standard practice from Punchdrunk's masked productions, where stewards in black masks guard no-access passages and occasionally intervene to guide audience behaviour. On the stewards as devices which break audience immersion and curtail agency, see Luckhurst (2017).

singular and fixed, unless a spectator defied invitations or instructions.[38] As such, *Kabeiroi* did not grant full agency to its audience, but rather a different form of agency to that of Punchdrunk's masked performances.

Although *The House of Oedipus* and *Kabeiroi* are both cross-referenced with 'failure' in Punchdrunk's encyclopaedia, as their value for Barrett and the company was in the lessons they taught rather than in their critical success, in both instances ancient literature served as the medium for experimentation that would shape the company's next phase of work. The same can be said for the company's turn to the classics for their enrichment work with primary school children in *The Oracles*.

The Punchdrunk Enrichment arm of the company commenced in 2008 with the primary school project *Under the Eiderdown*. Today, Punchdrunk Enrichment are an independent charity separate to Punchdrunk themselves, but at the time of *The Oracles*, the Enrichment activities were still part of the wider Punchdrunk organisation. Enrichment projects initially attempted to 'translate the awe and wonder generated in the masked events into a primary school setting', before later expanding this focus to a broader range of community settings such as care homes.[39] The projects involve the same standard of design and installation as Punchdrunk's work for adults, but follow an applied theatre practice and ideology and operate on more durational time scales, with the seeds of each project planted in, for example, school curricula weeks before a Punchdrunk experience appears in situ.[40] Since *Under the Eiderdown*, Punchdrunk Enrichment has delivered over twenty-two projects for over 100,000 participants. *The Oracles*, developed in 2017, was project number twenty-one and was a cross-platform storytelling experience aligned with the Key Stage 2 maths curriculum.

The Oracles was directed by Punchdrunk Creative Associate Matthew Blake and was created in partnership with Google's Creative Lab. It is significant to Punchdrunk's history as it involved the piloting of a series of technologies with the intention of, if the pilot was successful, scaling these technologies for Punchdrunk's public-facing work.[41]

---

[38] For an example of a spectator going rogue in *Kabeiroi*, see Saville (2017). See Myers (forthcoming) for a comparative example in the Odyssey-inspired *Nobody's Home*.

[39] Machon and Punchdrunk (2019: 282).

[40] See Machon and Punchdrunk (2019: 96).

[41] See Temperton (2017) and Machon and Punchdrunk (2019: 213).

The Oracles commenced in Haringey classrooms, where an actor, performing as a game designer, appeared before students to test a new game in class. The game featured Hercules, here mayor of the village Fallow Cross, and the witch Circe, who was laying siege to the village. At the end of the game, the students received a call for help from the village, following which (at a later date) they were taken on an excursion to Punchdrunk's site in Tottenham Hale where Fallow Cross came to life. At Fallow Cross, the students became the game's protagonists and were tasked with completing locked-room-style maths-based challenges with the assistance of a group of villages known as 'The Oracles'. The locked-room challenges involved the students uncovering the twelve labours of Hercules and piecing together his shield to protect the village.[42] The students carried lanterns, which were equipped with hidden positional tracking technology and operated as 'magic touch' devices which enabled them to, for example, open locked doors once they had successfully completed an activity; Peter Higgin summarised that they allowed participants 'to trigger a theatrical cue with a touch of your hand'.[43] The lanterns worked by sending a signal through the body which interacted with a sensor-based installation. The technology ensured that it was the participant's touch that was central to the experience, rather than the lantern needing to be swiped against an object. Across seven episodes (three in-person at Fallow Cross, three classroom sessions, and a final culminating video), the two platforms mutually developed based upon player interactions, with objects found in Fallow Cross, for example, later appearing in the game. Punchdrunk's augmenting of the physical space with the digital and vice versa piloted ideas surrounding connected, visceral and virtual forms of storytelling and the way technology assists the feedback loop between worlds in cross-platform mediums.

The underpinning classical material in *The Oracles* held a different function to the tragic source texts behind *The House of Oedipus* and *Kabeiroi*. Although Hercules' labours are recounted in numerous ancient literary sources, such as the *Bibliotheca* of Apollodorus, Punchdrunk did not adapt these texts but worked from secondary sources. *The Oracles* is consequently a reception of classical myth in general, rather than Greek literature specifically. Furthermore, it received Greek myth in a loose,

---

[42] Punchdrunk Enrichment (2023b).

[43] Higgin, quoted in Punchdrunk Enrichment (2018: 12). See also Temperton (2017).

rather than an engaged sense. The overall experience involved an amalgamation of classical references and did not aim for mythological accuracy or consistency. Alongside using the names of Hercules and Circe as references, and the twelve labours as a structuring device, other mythological references peppered the experience including a challenge requiring the children to navigate through a 'Forest of Cerberus', and a final message of thanks acknowledging the children's 'epic herculean journey'.[44] In *The Oracles*, the classical material did not unlock anything for Punchdrunk in terms of performance possibilities, and nor does the experience transform our understanding of the classical material. Yet it is still noteworthy that Punchdrunk turned to antiquity, even if only as a background reference for the students, when experimenting with pioneering cross-platform methodologies and technological innovation. *The Oracles* further showcases the centrality of the ancient world to Punchdrunk's research and development process, and to the company's history, and is an indication of the potential of the ancient world for creating different forms of immersive experiences.

Although *The Oracles* marks Punchdrunk's final classical reception prior to their twenty-twenties offering, Maxine Doyle's *Deo* for the Martha Graham Dance Company is a further production of relevance to my overview (Fig. 2.3). Doyle is Punchdrunk's choreographer, associate director, and the co-director of all masked productions from *Sleep No More* (2003) onwards, up to and including *The Burnt City*. She also works as an independent choreographer. *Deo* was a collaboration between Doyle and American dancer and choreographer Bobbi Jene Smith, which premièred in 2019 at the Joyce Theatre in New York. The piece was based upon the myth of Demeter and Persephone, and in particular Demeter's search for her daughter after Persephone's abduction by Hades as depicted in the *Homeric Hymn to Demeter*. *Deo* was not a research and development exercise for *The Burnt City* but rather an entirely standalone work, created in a movement vocabulary to suit the Graham company. However, the *Homeric Hymn* was in the background of *The Burnt City* (and was actively drawn upon during the production's development), as *The Burnt City* was set in the Underworld and featured both Hades and Persephone as characters. Doyle's engagement with antiquity in *Deo* is thus of direct relevance to the history of Punchdrunk's work, as it shaped

---

[44] Punchdrunk Enrichment (2018: 18–19).

the thinking of *The Burnt City*'s choreographer and co-director in the lead up to the production.

Deo was a twenty-minute dance piece for an ensemble of eight women. It was commissioned as part of the Graham Company EVE project, which commemorated the centenary of the nineteenth amendment giving women in the United States the right to vote. The EVE project focused on female progress and pressing conversations about gender and power. Doyle used *Deo* to explore the *Homeric Hymn* themes of separation, rage, and grief as part of the EVE project.[45] The dance did not tell the narrative of the *Hymn* but was structured around a series of episodes exploring, for example, the individual stolen Persephone and the searching Demeter, and the ritual prayers and mourning of the collective group of women hoping for mother and daughter's reunion. Doyle noted that she turned the myth into dance through 'a process that is about using dramatic tone and physical tensions in the body to tell stories and express emotion', and in a telling direction to her dancers was quoted as interrogating 'if you could try dancing your feet through the floor to try and bring Persephone back up, what would that dance be?'.[46] Lesley Flanigan composed an experimental electronic score for the work, which varied between eerie and ritual-like music to overwhelming and ominous bass-heavy soundscapes. Golden-toned lighting created the impression of the women dancing in candlelight and threw heavy shadows across the stage. Translucent costumes, in the form of simple tulle tunic dresses with a geometric pattern were at once sensual and feminine, while also amplifying the strength and muscularity of the dancers. The dresses were simultaneously classical and modern, with the tunic design and geometric pattern recalling ancient iconography while the fabric and the design inspiration, namely Levi's 'Heirloom Dress' from their 2018 *Made and Crafted* collection, provided a decidedly contemporary edge.[47]

Unlike Punchdrunk's engagements with antiquity, which innovated with audience engagement and projected the company into new terrain, *Deo* looked back towards the history of modernist dance engagements with antiquity and served to sharpen Doyle's focus on feminism and the classics. Doyle's research process and the creative development for *Deo*

---

[45] Grills (2019) and Kourlas (2019).

[46] Doyle, quoted in Kourlas (2019) and in Boguszewski (2019).

[47] Martha Graham Dance Company (2020).

Fig. 2.3 Martha Graham Dance Company in *Deo*. Choreography by Maxine Doyle and Bobbi Jene Smith. Image credit: Brian Pollock. Courtesy of the Martha Graham Resources

unlocked a focus on the mother–daughter relationship of Persephone and Demeter, and on the psychology of Persephone in the Underworld. Her work in *Deo* coloured the character treatments and choreography employed in *The Burnt City* and represents a further instance of the classics being central to the development not only of Punchdrunk as a company, but to the corpus of the individual creatives that constitute Punchdrunk as well.

Punchdrunk's three historic engagements with antiquity resulted in pioneering immersive experiences that were formative to the company's development. *The House of Oedipus* consolidated the loop structure of Punchdrunk's large-scale masked work and was decisive in shaping the style of audience mask and performance venue for which Punchdrunk would later become known. *Kabeiroi* was an experimental research and development exercise that took the company in a new direction. It explored both the possibility of utilising fragmentary Greek tragedy for immersive experience, and the ability to 'deepen' audience immersion by creating a durational experience which blurred the lines between performance and reality. *The Oracles* experimented with using Greek myth for cross-platform immersive experiences and in technologically enhanced performance spaces. During this time Maxine Doyle was also delving into the classics for *Deo* and exploring the potential to translate the Demeter and Persephone myth into dance. It is no surprise, therefore, that at the start of the twenty-twenties, when the company was again embarking upon a new direction of work, that Punchdrunk turned to Greek literature again. The company's current phase of work aims to bookend their large-scale masked work and to launch the company in a new direction, and they have turned to Greek literature for their first major output of this cycle. My subsequent chapters highlight the contours of Punchdrunk's engagement with classical literature in this next stage of the company's history.

Works Cited

Beard, Mary. 2011. Live Classics, or, "What's the Use of Aeschylus in Darfur?". In *The Public Value of the Humanities*, ed. Jonathan Bate, 17–29. London: Bloomsbury.

Biggin, Rose. 2017. *Immersive Theatre and Audience Experience: Space, Game and Story in the Work of Punchdrunk*. Cham: Palgrave Macmillan.

Boguszewski, Theo. 2019. Day in the Life of NEW@Graham: "Deo" by Maxine Doyle and Bobbi Jene Smith. *The Dance Enthusiast*, March 29. https://www.dance-enthusiast.com/features/day-in-the-life/view/NEW-Graham-Deo-Maxine-Doyle-Bobbi-Jene-Smith. Accessed 5 June 2020.

Cole, Emma. 2021. Fragments, Immersivity, and Reception: Punchdrunk on Aeschylus' *Kabeiroi*. *International Journal of the Classical Tradition* 28: 510–525. https://doi.org/10.1007/s12138-020-00578-9.

Frontisi-Ducroux, Françoise. 1995. *Du Masque Au Visage: Aspects de L'Identité en Grèce Ancienne*. Paris: Flammarion.

Gordon, Collette. 2012. Touching the Spectator: Intimacy, Immersion, and the Theater of the Velvet Rope. *The Journal of Shakespeare and Appropriation* 7: 2: 1–12. https://borrowers-ojs-azsu.tdl.org/borrowers/article/view/109/216. Accessed 2 March 2023.

Grills, Kelsey. 2019. Bobbi Jene Smith and Maxine Doyle Talk Instinct and Trust in Collaboration. *Dance Magazine*, January 8. https://www.dancemagazine.com/smith-and-doyle-2625359697.html?rebelltitem=1#rebelltitem1. Accessed 5 June 2020.

James, Anna. 2022. Punchdrunk's Felix Barrett and Maxine Doyle: "This Place is on a Scale that is Truly Mythic". *The Stage*, April 7. https://www.thestage.co.uk/long-reads/punchdrunks-felix-barrett-and-maxine-doyle-this-place-is-on-a-scale-that-is-truly-mythic-the-burnt-city. Accessed 12 May 2022.

Kourlas, Gia. 2019. Odysseys Into Martha Graham World, One Dramatic, the Other Abstract. *The New York Times*, April 2. https://www.nytimes.com/2019/04/02/arts/dance/martha-graham-pam-tanowitz-maxine-doyle.html. Accessed 5 June 2020.

Luckhurst, Mary. 2017. Punchdrunk, the Immersive and Gothic Tourism. *About Performance* 14–15: 7–18.

Machon, Josephine, and Punchdrunk. 2019. *The Punchdrunk Encyclopaedia*. London and New York: Routledge.

Martha Graham Dance Company. 2020. Deo. *Martha Graham Dance Company*. https://marthagraham.org/portfolio-items/deo/?portfolioCats=21%2C18%2C20. Accessed 5 June 2020.

Myers, Misha. Forthcoming. The Voice of Gods in Your Ear: Becoming the Avatar in Immersive Performance. In *Experiencing Immersion in Antiquity and Modernity: From Narrative to Virtual Reality*, ed. Emma Cole. London: Bloomsbury.

Nield, Sophie. 2008. The Rise of the Character named Spectator. *Contemporary Theatre Review* 18: 4: 531–535. https://doi.org/10.1080/10486800802492855.

Parker, Robin. 2023. How Porsche Got Playful with its Money-can't-buy Punchdrunk Experience. *Robb Report*, May 13. https://robbreport.co.uk/motors/cars/porsche-gets-playful-with-its-money-cant-buy-punchdrunk-experience-1234698810/. Accessed 25 July 2023.

Price, Ludi. 2014. Excerpts from "The Drowned Man" Pre-show Talk, December 1st 2013: Meet the Directors. *The Fan LIS Scholar*. https://blogs.city.ac.uk/ludiprice/2014/04/25/excerpts-from-the-drowned-man-pre-show-talk-december-1st-2013-meet-the-directors/. Accessed 2 March 2023.

Punchdrunk Enrichment. 2018. *The Oracles Final Report: Mapping the Affect and Effects of Immersive Play in Key Stage 2*. https://www.punchdrunkenrichment.org.uk/content/uploads/2019/10/The-Oracles-Resource-Pack.pdf. Accessed 2 March 2023.

———2023a. Kabeiroi. *Punchdrunk Enrichment*. https://www.punchdrunkenrichment.org.uk/project/kabeiroi/. Accessed 2 March 2023.

———2023b. The Oracles. *Punchdrunk Enrichment*. https://www.punchdrunkenrichment.org.uk/project/the-oracles/. Accessed 2 March 2023.

Saville, Alice. 2017. Kabeiroi: A Post Mortem. *Exeunt Magazine*, November 6. http://exeuntmagazine.com/features/kabeiroi-post-mortem/. Accessed 5 June 2020.

Shearing, David. 2015. Intimacy, Immersion and the Desire to Touch: The Voyeur Within. In *Theatre as Voyeurism: The Pleasures of Watching*, ed. George Rodosthenous, 71–87. Hampshire and New York: Palgrave Macmillan.
Sommerstein, Alan. 2009. *Aeschylus: Fragments*. Cambridge, Massachusetts, and London: Harvard University Press.
Statt, Nick. 2020. Niantic Partners with Sleep No More Creator to Build Immersive AR Theater Experiences. *The Verge*, June 30. https://www.theverge.com/2020/6/30/21307285/niantic-punchdrunk-ar-immersive-theater-sleep-no-more-pokemon-go. Accessed 16 December 2022.
Temperton, James. 2017. Punchdrunk's Next Great Act. *Wired*, December 22. https://www.wired.co.uk/article/punchdrunk-kabeiroi-felix-barrett-interview-sleep-no-more-2018. Accessed 5 June 2020.
Waite, Thom. 2022. Inside Punchdrunk's Radical Immersive Theatre Show, The Burnt City. *Dazed*, March 21. https://www.dazeddigital.com/life-culture/article/55727/1/inside-punchdrunks-monumental-immersive-theatre-show-the-burnt-city. Accessed 12 July 2022.
White, Gareth. 2009. Odd Anonymized Needs: Punchdrunk's Masked Spectator. In *Modes of Spectating*, eds. Alison Oddey and Christine White, 219–229. Bristol and Chicago: Intellect.
Wiles, David. 2007. *Mask and Performance in Greek Tragedy: From Ancient Festival to Modern Experimentation*. Cambridge: Cambridge University Press.
Wyles, Rosie. 2011. *Costume in Greek Tragedy*. London: Bloomsbury.

CHAPTER 3

The Burnt City in Development: Rehearsal as Mythopoiesis

Punchdrunk planned to open *The Burnt City* in November 2020. The production was cast, the budgets drafted, and the design well underway. In the week commencing 13 January 2020, I joined the company for the first of six weeks of Research and Development (R&D) in their new space in Woolwich, South-East London, in what would ultimately become the home for *The Burnt City* and a new, high-spec office space for Punchdrunk. In 2022, journalist Dominic Maxwell described Punchdrunk's new, glass-walled meeting room, complete with a skylight and wood-panelled flooring, as akin to 'a Silicon Valley HQ, or a starter-level Bond-villain secret base', but in January 2020 we were working in the unrenovated building with the bare minimum of butchers paper, markers, and a single electric heater.[1] The creative team was full of energy and optimism, as Punchdrunk geared up to launch not only *The Burnt City* but also their first television show, *The Third Day*.[2] On 14 January 2020, at the first Woolwich production meeting, Punchdrunk Artistic Director

---

[1] Maxwell (2022).

[2] *The Third Day* was co-created by Dennis Kelley and Felix Barrett and produced in partnership with Plan B Entertainment. The show starred Jude Law and Naomi Harris. The theatrical broadcast component of the show ('Autumn') was co-directed by Barrett and Marc Munden and was nominated for a BAFTA. On the TV show, see Punchdrunk (2023) and on how the coronavirus pandemic impacted the planned Punchdrunk live-event component, see O'Mahony (2022).

© The Author(s), under exclusive license to Springer Nature Switzerland AG 2024
E. Cole, *Punchdrunk on the Classics*,
https://doi.org/10.1007/978-3-031-43067-1_3

and *The Burnt City* co-director Felix Barrett commented to everyone that it felt as if they had 'gone into real show mode', following which the communications team presented a year-long strategy encompassing key messages, graphic design direction, and marketing opportunities. Yet just over two weeks later, on 31 January 2020, the first case of COVID-19 was reported in the UK, and by the end of February there had been twenty-three positive diagnoses. In early March, we were articulating the growing threat within the R&D rooms, booking grocery orders on our phones due to the increasingly spartan appearance of supermarket shelves and visiting the pharmacy to buy hand sanitiser and children's paracetamol during our lunch breaks. By the final week of the R&D period, the impact of the pandemic was professional, rather than personal. Punchdrunk were now one month away from announcing the show to the press and commencing ticket sales, yet their other projects were dropping like flies; *Sleep No More* Shanghai had temporarily closed, and *Sleep No More* New York was being adapted and downsized.[3] Fundraising meetings were cancelled as potential *Burnt City* sponsors started to work from home. The launch timeline was postponed, and the final day of in-person creative development was cancelled. Less than a week later, on Friday 20 March, schools closed indefinitely. As rumours of a London-wide lockdown began to circulate, it became obvious that the set construction and performance schedule could not go ahead as planned, and on the evening of Wednesday 8 April the producers announced a formal delay.

This chapter begins to tell the story of the research, development, and rehearsal phase of *The Burnt City*. It consists of a critically grounded rehearsal study based upon a Spectator-Participation-as-Research methodology and features thick descriptions of key moments of the development

---

[3] *Sleep No More* New York would eventually close until 14 February 2022; on the show's hibernation, see Soloski (2022). The Shanghai production would reopen in 2020 with a reduced capacity, only to close again for a subsequent lockdown and reopen in mid-2022. Although *The Burnt City* had not yet been announced, meaning the pandemic's impact upon the production was not documented within the press, one can trace the difficulties that the period placed upon other, non-Punchdrunk projects planned for late 2020 in the press coverage of, for example, Andrew Lloyd Webber's *Cinderella*, which was due to open in London's West End in August 2020. *Cinderella* was initially delayed until October 2020, and then further delayed until July 2021. The July opening was then postponed by a further month. The performance opened in August 2021, but closed again between December 2021 and February 2022. On the first delay, see Snow (2020), and on the 2021 delays, see Bahr (2021) and Lewis (2022).

process up until and including the commencement of preview performances. The rehearsal study is a theorised, after-the-fact analysis. On one occasion, I include unedited field notes, which are set out as a stand-alone italicised quotation. My approach enables a tacking back and forth between broad brushstroke, big-picture information about how *The Burnt City* was created, and close-up, illustrative examples of individual moments of rehearsal to showcase Punchdrunk's specific approach to transforming and supplementing Greek literature to create an immersive experience. The chapter is not intended to be a how-to guide to developing an immersive theatre production, and nor is it an attempt to offer a totalising rehearsal study; indeed, as will become clear within the chapter, an exhaustive record of Punchdrunk's process by a lone ethnographer is impossible due to the company's approach to creating immersive theatre. Rather, the chapter zooms in to key moments, in chronological order, of the R&D period and rehearsal process. My approach has two aims. Firstly, to offer instructive instances for beginning to think through how the classics can be transformed into immersive experiences, and secondly, to showcase some of the practical constraints, such as the pandemic-induced delay detailed in the opening of this chapter, that governed the work's creative development and shaped decisions that might more traditionally be considered through the lens of artistic vision or intentionality. The impact of the coronavirus pandemic upon the creation of *The Burnt City* is representative of how practical considerations shape artistic output; one of the central claims of this book is that, when it comes to classical performance receptions, process informs product and is an understudied component of the field. At the conclusion of the chapter, I suggest that Punchdrunk's process of braiding together multiple strands of material in the R&D phase and the rehearsal period to create *The Burnt City* equated to a form of contemporary mythopoiesis, or mythmaking.[4] *The Burnt City* was not a form of mythic revisionism, but involved the creation of a new, original mythic universe. The range of intertexts woven into *The Burnt City* resulted in a work of such complexity that the final production became its own megatext, featuring interconnecting, vast narratives and facilitating (or having the potential to facilitate) the type of fandom associated with other forms of contemporary mythopoiesis. *The Burnt City* consequently treads a unique line within classical performance

[4] I am indebted to Vanda Zajko's article on Neil Gaiman's work as a form of contemporary mythopoiesis in helping me to develop this idea. See Zajko (2020).

reception and is both a reception of ancient tragedy and an example of contemporary mythopoiesis.

Origins of *The Burnt City*

I arrived at Punchdrunk's Tottenham Hale offices on 22 July 2019 for a full day of creative meetings with a series of key Punchdrunk staff members, including designers Livi Vaughan and Beatrice Minns, director Felix Barrett, and associate directors Kath Duggan and Elgiva Field.[5] The project we were discussing did not yet have a fixed name, and the location in which it would première had only recently been confirmed as two Grade-II listed former munitions factories in Woolwich's Royal Arsenal, Greater London. Nevertheless, two things were certain: the show would be Punchdrunk's long-awaited next major masked production, and it would use Aeschylus' *Agamemnon* and Euripides' *Hecuba* as its source texts.[6]

The walls of our meeting room were littered with blu-tacked images. Underneath a sign that read 'finale' were two A4 printouts of the right-hand panel from Hans Memling's triptych *The Last Judgement* (1471), which showed ghoulish souls of the damned descending to hell. Adjacent were a pair of photographs depicting a cluster of around a dozen bodies balanced upon and hanging off a vertical frame; the position of the bodies varied slightly across the two images, giving the impression that they were stills from a physical animation of Memling's painting. A copy of a similar painting, namely Dirk Bouts' 1470 *The Fall of the Damned*, would ultimately hang in Hades' office in the set of *The Burnt City*, and the finale would indeed seek to bring the painting to life, featuring near-naked bodies tumbling down the grand staircase from the mezzanine to the ground floor in one of the munitions factories that became home to the show. Rehearsal director Carl Harrison later described the action to the cast via emailed rehearsal notes as moving down the stairs while

---

[5] Field worked with Punchdrunk from 2014 to 2020 and was involved in *The Burnt City* R&D phases. The July 2019 meeting marked my first formal involvement with *The Burnt City* as dramaturg and embedded researcher; for more on my position within the creative process, see Chapter 1.

[6] Although this meeting represented my first formal involvement in *The Burnt City*, the concept of a masked production based upon select Trojan War tragedies, as discussed in my previous chapter, had been on the cards for close to a decade.

wanting to return to the top, which 'creates a good tension/torsion in the body - the two equal opposing forces resulting in a live stillness which is the image of the painting'. Elsewhere in the meeting room were clusters of printouts, including a photograph of a bombed train station in France from the First World War, and stills from the 1927 Fritz Lang film *Metropolis*.

Two of the other walls were dominated by separate poster-size charts filled with colourful, curling post-it notes. The first featured a column of room names, with each name corresponding to a row of design features variously categorised as 'Greek', 'Metro/Future', 'Underworld', 'Bluebeard', 'Abstract', 'War', 'Purgatory', and 'Gods'. The second, I shortly learned, was the draft loop chart. The loop chart was the closest thing that *The Burnt City* had to a script and was a matrix for the performance that documented the cast of characters and what they were doing and with whom during each five-minute scene of the show. It got its name from the fact that the content of the table played, on a loop, three times per performance, offering the free-roaming promenade audience the opportunity to witness a cross-section of what different characters were doing in up to three different areas of the venue at the same moment of the loop. Before rehearsals commenced, so-called travelling characters (dance-heavy roles) had some of their arc plotted in the space so that the creative team knew when characters would come together and create audience hotspots, while the 'resident' characters, whose roles included less choreography, usually resided within a smaller portion of the set and may have had only a few key scenes sketched out.[7] *The Burnt City* choreographer and co-director Maxine Doyle previously explained the chart in *The Punchdrunk Encyclopaedia* as:

> a formula, a process of working out from the main characters, those that we have more information about in the text, plotting their journey through the space; writing treatments for their scenes, and then gradually filling out a grid. As the grid gets further away to the characters that live on the edge of the space, their stories are much lighter. When we begin the rehearsals on site we give characters loads of information, resources, stimuli and a

---

[7] For details on the travelling and resident characters in *The Burnt City*, see Chapter 1.

sheet of paper with scenes one to twelve on and a location and a starting point for the scene ... often the journey is mapped but the content isn't.[8]

On 22 July, *The Burnt City*'s loop chart was something of a skeleton. Twelve character names were written in pen, the majority of which came from the two source texts. Somewhere between a half dozen and a dozen additional names were written on post-it notes. Already, the chart marked the characters who would come together for the key moments from the source texts, such as the fall of Troy or the death of Agamemnon, and the blanks in between where Punchdrunk would exercise artistic licence. All scene markings were done on post-it notes, revealing that even this faint structure was entirely in flux. Ultimately, due to the length of the finale, the loop included eleven, rather than twelve scenes. Not even all the character names written in pen would appear in the final show.

My focus with the company in July was to help them begin to flesh out how the Underworld might relate to their vision for the show. Punchdrunk always set their source texts in an unexpected location and introduce what they term 'collision' sources to thicken the psychological and emotional complexity of the narrative world in which audiences become immersed. For *The Drowned Man* (2013–2014), they spliced a narrative drawn from Georg Büchner's nineteenth-century *Woyzeck* with elements from Nathanial West's *Day of the Locust* and set the resulting loop in the final days of the studio system, partially in a Hollywood film studio and partially on its desert outskirts. For *The Burnt City*, the collision source was a range of dystopic science-fiction texts including Lang's *Metropolis*, and the unique spin was that the show was set in the Underworld, although what this meant in practice and the degree to which it would be obvious to the audience was yet to be determined.[9] I had come prepared to talk to the team about Tartarus and the purgatorial tales, as

---

[8] Doyle, quoted in Machon and Punchdrunk (2019: 173). See also p. 76 for performer and rehearsal director Fernanda Prata's take on crafting the loop structure.

[9] The *Metropolis* intertext played a more substantial role in *The Fates and the Furies* version of the show, and indeed in the 2019 R&D period for *The Burnt City*, with a travelling character named Freder on the loop chart drawn from *Metropolis*. In the final production, the impact of *Metropolis* was primarily felt through the design of Troy, which contained Weimar-era features in, for example, the costume design (including hair and make-up), and the set design (including lighting fixtures and set dressings such as concert posters). No characters were explicitly drawn from *Metropolis*, although Polymestor worshipped Moloch, a bull-headed idol akin to a Minotaur who appears in Lang's film.

the designers were considering creating a tenement structure based upon Tartarus, with different apartments designed as if the homes of its mythological residents. Meanwhile, Barrett, Duggan, and Field were considering adapting the repetitive purgatorial acts of Sisyphus, Tantalus, and the like into army training exercises. Although the training exercises did not materialise in the final production, the tenement structure did, with rooms associated with the Titan Kronos, the 49 Danaids, Tantalus, Salmoneus, and Phlegyas all found in the set.

Although this was not my first experience of working with Punchdrunk, it was my first time embedded within the team in the knowledge exchange agreement that saw me work as dramaturg on *The Burnt City* while completing fieldwork for this book. Unlike my prior collaboration with Punchdrunk on *Kabeiroi*, where I was brought in as an academic consultant and sat outside of the process, here I was embedded within the team for designated windows during the R&D period. My experiences in July were in stark contrast to the solitary desk-based research I usually conduct. Silent agonising over turns of phrase and 'al desko' lunches were replaced with collaborative discussions and invitations to lunchtime bootcamps, but while at times exhilarating (and bewildering) I was well aware that this was not a workplace utopia but a creative approach to making high-stake decisions about the 'build' of the show, in terms of set construction (involving drafting building plans to fill two separate warehouses, covering approximately 100,000 square feet of performance space), design, character, and story arc, all of which fed into an ever-evolving budget. Decisions made in July reverberated long after the show's opening; Doyle commented in 2022, for example, that 'We have ridiculous discussions about how many square metres we can afford for an ash fall and how much our blood budget is because we spent it all on the building'.[10] The challenge in July was to ensure that performance possibilities stayed available before the company definitely knew what they needed, and to prioritise the concept and aesthetic. This early meeting, therefore, offered insight into how the jigsaw of an immersive world began to be assembled, with the foundational building blocks from source texts, performance space, and design plans providing the scaffold around which later decisions revolved.

---

[10] Doyle, quoted in James (2022).

The Burnt City in Development

By January 2020, when I arrived at Punchdrunk's new Woolwich headquarters in those early days of the pandemic for an intense period of R&D with Barrett and Doyle, the show's development had picked up apace. The building we were working in, Building 18, ultimately became offices and backstage for *The Burnt City*'s show operations team, with the room we were based in destined to be a performer dressing room. Downstairs we had direct accesses to Building 17, which still appeared as a light-filled, industrial warehouse but would become home of Greek Mycenae within the show. Next door, in Building 19, was a live construction site where the internal infrastructure of Troy, and the purpose-built link structure that would connect Greece to Troy and close down a Woolwich street, was slowly materialising. Our title was now confirmed as *The Burnt City*, inspired by Heinrich Schliemann's term for the settlement he excavated at Hisarlık, Turkey, in the 1870s and which he erroneously claimed was Homeric Troy.[11] Inspiration struck when Barrett visited the British Museum's *Troy: Myth and Reality* exhibition, which used the term regularly in the signage devoted to Schliemann's discoveries and which the creative team visited in a private viewing on 27 February.

Since I last visited Punchdrunk, building plans had progressed and construction had commenced. Barrett, Doyle, and I, along with the design team, were regularly permitted to enter the construction zone for site visits with Head of Production Andrea Salazar for time-limited periods (usually one hour) and while wearing full personal protective equipment (PPE) including hard-hats, gloves, and steel-capped boots. During these visits, Punchdrunk staff made quick-fire decisions to modify the architecture of the space and to decide which item from a wish-list they might prioritise for construction. On one site visit, for example, a small corridor was added (although then later removed) near where Polymestor's office would be to allow for windows looking down into Troy. The character list, while not complete, had expanded and the priority was now to give flesh to the characters by writing short biographies and adding as much detail to the loop chart as possible. The biographies were straightforward for those characters, such as Agamemnon or Hecuba, who

---

[11] On Schliemann's use of the term, see his 1880 publication about the excavations, and in particular Rudolph Virchow's preface to the volume, in which Virchow refers to the site as the 'Burnt City' five times. See Virchow (1880: ix–xvi).

were drawn directly from the tragedies, and more complex for those taken from collision sources or envisaged as a fusion of different roles, such as Neoptolemus, Patroclus, and the Watchmen, all of whom stood in for a suite of Greek soldiers from the source tragedies and wider Trojan War mythology. The discussion was still big picture, thinking about overall journey rather than at the level of specific action, but it had turned firmly towards narrative, character, and the question of abstraction.

Abstraction is signature to Punchdrunk's work and refers to the company's process of drilling down to the core of a concept and abstractly rendering it within their immersive worlds. It most frequently refers to the company's conceptualisation of design and their choreographic approach; for example, during *The Burnt City* R&D window Barrett, inspired by the three-legged pots that Schliemann excavated from Hisarlık, floated (or jested) the (not realised) possibility that all the furniture in Troy might have only three legs. Examples that were realised in *The Burnt City*, as my subsequent chapters discuss, include morphing almost the entirety of Clytemnestra's narrative arc from *Agamemnon* into wordless contemporary dance, and turning the infamous purple carpet that Clytemnestra lays out for Agamemnon into a billowing silk cloak, which Clytemnestra and Cassandra placed on Agamemnon's shoulders as he climbed the staircase to his Palace, appearing akin to a river of blood as it flowed behind him.

The room in which Barrett, Doyle, and I were based was filled with visual representations of our ideas and discussions until this point. In the centre of the room was a collection of tables which were pushed together to create a make-shift board table, most of which was taken up by the still skeletal loop structure as an ever-present reminder of the enormity of our outstanding task. Fast-forward to 3 March 2020 and we were working on creating one A2 page per character, which we stuck, gallery-wall style, onto two of the room's walls. Underneath each character's name were numbered rows for the character's scenes, alongside a space for listing key sources and a 'life quest'. Barrett had previously noted how he was 'spoilt for information' almost to the point of being overwhelmed by the amount of detail we could draw from the mythological and tragic sources at our disposal, explaining that his process was not solely in doing the 'excavation' of these sources but also in 'bringing the abstraction, bringing the opposing sources that make it cackle'. Doyle, conversely, was enthused by the opportunities that the material presented and eagerly delved into the mythological variants surrounding each of the characters from the source tragedies. While Barrett moved between meetings for Punchdrunk's television project *The Third Day* and *The Burnt City*'s R&D room, Doyle and I added smaller pages to each character's master sheet, complete with background information, timelines, family trees, and story beats. Doyle's interests ranged from the tragic source texts through to more obscure cult associations, and she jumped at the chance to document ideas for multi-scene journeys for those characters still awaiting content for their loop.

The character of Iphigenia was one such character who required a substantial amount of narrative content at the R&D stage. Iphigenia is not an onstage character in either of the tragic source texts, but she is evoked in a powerful analeptic choral ode in *Agamemnon* which describes her sacrifice at the start of the Trojan War [105–257]. As Punchdrunk's masked performances are largely wordless and are instead predominantly enacted through the medium of dance, Iphigenia was to become part of the dramatis personae within *The Burnt City* and her sacrifice was already positioned as occurring during Scene Four of the loop. A wedding breakfast scene was mooted for Iphigenia's Scene Three, in a nod to Agamemnon's ruse of an engagement to Achilles, which is deployed in Euripides' *Iphigenia at Aulis* to lure Iphigenia to her sacrifice. For Scene Five, a post-it note suggested 'rebirth: deer', in a reference to the interpolated ending of *Iphigenia at Aulis* in which a Messenger reports how a deer replaced Iphigenia on the altar during her sacrifice [1532ff]. Aside from this note, Iphigenia's loop was blank. When we got to rehearsals, Doyle stressed the significance of Iphigenia and Clytemnestra's early scenes to the performers, saying that 'we have fifteen minutes to establish the relationship between Clytemnestra and Iphigenia. It isn't long, but we need that time to count to give Clytemnestra's revenge weight'.[12] In the March R&D window, during Doyle and my discussions about Iphigenia's wider mythology, Doyle became intrigued by my mention of Iphigenia's association with the Sanctuary of Artemis Brauronia in Attica. Euripides' *Iphigenia among the Taurians* records the establishment of Artemis' sanctuary [1462–1474]. The mythology tells us that after Iphigenia escapes

---

[12] There is a wider trend, dating back at least to Ariane Mnouchkine's 1990 *Les Atrides*, towards staging the *Oresteia* with *Iphigenia at Aulis* as a prequel, to give Clytemnestra's murder of Agamemnon weight and (psychologically realistic) motivation. Punchdrunk's inclusion of Iphigenia's sacrifice can be considered part of this wider tradition, as well as being understood as a product of their innovative performance structure.

from Taurus with her brother Orestes, where she had been living as a priestess following her sacrifice (averted due to the deer substitution), she became Artemis' temple warden at Brauron, where she later died and was buried. Historically, Brauron was an important Attic cult site. It was home to the penteteric Brauronia festival where Athenian girls between the ages of five and ten would complete a maturation rite in preparation for marriage and to mark the transition from *parthenos* (girl) to *gyne* (woman). The chorus of women in Aristophanes' *Lysistrata* refer to 'shedding my saffron robe' and being 'a Bear at the Brauronia' [645] as one of four potential (and sequential) rites-of-passage for young Athenian women.[13] Black- and red-figure pottery fragments of fifth-century *krateriskoi* from the sanctuary depicting the *arktoi* (bears) dancing and/ or running have led some to posit that during the rite not only did the women act as bears in honour of Artemis, but that they also danced in her honour as well.

In 2021, Doyle commented to theatre critic Lyn Gardner that dance in antiquity was a source of inspiration for her direction and choreography in *The Burnt City*, noting that the Greeks 'used dance in many ways including as worship, ceremony and to bring them closer to the gods in ecstatic dance'.[14] Doyle's eagerness to incorporate as wide a range of references as possible not only to the relevant mythology, but also to ancient dance practice, was immediately apparent in how Iphigenia's link to the Brauronia sparked her interest. The evidence for the style of ritual dance possibly performed at Brauron is exceedingly small and consists of a mere handful of krateriskoi fragments showing either a single naked initiand dancing, or a group of clothed older initiands dancing.[15] Lilly Kahil interprets the broken pottery fragments as perhaps showing a 'slower ritual dance', while Christiane Sourvinou-Inwood considers the arrangement of arms surrounding a central figure on comparable fragments (the rest of the bodies are lost) as depicting 'probably a rather fast' dance.[16] In Richard Hamilton's analysis of krateriskoi from a range of Greek sanctuaries, including Brauron, he does not go as far as suggesting

---

[13] On the *arkteia,* see Sourvinou-Inwood (1988). The scholia to Aristophanes' *Lysistrata* provides further details of the ritual.

[14] Gardner (2021).

[15] On the material evidence, see Sourvinou-Inwood (1988: 65 n. 314).

[16] Kahil (1983: 237) and Sourvinou-Inwood (1988: 104).

the pace or style of dancing but does claim that the fragments depict dancing (rather than running) 'when there is no full forward motion and when there are attributes appropriate to dancing', such as holding hands, having a dress ballooning out as if the dancer is spinning around, having arms bent and the head thrown back, or the head thrown back and the foot visible in a 'kick' reminiscent of the *skinnis*.[17] For Doyle, the lack of information was not problematic, as she was not interested in creating a reconstruction. The link between Iphigenia and Brauron, plus the fit between the Brauronia as a potential marriage preparation rite and Iphigenia's status as betrothed during the first scenes of the production, provided an opportunity to incorporate references to ancient cult activity and dance in ritual worship as part of Iphigenia's loop, and to layer historical notes into the production to be unearthed by the company's detective-like superfans. Our discussions about *Iphigenia among the Taurians* and Artemis Brauronia manifested in *The Burnt City*'s first two scenes: Iphigenia's Scene One included a preparation scene in her bedroom, where together with Clytemnestra and a third character (the Oracle) she prepared for the ritual, practising slow and solemn dance moves, before the women journeyed together to a shrine to Artemis where Clytemnestra poured a libation and Iphigenia danced hypnotically, in a full-length bear costume, for Scene Two (Fig. 3.1).

Although the spectre of COVID-19 haunted the creative development process in early 2020, key components of the initial process of turning Greek literature into immersive experience were nevertheless apparent. The company 'excavated' not only the two core tragic sources, but also the surrounding tragic and mythological texts that held character and/or narrative connections to the core tragedies, alongside any other literary or historical sources and relevant material evidence. Although many of the sources and scene ideas floated during these weeks were not realised during the final production, traces of various conversations did become concrete scenes, such as the link between Iphigenia and the festival of Artemis Brauronia. The company's process of fleshing out the loop chart by finding the seeds of new scenes in a variety of sources, to ensure a depth of material and in turn opportunities for audiences to unearth additional layers of information, demonstrates how closely the company depended on research, in this case into the ancient world, to build their

---

[17] Hamilton (1989: 454). On the dancing at Brauron, see also Perlman (1989).

Fig. 3.1 Stefanie Noll and Omagbitse Omagbemi as Iphigenia and Clytemnestra in Scene Two, ('Bear Dance') of *The Burnt City*. Image Credit: Julian Abrams. Courtesy of Punchdrunk

masked show. Doyle and Barrett's engagement with the ancient world beyond *Agamemnon* and *Hecuba* involved doing deep dives into points of connection between their core sources and wider antiquity which sparked their creative imagination. The breadth of material they incorporated was not randomised but was rhizomatic, creating a densely criss-crossed network of characters and narratives essential for the creation of an independent secondary storyworld. The conglomeration of sources involved in developing *The Burnt City* makes the work difficult to conceptualise as a classical reception of any fixed number of texts or artefacts. The production instead created a multifaceted dialogue with antiquity of an entirely original kind and scale.

The Pandemic

From March 2020, as the UK moved in and out of lockdown and between varying levels of COVID-19 restrictions, producers Lucy Whitby and Lauren Storr drafted remobilisation plans for *The Burnt City*. Although the bloated timeline was never anyone's wish, it provided time for ideas to percolate and gave the cast more opportunities than ever before to interrogate their characters and become accustomed to Punchdrunk's style of performance. Barrett and Doyle met for another four-week creative development period in June 2021, with the goal of edging towards completing the loop chart and writing *précis* for each character's eleven scenes (Doyle later described these to the cast as 'less provocations, more inspirations'), which included a location for each scene and a short guide as to what the performers might devise. Several scenes, however, remained blank right up until mid-rehearsals, particularly for resident characters.

In September 2021, Barrett and Doyle added the UK and EU-based members of the performing company for *The Burnt City* into their creative development process for four weeks of studio-based workshops. The focus was on finding a common movement language. Around three fifths of the cast were veteran Punchdrunk performers, with several having appeared in both the Shanghai and New York *Sleep No More* productions, London's *The Drowned Man*, and some even in Punchdrunk's earlier works going right back to the 2003 London version of *Sleep No More*.[18] The other cast members were new to Punchdrunk's style of performance and way of developing work, although some of the dancers had worked with Doyle on non-Punchdrunk projects before. Irrespective of their prior exposure to Punchdrunk's way of devising theatre, the cast needed time to start learning the ecology of the show. The choreographic style of *The Burnt City* was shaped by the specific source texts being utilised and the cavernous warehouse venue in which the show was performed, which invited a particular scale of movement due to the height of the central spaces and the possibility of elevating action for improved sight lines. The bespoke movement vocabulary of *The Burnt City* was coupled with

---

[18] Sarah Dowling and Rob McNeill, who co-devised the parts of Hecuba and Agamemnon respectively, were both part of the original London 2003 cast for *Sleep No More*. On their history of working with Punchdrunk, see Machon and Punchdrunk (2019: 59–61) (Dowling), and Machon and Punchdrunk (2019: 254) (McNeill).

Punchdrunk's trademark mix of character types, which included not only their traditional travelling and resident character roles but also a hierarchy of divine, royal, and mortal character types as well.

Honing a shared movement language and a unified approach to collaborative creation was essential during these early workshops due to the significant time pressure placed upon the creative process during the formal rehearsal period. Punchdrunk's masked productions are so complex that what initially appears to be an enormous rehearsal window evaporates quickly under the pressure of building a show. For *The Burnt City*, previews commenced in week nine of rehearsals and lasted for an entire month; this equated to a rehearsal period that was several weeks longer than most of Punchdrunk's West End contemporaries. With eleven scenes and a finale to create, involving 28 separate characters working across two warehouses, the cast and creative team built the equivalent of multiple separate performances at once. Punchdrunk employed a large creative team to help oversee the development of the show. In addition to Barrett and Doyle operating as co-directors and, in Doyle's case, choreographer, Kath Duggan held the position of associate director, which was the most senior directorial position under Barrett and Doyle and involved Duggan collaborating on *The Burnt City* from the earliest R&D phase of the production. Duggan worked closely with the cast on individual scenes during the rehearsal period and was a key point of contact for cast queries once the production opened. Alongside Duggan, Punchdrunk also employed a team of five rehearsal directors. Rehearsal directors are common within dance-based practice and involve interpreting and communicating a choreographer's vision to an ensemble, working with the performers during rehearsals, and liaising with the cast day to day during the run of the production. *The Burnt City*'s rehearsal directors split their time between working as an 'RD' and performing in the show; once the production opened, they observed the shows in which they were not performing, noting the work to ensure quality consistency and running subsequent rehearsals to input any changes required as the performance evolved or as new performers joined the cast. The entire team of eight creatives met daily during rehearsals. Yet even with a core creative team of such size, many performers still devised and rehearsed scenes without immediate directorial oversight. Solidifying the movement vocabulary during these early workshops was thus of vital importance.

On 6 September 2021, I joined the creative team and performing company to give two lectures, the first on the Trojan War and the second on both death in antiquity, and the mythological Underworld. Before my first lecture, Doyle led the performers through a movement workshop, which took place on the ground floor of Building 17. Building 17 featured a mezzanine, with a grand staircase connecting the two levels. The cavernousness of the space and its architectural features were all retained for the performance, with the action in Greece site-sympathetic to the built environment. The specific bit of floor on which the cast were working later became No Man's Land within Greek Mycenae, but in September 2021 the set installation was yet to begin. The cast had just returned from their lunch break and were barefoot and in sweats. Some walked around the space while others sat in small groups talking until Doyle turned on some music, cuing the performers to come together in the space. They eased into moving, shifting their weight around and loosening their limbs wordlessly. The diverse group ranged in age from their twenties to their forties and mainly included professional dancers, although some self-classified as actors. One performer, who I later learned was the Brazilian Joaquim de Santana, a veteran Punchdrunk performer who was then slated to play Apollo, danced with a beanie pulled down over his face, the movements of the ensemble being so contained and their proprioceptive awareness so great that he could close off his vision and still warm-up safely.[19] Doyle tinkered with the volume of the music and called out to the performers to 'turn up the listening. Listening through the skin'. The performers' movements rippled through their limbs on increasingly larger scales as the volume increased, moving from waves in the fingers ('hands are storytellers', Doyle interjected at one point) through to the elbows and knees. Doyle encouraged contact, inviting the cast 'not looking, not searching, just being available for very light touch'. As performers brushed up against one another, they occasionally leaned into each other's limbs and torsos, momentarily and lightly taking on some of another's weight before the other performer reciprocated, modulating the dynamic between the two. At one point, the music ceased all together and Doyle instructed the cast to continue moving through 'listening to the room'. The music, a bespoke mix that Doyle adjusted while the performers moved, reappeared, and grew in volume with added bass. The cast, previously spread across the full space, slowly swarmed together in the corner of the floor closest to the speaker. As

---

[19] De Santana returned to Brazil later in 2021 and was not part of the original performing company of *The Burnt City*.

the sound grew louder and louder, they undulated and bounced joyously, individually but with a group dynamic, with Doyle directing the transition through the musical changes alone. Watching from the side-lines, I could not help but smile as this moment of revelry came together before my eyes. As the volume decreased and the scene dissipated Doyle called out 'keep the memory of that. Don't drop it'. Although we were several months away from the rehearsal period itself, even in this early workshop a 360-degree performance style was being crafted, with a firm emphasis on the ensemble rather than the individual. The performers had to listen and respond to the room, to the music, and to each other to craft a choreographic style which was collaborative and responsive. There was no taught choreography or overt direction, but instead the performers were empowered to find shapes and dynamics themselves which Doyle then tuned like an instrument. The DNA of *The Burnt City*'s performance language was built from this moment on.

HIDE AND SEEK

By the time rehearsals commenced in 2022, a shared movement vocabulary had been honed. The company's attention now turned to building the show in dialogue with the space. The cast's first day of working in situ occurred on 31 January 2022, one week into rehearsals and following five days of work in an adjacent studio space. The cast had warmed up and, having been divided into groups of 15, were stood queued outside a door on which an A4 piece of paper read 'Entrance to Greece'. We were here for Hide and Seek, the first on-site rehearsal exercise that Barrett runs for all Punchdrunk site-based performances. Barrett stood at the doorway, ready to let the company into the performance space one at a time. None of the cast had seen the space since the September workshops and the commencement of the design installation. Barrett instructed the company to explore the space and to be the hider as well as the seeker, to discover up to sixty written prompts in the space, and to do three specific things: find your safest space, your most threatening space, and the space where you feel closest to the gods. The aim was to try not to be witnessed by anyone else playing the game and to remain aware of the significance of this first introduction to the space, which was the closest experience that one would have to the virgin audience member entering *The Burnt City* for the first time. The performers' emotional responses to the space in Hide and Seek would go on to inform any future material that they devised.

The darkness upon entry to Greece was utterly enveloping. The soft yellow glow of smart tealight candles, here encased in torn pieces of paper depicting maps of the ancient world, illuminated small pockets of the building, but I was otherwise in a complete blackout and needed to use my hands to feel along the walls to find my way. A soft, drone-like soundscape provided a haze of noise in the background and was returned to during countless future rehearsals when workshopping choreography for scenes yet to have a completed sound design. As I edged forwards, I felt the floor change under my feet from solid ground to sand. The sudden unsteadiness I felt as I stepped onto a new surface for which I had no visual referent felt aptly representative of the experience. As I adjusted to the darkness, I slowly made out familiar sites from September, spying the staircase up to the mezzanine that I knew was to constitute the Royal Palace. At the end of a long plinth table in the Palace I spied a small bedroom, with the walls represented by fine hanging chains and with LED strip lighting illuminating the boundary from which the chains hung. I immediately identified the room as Iphigenia's bedroom due to my prior knowledge that this warehouse represented Greek Mycenae and thanks to the inclusion of set dressings which linked the space to that of a young girl's bedroom, including a doll's house, a dressing table, soft toys, and a single bed. I did not loiter, however, being exposed in this wall-less room. The instruction to remain hidden was a challenge throughout this entire building. Greece was vast, and I felt dwarfed by the warehouse and exposed in both No Man's Land downstairs and the Palace upstairs.

I made my way across Greece and pushed open the heavy fire doors, finding immediate comfort in the contrasting labyrinthine design and the brightly coloured fairy lights in the tat shop at the entrance to Troy. Unlike Greece, where I had been before, Troy was unfamiliar due to the level of construction that filled the warehouse, which created a density of design absent from Greece. I was immediately struck by the changing wall lights in each room and corridor I passed, and the bric-a-brac in the smaller rooms around the side of Troy. Books and notes had an emphasis on games, fate, and magic; I spied dice, checkers, chess, cards, and astrology books. In front of some of the smart candles lay individual provocations, written on small pieces of paper like a fortune from a cookie. I stopped to read each one I passed. Have you ever witnessed a miracle? Which god would you pick to worship? What would you ask for? Let the light fill you up. Can you channel it?

After close to an hour, music swelled and soared. The sound encompassed the warehouse completely, becoming an active presence in the space rather than a mere backdrop. It was impossible for me to continue to ferret around the games and books of Troy for these two minutes; instead, I remained still, listening to the music reverberate around the darkened space. In our afternoon meeting when we shared our discoveries from Hide and Seek, many identified this moment as when they felt closest to the gods, while the safest and most threatening spaces were usually identified as linked to the tasks. The scenography was in some ways a blank canvas, waiting for the performers to build into and complete, despite the differing energies that each building embodied and the level of set dressing already present.

Barrett developed a version of Hide and Seek during his finalist undergraduate production of *Woyzeck* at Exeter University and has since employed a version of the game for all Punchdrunk site-based performances.[20] His aim is that Hide and Seek represents the very first time that the cast experience the performance space, although the September studio rehearsals and the presence of the Punchdrunk offices in the same site as the performance space meant that the experience was not as 'pure' in this instance as in others. Despite having some prior exposure to the venue, I still found encountering the space in darkness an adrenaline-filled experience. Veteran Punchdrunk performer Conor Doyle, although not involved in *The Burnt City*, similarly records his embodied experience of Hide and Seek in his entry to *The Punchdrunk Encyclopaedia*:

> I remember being quite scared, in a heightened state of awareness. My skin was on fire, my hearing was acute, I could feel everything with a readiness to move in quite a primitive way. There was a sense of my body being not at all casual, of being alive in my body and being aware of the possibilities for that as a performance mode. Imagination-wise that exercise feeds you and it opens up your own fantasy world. It makes you connect to something instinctive, innate, something very pure.[21]

---

[20] See Machon and Punchdrunk (2019: 134) for an excerpt of Barrett's *Woyzeck* support portfolio, which details this first iteration of the hide-and-seek exercise.

[21] Doyle, quoted in Machon and Punchdrunk (2019: 19).

The provocations employed in Hide and Seek were customised to *The Burnt City*. Just as Doyle's movement workshop in September facilitated the cast developing the production's choreographic mode of listening through the body, of giving and responding within the ensemble rather than performing in a presentational manner to an audience, and of a range of movement stretching from the pedestrian through to the Dionysiac, so too did Hide and Seek help create a specific repertory of embodied, place-based memories from which the performers drew during the rehearsal process. The inclusion of scenographic materials relating to fate and fortune and the provocations linked to the divine fused connotations between the space and a vocabulary of divine plans and interventions and facilitated the sensation of being in a universe defined by awe and wonder. Whether vulnerable in the vastness of Greece, or hidden nestled in the scenographic cacophony of Troy, the individual was always a small cog in the machine of the larger forces at work in this new Punchdrunk world.

On-site Rehearsals

On 1 February 2022, Punchdrunk commenced what became the standard schedule for on-site rehearsals. This meant that the performers gathered each day in the rehearsal room for a one-hour warm-up, before working in the performance space for the remainder of the day. Initially, the company worked on one scene per day, going sequentially from Scene One to Scene Five. The space was constantly busy, with the performing company numbering fifty and consisting of two casts, known as the 'red' and 'blue' casts, who after opening alternated performances, as well as an ensemble of swings who understudied several parts (and in some instances played a central role in devising a role or roles, too) and prepared to 'swing in' to roles to cover periods of leave, or even mid-performance in the case of injury. Most full-time cast members had roles in both casts, alternating between a travelling part in one cast and a resident part in the other cast; Sam Booth, who developed the role of Hades, unusually played the same role in both casts, as he did in Punchdrunk's prior production *The Drowned Man*. On 1 February, Doyle cautioned that for those new to working with Punchdrunk these early days could feel light and empty, and to remember that the objective for each day was just to 'push out a sketch of the scene'. Often, she would supply some guiding phrases and key words to the cast as they commenced these initial attempts at devising scenes. Here, for example, she informed the Clytemnestras and Iphigenias who were working on the first scene of their loop in Iphigenia's bedroom, 'prep for bear dance', that the focus was on 'images that tell stories' and that the musical palette of the scene was 'heavy' and 'thick'. Later, when rehearsing Scene Seven ('wine to blood') with Agamemnon, Neoptolemus, and Cassandra, Doyle suggested that the key choreographic mode was 'high tone, stamp, bravado'.

Once the first five scenes were sketched out, the company moved on to recapping two scenes a day before doing a run of the first half of the loop at the end of the second week of rehearsals. Usually, the directors had already designated the location of each scene. Senior State Manager Hetti Curtis' daily call sheet stipulated where in the set cast members were to rehearse, which would be in the predetermined location for their scene as everything was devised in situ, in response to the building and the design installation. During each rehearsal, a member of stage management was on hand to assist, cueing music and filming choreography. Some scenes nevertheless relocated as the show took shape and as the audience's flow through the space became apparent. During rehearsals, the directors (including rehearsal directors) worked their way around to as many performers as possible. Major scenes involving multiple travelling characters such as the fall of Troy or the blinding of Polymestor inevitably required a full or half day's directorial attention, meaning that the casts who were devising duets or solo scenes elsewhere in the set often had considerable autonomy.[22] Among all this action, the build of the performance space continued. Large swathes of design were still being created and installed, while substantial levels of construction and painting were also taking place. Each day had different no-entry zones for the cast and creative team due to production requirements. Everyone present added a different quality to the ambient soundscape in which we were working and another piece of the jigsaw that ultimately became *The Burnt City*. The 'blueprint' I took of the space in my field notes on 17 February, when the cast were working on Scene Ten, provides insight into the dynamic of a typical day on the set of *The Burnt City*:

---

[22] Doyle has elsewhere detailed the amount of autonomy Punchdrunk performers have, and the way she and Barrett need to empower their performers so that they generate the required content; see Doyle, quoted in Machon and Punchdrunk (2019: 173).

I start my observations in Greece, from upstairs in the Palace, where I can see a suite of scenes being workshopped. The red and blue cast of Aegisthus, Clytemnestra, and Agamemnon are rehearsing an abstracted, dance-based massage on the plinth; the Cassandras are improvising their stair solo, with today's choreography including a backbend and a frankly scary looking slide down the banister of the stairs; the two casts of Neoptolemus and Patroclus are rehearsing the 'berserk' duet; and Milton as the Watchman plays with ideas for a durational on the watchtower, finding shapes in the space which Assistant Stage Manager Lily films.[23] Jane as the Oracle is by the shower working on another scene, and the Iphigenias are also in the space. Alongside this plethora of cast devising the show there is a huge amount of construction occurring, including a second cage containing bunk beds being constructed opposite the Watchman's cage. As I walk the space downstairs I get the impression that even two weeks into our on-site rehearsals, entirely new spaces are still being created. What is to the right of the Watchman's cage, behind the tents? A maze?

As I walk through to Troy I'm met by construction noise and the smell of paint fumes as corridors are painted black to plunge the set into eternal night. I go up some stairs and I don't even know where I am, ending up in a space which is unfurnished, with painting and some construction materials in it. How is this still happening?

As I continue my walk-through I enter the bar, where RD Carl is rehearsing the bar host routine with performers Ali and Kat, while Nathan, here as Orpheus, is in the corner with a group I don't recognise (perhaps a vocal coach, or the magic expert?). Anna and Sam (Persephone and Hades) are in the Town Square with another man I don't recognise – a tango coach, perhaps? I see spaces still un-utilised and being built; there is a real sense of how the performance could still grow through unlocking extra square footage within the space. I walk through the love hotel and notice new, identical rotary phones with pink sparkly cords with Aegean numbers on the dial. Every time I do a walkthrough such as this I notice new details being added, not just in quantity but in quality, with the scenography further thickening the world by adding new notes of interest, such as the Aegean numbers. As I near the end of my walk I come across two final scenes: firstly, I see the Hecubas in Polymestor's office, who had a blank in my current version of the loop chart

---

[23] Punchdrunk performers often referred to 'going into a durational' as a shorthand for resident scenes involving minimal choreography or narrative. 'Durationals' are a mainstay of resident character loops; in their encyclopaedia, Punchdrunk highlight their significance to the ecology of their immersive worlds, noting that 'the tempo and tracking of the most pedestrian of actions, becomes a rhythmical layer of the world and a potent holder of time … the pedestrian becomes poetic'. See Machon and Punchdrunk (2019: 95).

for Scene Ten but who today are experimenting with trashing the office; and secondly, downstairs in Trashcan Alley, I find the two furies—the resurrected Polyxena and Polydorus—who will be chasing Polymestor in a parkour-style Scene Ten. They agilely experiment with levels, climbing on platforms and street signs in the alley and criss-crossing one another in its bends, while the other cast, alongside the swings and RD Eric, are bunched together below, watching their improvisations and advising on routes and handholds. Hard work in a tight space.

I end back in the Palace, where I find a discussion taking place about Agamemnon's robe and the possibility of poisoning it like Medea and Deianeira poison robes in other tragic texts. I supply these intertexts to the team, becoming distinctly aware that the creation and recreation of scenes is a long way from complete.

Gay McAuley describes rehearsals as 'hard graft' and uses the Brecht quotation 'And let him observe/that this is not magic but/work, my friends' as an epigraph to her rehearsal study.[24] The graft required to create theatre is particularly true for a project the scale of *The Burnt City*. With so many interlocking gears working together to create the production, there was a real sense of always needing to push forwards; if one component fell behind schedule, there was a risk of destabilising the whole operation. The preview period was considered part of the rehearsal window, with content still awaiting creation once the company experienced both the audience's movements and the timing of characters' journeys through the space. Nevertheless, a strict adherence to the schedule was required so that a baseline version of the show was ready for paying audiences. This meant that when cast members became infected with COVID-19, for example, swings stepped up to devise scenes for characters who were not, until that moment, considered to be their priority, gaining additional creative autonomy as the show simply had to go on. Curtis ensured that the company followed the daily rehearsal calls with military precision, and no time was ever wasted. On the one hand, then, Punchdrunk's rehearsals were certainly not magic but work, not only in terms of the demanding performance style of Punchdrunk's immersive theatre, but also in terms of the intensity of the schedule required to co-create such a multidimensional universe. But on the other hand, moments of magic peppered the creative process, and on occasion,

---

[24] McAuley (2012: 27).

I found myself overwhelmed by the intensity of the performers' work as I watched an entirely new version of well-trodden classical myths unfold before my eyes.

One such example of the magic created through the cast and creative team's hard work came at the end of the first week of on-site rehearsals, on Friday 4 February. The company were up to devising Scene Four, and I was based in No Man's Land with the group of performers involved in creating the sacrifice of Iphigenia. Iphigenia's sacrifice had been mooted for Scene Four since the early R&D phase. Barrett and Doyle had a strong vision for the scene, which included both a soaring orchestral score ('Every Reborn' from *V for Vendetta*) which grew in pitch and volume until a climactic peak, at which point the sacrifice would take place. Agamemnon was to sacrifice Iphigenia at the apex of one of two tank traps in No Man's Land, elevated for ideal sightlines in a tableau that was already depicted on a mock terracotta red-figure krater that the company had commissioned from a potter as part of their set design. The vase would ultimately be displayed as an artefact in the museum cross-fade entrance experience, with the illustration and its caption foreshadowing the upcoming plot of the performance.[25]

We started the rehearsal walking through a rough structure for the scene, mapping out where characters were both coming from and going to and the key narrative beats. The sacrifice was to take place on the high point of the tank trap closest to Troy. The sequence involved Neoptolemus, Iphigenia, and Agamemnon on the tank trap, with additional support provided by Patroclus and Artemis who were also present in No Man's Land. Most of the sequence was set out in the first two hours under Doyle's direction with a focus on nailing the mechanics of the scene. No backing track was used while the scene was worked through. Safety was paramount, with a crash matt positioned under the tank trap. The initial practice involved trying to create the shape of Iphigenia (Dafni Krazoudi) leaning back as she walked up the trap, creating the sensation that a force

---

[25] The fact that the vase was painted before the scene was devised did result in minor discrepancies between the pottery and the performance. On the vase, Iphigenia is sacrificed at the mid-point of the tank trap and has her neck slit with an arrow. In the final performance, Iphigenia was sacrificed at the high point of the tank trap and no weapon was used. On Barrett and Doyle's decision to remove weapons from the production and abstract the violence, see Waite (2022). The other vases in the museum entrance experience were painted during rehearsals and were thus more accurate reflections of the way the scenes were staged.

was pulling her backwards as she climbed. The male soldiers involved in the scene experimented with holding her feet down, acting as stirrups, while she ascended the trap on an angle; however, this was abandoned as the soldiers could not reach her feet at the high point of the trap. When they re-rehearsed with Krazoudi climbing the tank trap by herself, Doyle directed Krazoudi to 'feel that she is floating, that's the sensation', and then later: 'that's the image' as Krazoudi leant back at the moment of sacrifice, vulnerable and exposed.

With Iphigenia's ascent up the tank trap set, the performers moved on to block her meeting with Neoptolemus, who Luke Murphy was playing in this rehearsal. In the sources which use the ruse of an engagement to lure Iphigenia to Aulis, it is Achilles, Neoptolemus' father, who is Iphigenia's fiancé, but in *The Burnt City* Neoptolemus held this function due in part to the cast size, with Neoptolemus covering both the role of Achilles during Iphigenia's storyline and his own role during Polyxena's sacrifice, and in part due to the 'weight' of Achilles' name and the potential for confusion given that Punchdrunk were not staging the part of Achilles' narrative made famous from *The Iliad*. Murphy, as Neoptolemus, started the scene standing at the apex of the tank trap, facing towards the stairs leading to the Royal Palace. Considerable time was spent fixing exactly how Murphy mounted and then balanced on the trap, so that he was secure and comfortable; stage management supplied shin pads and foam wedges so that he could 'lock' his feet into the gaps within the steel beams. As Krazoudi approached Murphy, she went to embrace him but he, almost in slow motion, lowered himself off the trap and down into Patroclus' (here played by Fionn Cox-Davies) arms. Again, the emphasis was largely on the mechanics of the scene, here of Murphy's assisted dismount, with Doyle happily leaving Murphy and Cox-Davies to work elements like this out without her intervention. The next step was to work out the blocking of the actual sacrifice.

As the narrative beats of the sacrifice scene were minimal, including a moment of affection between Agamemnon and Iphigenia, a moment of realisation from Iphigenia, the sacrifice, and Agamemnon's retreat, the rehearsal focused on timing and imagery. Vinicius Salles as Agamemnon slowly walked towards the now isolated Krazoudi. She sat down and they embraced, Salles' hands touching Krazoudi's face, before Salles pushed her head back and stabbed her in the neck with a long, retractable golden arrow. Krazoudi led this moment of rehearsal based on her safety and comfort, adjusting the placement of her body on the tank trap and her attachment to Salles. Doyle then advised how the performers could add in negative space to crispen the image. With a few angles set, the performers rehearsed Krazoudi shuddering, lying back on the trap, and then hanging limply, before Salles' dismount (here a slide down the tank trap) was practised, which led into a pre-rehearsed piece of choreography representing the winds returning to Aulis.

Once the mechanics were set, Barrett joined the rehearsal to watch a run through of the scene from beginning to end. The performers moved through the actions with the house lights on and in silence, with Doyle clicking the beats and occasionally offering spoken clarifications. Barrett and Doyle offered precise guidance on angles and pacing, particularly in relation to how to make the image painted on the red-figure krater come to life, which Curtis brought into the rehearsal for reference. Krazoudi and Salles transitioned to the crash mat to rehearse the positions in a safer environment, before Barrett introduced the music, cautioning that the scene now 'could be a tear jerker'. As soon as the music was played, which set the pacing of both Iphigenia's and Agamemnon's ascent, it became obvious that a pause in Agamemnon's climb was essential to match the slight diminuendo and series of pauses in the music before it gathered pace and volume and swelled to a more consistent rhythm. Salles and Rob McNeill (the 'red cast' Agamemnon) rehearsed pausing midway up the trap during this point in the score, looking away from Iphigenia in a moment of doubt, either up towards Clytemnestra at the Palace, or down and behind towards No Man's Land. The pause built dramatic tension and further layered the dramaturgy of the scene; for me as a witness to its creation, I felt a sudden sensation as the Agamemnons rehearsed this pause that I as audience was being cast as one of the restless troops at Aulis, hungry for war and holding Agamemnon hostage to the sacrifice.

With the timings now set to the music, the performers ran and re-ran the scene. Doyle and Barrett continued to shape the scene's colour and emotional impact, calling out that 'the language is Caravaggio' but that there should be 'no acting. Trust the pot'.[26] Doyle cued the scene

---

[26] The direction to avoid acting is a recurring note that Barrett and Doyle gave to performers throughout the rehearsal process. When rehearsing Scene One 'prep for bear dance', for example, Doyle instructed the performers 'Don't worry about acting, just find the actions', while in a rehearsal for the character of Laocoön (then called Calchas) in late February, Barrett cautioned the performers to avoid showing any comedy in their hands or face but to keep humour in the body.

as freeze frames, showing the narrative as snapshots and reminding the performers that they are 'in the same picture'. The red and blue casts shared precise notes about their physicality with one another, with Salles, for example, advising McNeill of the exact angle of their knee and toe when sliding down the tank trap so that they had control over the movement. As the scene was consolidated, Barrett and Doyle's notes became manifest, with a striking image of tenderness between Iphigenia and Neoptolemus disintegrating as the artifice of the engagement dissipated, and a moment of love between father and daughter rendered horrific through the vivid and graphically violent sacrifice.

An enormous number of hours of preparation went into this moment behind the scenes, from Stephen Dobbie selecting the music as part of the sound design, to Barrett, Vaughan, and Minns deciding to incorporate tank traps in the set, and then Barrett and Doyle pre-determining the key tableaux between Iphigenia and Neoptolemus and Iphigenia and Agamemnon. Nevertheless, the way that the music and the performances came together here in one afternoon felt magical. In a matter of just a few short hours, the company created their own interpretation of a key moment from the tragic canon, rendered with such poignancy and lyricism that it acted as gut punch to those watching and a lightning rod for the characters within *The Burnt City*. The scene was noteworthy for the clarity of artistic vision surrounding it; indeed, it barely changed from this first rehearsal onwards, with the most substantial alternations being the removal of the arrow and implementation of a weapon-less sacrifice, and the inclusion of an additional narrative beat between Iphigenia and Neoptolemus, involving Neoptolemus placing a wedding ring on Iphigenia's finger before abandoning her to her sacrifice. In this instance, then, the process of transforming Greek literature into immersive experience was director led, with support from design and sound, and was about capturing a narrative plot point via a searing, 'money shot' image. The company stripped back the narrative of Iphigenia's sacrifice to a core image and then rebuilt it in dialogue with other intertexts and references. The clarity of artistic vision underpinning the scene, combined with the contributions of the performers, meant that the devising of the scene was about mechanics and logistics, which once ironed out left a scene of moving poetry and raw emotion, both magic and work.

Full Run

On Friday 25 February 2022, one month and one day since rehearsals commenced, Punchdrunk ran a full loop of *The Burnt City* for the first time. The day before, the company had recapped the eleven scenes of the loop, spending twenty minutes on each scene with an instruction from Doyle to 'remember, play, [and revise] safety mechanics'. On 25 February, both the red and blue casts performed a single loop in turn, with Doyle informing all that the run 'is about mechanics, music, finding connections in your show'. The run was a milestone, something between a rehearsal and a stumble through. Scenes One to Five had not been run together since a closed rehearsal on 11 February, and Scenes Six to Eleven had never been run together. The rehearsal thus represented several firsts: the first time the cast performed the transitions between more than half of the production's scenes; the first time that performers used blood and did aerial work across a suite of scenes; and the first time they were able to climb on the set pieces, which were only secured down after the performers had devised Scene Eleven. A few members of the cast wore pieces of costume, with Apollo (Steven Apicello) in gold hot pants and a gold silicon muscle top, and Cassandra (Yilin Kong) a white tulle rehearsal skirt and black long-sleeve leotard. The house lights were left on for the run, and some sound was played within the space, but approximately half of the venue (including most of Troy) remained entirely silent with the exception of a 'god mic' which announced the beginning of each scene and marked each minute to keep the performers on track ('Scene One, two, three, four five, Scene Two, seven, eight, nine, ten, Scene Three', etc.). Nervous energy filled the space; the two Hecubas, Emily Mytton and Sarah Dowling, told me that this was not a fun part of the process, while Milton Lopes, who devised the resident Watchman and Zagreus roles, told me that this run was not really for them [the performers]. The implication was that the run was aiming to expose the holes in the performance and highlight problematic scenes which would require reorienting, whether due to the action being too fast or slow and meaning the performers could not reach their next scene on time, or due to different groups of travelling characters intersecting and potentially creating a bottleneck of audience in the space. Running to unearth problems, rather than to polish material, does nothing to massage one's ego, but was a necessary part of the process; indeed, Doyle previously described the first run to me as necessary chaos which was full of moments of discovery.

Today's audience was made of up the cast and creative team, alongside associates, the company physiotherapist, and some members of production and company management. Most followed the tactic of observing one character per run; I followed Cassandra for the first loop and Aegisthus for the second to witness some of the scenes to which I had not yet contributed. The cast's stage presence went a long way towards bringing the production together, despite how far away the company were from having a performance ready for a paying audience, with outstanding tasks including finishing the sound design, fleshing out too-short scenes with added choreography, and finishing the build of the venue. The work achieved through performer presence was particularly evident when I observed veteran Punchdrunk performers, whom I saw employing crowd management strategies innately within their loops. Both Steven Apicello and Paul Zivkovich, playing Apollo and Aegisthus respectively, slowed their audience down by suddenly stopping in a hallway or pausing in a doorway and touching its architraves. Their techniques forced a moment of stillness to calm an energetic flock of audience or to adjust their own flow and timings between scenes when running ahead of schedule. Alternatively, when they needed to speed up to get to another scene in less time than anticipated, they draped an arm or traced a fingertip on the wall behind them, particularly when they rounded corners or disappeared through doorways mid-corridor, to provide a visual trail for the audience to follow even when it seemed that the performer was getting away. I again bore witness to the performers' audience management strategies when Zivkovich squeezed my shoulder, momentarily but with increasing and then decreasing pressure, to move me out of his path as he approached the shower during Clytemnestra's murder of Agamemnon (Scene Eleven). I later heard rehearsal director Emily Terndrup describe this approach to the cast as the 'skin-muscle-bone' technique, where one progresses from a light to a stronger pressure upon an audience member's arm or shoulder to communicate clearly through touch that the spectator needs to adjust their position in the space (or alternatively, that they should stay put). The embodied history of performing in Punchdrunk's immersive worlds equipped performers with crowd management strategies which were just as much of an influence in *The Burnt City* as the other source texts, intertexts, and choreographic language.

1:1

Following the full run, *The Burnt City*'s creative team commenced week six of rehearsals with a clear list of priorities, ranging from reconceptualising certain travelling roles, creating additional content for resident roles, and reorienting and re-blocking challenging ensemble scenes. Rehearsals were no longer structured around one scene per day, with all cast members working on the same scene at the same time. Instead, the cast were called to work on up to three specific scenes requiring attention per day. A priority encompassing both travelling and resident roles was the creation of one-on-one scenes, referred to by the shorthand 1:1, which until now had remained untouched. It became commonplace from this point forward for at least one performer to spend time devising a one-on-one experience each day.

One-on-one experiences are a signature of Barrett's work and involve performers selecting a single spectator from the audience and inviting them to a private part of the set (usually a room behind a locked door) for an intimate performance for that single spectator alone.[27] Within the one-on-one experience, which represents a scene (and is as tightly structured as any other) within a character's loop, the 'rules' of the performance are temporarily suspended; an audience member's mask is usually removed and they are sometimes invited to speak in the form of answering questions as part of a pre-scripted exchange. One-on-ones fall into two broad categories, depending upon the character's role in the performance, as summarised by previous Punchdrunk performer Katy Balfour who noted that 'If a travelling character has a one-on-one, this will have a specific function within their loop; a moment of confession or realisation that's central to the rest of their narrative. A resident character on the other hand has a less defined role and narrative'.[28] Zivkovich further clarified to me during rehearsals that both dramaturgical and practical reasons govern the decision behind which travelling characters conduct one-on-ones. Dramaturgically, there must be a justification for why a character suddenly sees and acknowledges an audience member within the narrative of the show to select them for the one-one-one, while practically, the number of audience members following a character must be taken into

---

[27] On how one-on-ones have become a core part of Barrett's practice since his Exeter experiments, see Machon and Punchdrunk (2019: 203–204).

[28] On Balfour's comments, see Machon and Punchdrunk (2019: 205).

consideration. Macbeth, Zivkovich pointed out, does not have any one-on-ones in *Sleep No More*, because 'can you imagine shutting a door in the face of one hundred and fifty people?'. The fact that in *The Burnt City* neither Agamemnon, Clytemnestra, nor Hecuba had one-on-one scenes was, by this logic, in part due to the sizeable audience numbers that these characters attracted.

The distinction between styles of one-on-one scenes gave residents slightly more space to innovate within their one-on-ones and to weave in other intertexts and create stand-alone experiences that could be repeated on multiple occasions within each loop. Despite these differences in content, there were structural similarities between travelling and resident one-on-one scenes. All one-on-ones usually lasted for three-to-five minutes, had bespoke soundtracks which the performers triggered through a mechanism when they wished to start the scene, and created an illusion of intimacy and improvisation even though they were in fact tightly structured and usually repeated multiple times per night. Although each one-on-one was seen by only a fraction of a performance's audience, Punchdrunk's fans highly prized the experiences and actively sought them out. Their creation was thus given just as much rehearsal time as any other scene within the performance. Their significance was felt within the ensemble, too, with Barrett referring to them as a 'theatrical gift' during rehearsals and Balfour writing movingly about the emotional experience of giving a one-on-one from a performer's perspective in *The Punchdrunk's Encyclopaedia*.[29] The importance of each one-on-one within the crafting of Punchdrunk's work is reflected in the fact that each scene requires a formal directorial sign-off, not only for the content of the scene but for safeguarding and caretaking purposes for each new performer who will take on the part and perform the scene as well.[30]

On Tuesday 1 March 2022, I joined performer Andrea Carrucciu and rehearsal director Eric Jackson Bradley to begin devising the one-on-one of the resident character Askalaphos (Fig. 3.2). Askalaphos does not appear in *The Burnt City*'s source tragedies, or even in Trojan War mythology, but is an Underworld figure most famous for revealing to Zeus that Persephone ate seven pomegranate seeds in the Underworld.

---

[29] Balfour in Machon and Punchdrunk (2019: 164).

[30] On safeguarding and caretaking during one-on-one experiences and the process of directorial approval, see Machon and Punchdrunk (2019: 207).

His revelation bound Persephone to spend part of each year in the Underworld. Ovid's *Metamorphoses* records how Demeter, in vengeance, went on to turn Askalaphos into an owl [5.538–550]. Askalaphos' loop in *The Burnt City* did not revolve around Askalaphos' whistleblowing narrative. Instead, Punchdrunk used the name Askalaphos to substantiate the Underworld setting of their Trojan War retelling. After the first 'sneak peek' (dress rehearsal with an invited audience), Barrett reminded the cast that the resident roles 'are created to hold the rhythm, they are the heartbeats of the space. You can always walk past and see them somewhere, [they are] familiar presences in a disorienting world'. Askalaphos reflected Barrett's conception of resident roles and could be found in a florist named Hesperides for much of the performance. His loop featured original narrative material that Punchdrunk interpolated into the Trojan War storyline. Within Askalaphos' loop, Barrett and Doyle left space for up to three one-on-ones, all of which were envisaged to be identical.

Although Askalaphos' loop did not tell the story of his whistleblowing, the one-on-one experience drew upon some of the character's mythology

Fig. 3.2 Jordan Ajadi as Askalaphos in Punchdrunk's *The Burnt City*. Image credit: Julian Abrams. Courtesy of Punchdrunk

and in particular Ovid's description of Askalaphos' transformation into an owl [5.534–50]. The rehearsal commenced with a visit to the one-on-one room. The directors had predetermined that the one-on-one would take place in the back room of Hesperides, which in a rare occurrence for such a room at this point in rehearsals already had its intricate set design installed within it. As *The Burnt City* was set in the Underworld, by Punchdrunk's logic this meant that there was nothing living in the set (except for two plants, which formed a crucial part of Persephone's narrative).[31] As such, the florist only sold fake flowers. The back room was designed as the space where Askalaphos dyed the flowers, with fake flowers hanging from the roof drying, alongside buckets of pre-made flowers, dyes, and feathers. Carrucciu also had some costume to work with, including a moth-holed vest with fake skin beneath the holes from which he would, after scratching, pull out some feathers in a *Black Swan*-esque moment. Having visited the space, work began on interrogating the text, mining Ovid's passage for language that could be translated into physicality. Both Bradley and Carrucciu were interested in the disturbing quality of Ovid's description of the transformation and wished to play with the idea of nails bending inwards and arms being immobilised, as well as the representation of the owl in the *Metamorphoses* as a vile creature, rather than an animal associated with wisdom.

The rehearsal continued in situ. The room had two entrances, one from within the florist where Askalaphos worked and one from 'Trashcan Alley' in the backstreets of Troy. The two entrances facilitated the audience member's entrance and exit from different locations. The room was an apt representation of Punchdrunk's design ethos, which preserves the mystery of a space by ensuring that one cannot view a space in its entirety from a single vantage point. To view Askalaphos' one-on-one space completely one needed to walk through the doorway from the flower shop, take a few steps in, and then turn right. Bradley and Carrucciu became immediately interested in the idea of Askalaphos getting wet, in a nod to Demeter cursing Askalaphos by flinging liquid lava from the river Phlegethon on him. They experimented with how water could drip on Askalaphos' forehead, either by having Carrucciu sit beneath the tap of a metal keg, by adding a hidden device in the room's benches which

---

[31] The idea that nothing grows in the Underworld is part of the dramaturgy of *The Burnt City* rather than Greek mythology, as within myth there are several living plants in the Underworld, including the meadow of asphodels.

could manually feed through to drip from the roof, or by utilising the faux flowers in the room, perhaps by holding a dripping wet flower above Carrucciu's head or having the audience dunk a flower in water and then pegging it up and having it drip on his head.

To begin to build the action of the scene, Carrucciu and Bradley then turned to the music. They had two possible soundtracks from which to choose; as they played the first option, which was the 'Porter' one-on-one soundtrack from *Sleep No More*, Bradley and Carrucciu simultaneously broke out in the monologue from this scene, having both performed the role before. One-on-ones clearly became woven into the embodied history of Punchdrunk's practice and a shared point of reference for performers who work on each production. Carrucciu began to improvise some material around the music, room, props, and costume. He walked through the beats of leading someone in, removing their mask, doing some business with the flowers, dripping water, scratching, and revealing the feather. Creating the scene was a dance between Ovid's text, the intricate design of the space, the storytelling facilitated by the sound design, and Carrucciu's emotional colouring and physical interpretation of the material, which from this rehearsal onwards went on to be honed in collaboration with the other directors and the performers who shared the role of Askalaphos. Although the narrative arc of the scene and the core imagery around the feather reveal remained the same right up until the performance opened, this moment of rehearsal just scratched the surface of what it took to create the scene. One-on-ones were not performed to paying audience members until several weeks into previews, when the precise emotional stages of each experience became fixed, when the performers had embedded a minimum of three 'invited nos' into the scene from their chosen audience member, and when the directors had formally approved each performer's staging of each scene. What was clear from this moment of rehearsal alone, however, was that one-on-ones within *The Burnt City* represented a more intimate, small-scale approach to transforming ancient literature into immersive experience, which was less about paring back a text to a core image and more about excavating language for both an overarching narrative 'reveal' and small-scale details that could add colour and dynamism to a scene. Rather than being director led, these scenes were collaboratively created and even performer led, and were a place where prior Punchdrunk experiences came into their own.

Finale

On 10 March 2022, when there was just one week until the first invited audiences arrived for a sneak peek dress rehearsal, attention turned to the finale. The concept for the finale, involving bodies cascading down the central staircase of Greek Mycenae in an echo of both the Memling and Bouts paintings, was established during the early R&D phase of the project.[32] Doyle, Harrison, and the cast then developed follow-on choreography for when the ensemble reached the base of the staircase during the September 2021 studio rehearsals, which the team regularly revisited during rehearsals. Stephen Dobbie designed the soundtrack for the scene, which culminated with an extract from Cherubini's 'Requiem in C Minor' and an ash drop in the centre of the space. Despite all this background information being known in advance of the March rehearsal, it would be a mistake to assume that the scene was near completion. Three large questions required resolving: how would the cast transition from Scene Eleven of Loop Three into the finale sequence? What would the choreography for the 'descent of man' stair sequence look like? And what would be the production's final tableau?

A large-scale finale sequence has featured in all Punchdrunk masked performances since the company's 2003 *Sleep No More*. The finales bring together the entire audience for a central, large-scale scene which provides a definitive conclusion to the performance and then helps transition spectators out of the immersive world through select audience members having 'walk outs' and being 'demasked' by performers in much the same way that the cross-fade facilitates their entry. Although only a few audience members experience a walk out, they lead the exodus from the performance space and facilitate the broader re-immersion back into reality.

The focus on 10 March was on the descent down the stairs, which was the component of the finale inspired by the Memling and Bouts paintings. The descent was the only part of the finale which drew upon an intertext explicitly about entering an Underworld; however, the concept behind the finale was that it would clarify to the audience that the characters were in the Underworld and make a broader statement about the

---

[32] Another key source for the finale concept was Ted Hughes' translation of Clytemnestra's final monologue during the first episode of *Agamemnon* [320–350]. The role of this intertext in the creation of the finale is discussed in Chapter 4.

impact of war. Barrett went on to describe *The Burnt City* to the press as, for example, 'a war requiem, it's about grief and the impact of conflict and loss'.[33] Although Punchdrunk's rehearsals often involved a large degree of performer autonomy, today's rehearsal had a strong directorial presence given the specificity of the vision attached to the scene and the large number of bodies involved in bringing the image to life. The rehearsal thus included not only Doyle and Barrett, but also rehearsal directors Kath Duggan and Eric Jackson Bradley. Duggan initiated the rehearsal with the instruction that today they would attempt 'to find more thickness in the finale in the movement, dig in, progress it forward'. The image of the Bouts painting was then circulated to the cast, with Barrett explaining that the audience would see the image incorporated into the signage within the museum entrance experience, and could also find it hanging in Hades' home within the set (although in a telling indicator of where we were at, the framed print of the painting for the set had not yet arrived). Barrett was also working with lighting designer Jeremy Lechterman (FragmentNine) to build flashes or strobes into the finale so that 'we see the image come to life as freeze frames, seared into the retinas'. In rehearsal, Doyle offered the clarification that we were 'not reconstructing the image - they [the audience] will instead get the feeling, sensation, [of the] image'. Before commencing work on the stairs, the directors gave the final instruction that, apart from the two queens, Clytemnestra and Hecuba, the rest of the cast should shift away from their character ('leave it at the top of the stairs') and were instead 'now leftovers of mankind frantically trying to escape damnation'. The task was set as to create a grieving, mourning ritual, rather than a linear narrative, with Doyle offering the final direction that the sequence 'is more of an existential piece on the impact of conflict, grief'.

The cast's work on the stairs commenced with an initial group of performers moving to the top of the staircase. The directors' first task was to determine how many bodies were needed on the stairs to give the sequence the necessary gravitas for a finale. Doyle started with twelve bodies, spaced at different intervals across the staircase, before playing

---

[33] Barrett, quoted in Waite (2022). See also Doyle, quoted in Hemming (2022), where she states that 'Before the invasion [of Ukraine] happened, we were already thinking of this work partly as a war requiem: a piece about all wars rather than one war [...] and Greece becomes our place of remembrance and contemplation. There's definitely a sense of loss and a sense that there are no victors in this world'.

the sound design on a portable speaker. The soundscape included nine dull sirens intermixed with a gong. Despite the abstractness of the soundscape, Doyle and Duggan clarified to the cast that the sequence could not be improvised but would consist of very precise choreography. Patroclus, here performed by Fionn Cox-Davies, led the stair descent, in part because of the role Cox-Davies played in developing the choreography from the base of the stairs and the need for him to lead the transition into the centre of the space and set the rhythm for the next sequence. Doyle stopped and started the siren composition, spacing out the bodies as the performers started their stair descent. The movement language already solidified through the early workshops and the daily hour-long warm-up classes meant that a broader gestural language of a lyrical, slow-motion descent came innately to the performers. Directorial notes were consequently about specific tweaks to physicality, including 'position your face more so we can see it', 'think about the angle of your arm', 'incline back further', and 'carry a shape more rather than move through'. At one point, to add another dimension to the finale, Doyle suggested that Cassandra enter the stair descent as the final figure and try her 'stair solo', which had until now been positioned in Scene Ten when she escaped back to Troy after arriving with Agamemnon at the Mycenaean Royal Palace. The more frantic, staccato movements of the Cassandra solo contrasted with the stillness and 'tension/torsion' of the descending characters and was a juxtaposition retained for the final performance. With the specific angle and positioning of each performer set, the directors began to add in notes about the way the group moved together such as 'when Harry does his drop we need to feel that ricochet through the group a little'. To my observing eye, the notes seemed so specific that running the scene and witnessing a fluid choreographic echo of the painting felt impossible, but that was precisely what occurred, with the performers, on Doyle's cue, running the full scene and then handing over the detail of their choreography to the second cast.

It seemed that in one ninety-minute rehearsal the stair sequence quickly came together and the finale became substantially closer to completion. However, the end of *The Burnt City* was still a long way from finished with various aesthetic decisions still pending, including the finale costumes, the lighting design, the possibility of an ash drop, and the finessing of the choreography. Additional hours of rehearsal during the next two weeks solved most of these outstanding queries, but the idea of the scene reaching completion remained a fantasy until after the arrival of the audience and the adjustment of the scene in response to their presence.

Two 'sneak peek' dress rehearsals took place on 17 and 19 March 2022. These sneak peeks represented the first time each cast did a full run of the production for an audience. *The Burnt City* still had many pieces of its jigsaw missing, but the broad outline of the performance was in place and ready to be tested out in relation to audience flow. The sneak peeks had a reduced audience capacity of five hundred, as opposed to the full capacity of six hundred. Even with these smaller numbers, issues with the finale were immediately apparent. Some of the performers coming from Troy, and in particular Polymestor, who came from being blinded in the Klub at the conclusion of Scene Eleven, were struggling to get to the top of the staircase in good time, and for the audience waiting at the bottom of No Man's Land, sight lines were an issue. Standing in the middle of No Man's Land during the first sneak peek, for example, I had a clear view of the staircase for the descent, but once the performers reached the base of the stairs I found myself unable to see their transition to the centre of the space, while those closer to the stairs found themselves unable to see the circular choreography that took place in the centre of No Man's Land or the (then current) final image of Hecuba and Clytemnestra coming together in a moment of shared humanity and understanding. After the first preview, on 22 March 2022, the sightline issue was compounded with challenges around the audience's exit, with an enormous bottleneck created as hundreds of audience members were funnelled through the small doorways between No Man's Land, the Barracks, and the Bar. The finale was clearly unworkable; rectifying it was now the number one priority.

During the morning notes session which kick-started rehearsals on 23 March 2022, Barrett and Doyle informed the cast that a second finale would take place in the Trojan Town Square to weave in the requirements surrounding audience flow and visibility and share the audience across the two warehouses. A Trojan finale had been raised as a possibility early in the creative development of *The Burnt City*, so although practical constraints governed the decision they were not in opposition to the directors' creative vision. The concept that Barrett and Doyle presented was for a version of the blinding sequence as the Trojan finale, relocated to the Town Square from the Klub with additional characters to heighten the scale of the scene and the degree of spectacle. The blinding scene usually took place in Scene Eleven of the loop and used the conclusion of Euripides' *Hecuba* for its narrative, in which Hecuba and the other Trojan female captives blind Polymestor in revenge for his murder of Hecuba's son Polydorus. In *The Burnt City*, the company spliced Polymestor's blinding together with the sense of a *sparagmos* (ritual tearing apart) drawn from Euripides' *Bacchae*.[34] Hecuba delivered an incantation and called upon the furies and her allies to enact their maenad-style revenge in Scene Ten, with the blinding in Loops One and Two involving the reincarnated Polyxena (now a fury), alongside Cassandra and the resident characters Kampe, Luba, and the character later known as Macaria. The Loop Three version added in Eurydice (later renamed Eury), Polydorus, and a bar host. The image of the two queens coming together in Mycenae to conclude the performance was removed, and instead, the production had mirror images of the two queens in the two finales, with Hecuba staying in the Town Square where she looked up into an ash drop as the same extract from Cherubini's *Requiem* played.

The afternoon's rehearsal schedule was amended to allow time to rehearse the new finale, with the company intending to perform the production with both finales for the second preview in two days' time, on 25 March. Just like the stair descent sequence, there was again a large directorial presence at this rehearsal, with Bradley, Harrison, Doyle, and Barrett all in the space. Doyle led the beginning of the session, setting the big-picture agenda: 'today, our aim is to find a moment to bring in the Cherubini, to allow Hecuba to finish her story, and have that simple concluding moment currently present in No Man's Land'. There were also several practicalities, including relocating Hecuba's incantation, which took place in Polymestor's office in Loops One and Two, and reconfiguring the blinding choreography, which took place in the round in the Klub. The cast of performers involved in the original scene commenced work altering their choreography to suit the natural architecture of the space, which included the original steel beam of the building which cut across the square in parallel to the end of the warehouse. It became clear that the challenge was not the relocation of the choreography per se but reconfiguring the interaction between the 'maenads' and

---

[34] Although Euripides' *Hecuba* pre-dates *Bacchae*, Euripides' refers to Hecuba and the Trojan women as 'Bacchants of Hades' [1076], and Segal (1990: 119) notes that the 'pattern of Maenadic violence was sufficiently established in myth and art to serve as a model for the Trojan women'. As such, there is a textual precedent for Punchdrunk's interpretation.

Polymestor, with Polymestor weaving between and being passed around the women before his ultimate blinding. The performers moved across the plane in a circular, weaving motion, setting the location of each beat of movement and the order in which Polymestor was passed through the group, with Doyle noting that the sequence needed to be clean and energised or it would become a blur of movement. With the locations blocked out, the performers involved in the Loops One and Two blinding sequence then taught the choreography to the additional cast who would now be incorporated into the Trojan finale, which was performed (in all loops) to the techno track 'Confusion' by New Order from the *Blade* soundtrack.

The addition of a second finale involved performers losing material as well as creating it, with some of the cast members who had previously been involved in the stair descent sequence handing over material devised on 10 March to other performers in service of the bigger picture. When the second preview took place on 25 March, it included not only the addition of a new, second finale (a moment from which is pictured on the front cover of this volume), but also new cast members performing parts of the original Greece finale. Performers had as little as thirty minutes to rehearse these new scenes in show conditions (i.e. with lighting and sound cues), reflecting just how alive, pressured, and precious the rehearsal period was during Punchdrunk's preview process and the efficiency required to rehearse the essentials in the time available. Although the audience was the final source of meaning in *The Burnt City*, generating and shaping content and becoming an active player within the space of the performance from previews onwards, their impact as a collective entity upon the conclusion shows that they were by no means the least important. The wider structures of performance and the tracks of each character all bent to accommodate the audience's needs.

* * *

This chapter has sketched out the development process of *The Burnt City* as I had access to it through my work as dramaturg and embedded researcher. Through thick descriptions, in chronological order, of the development of the project from the summer of 2019 until April 2022, I have offered glimpses into how Punchdrunk responded to ancient literature when developing the loop structure for *The Burnt City*, and how the company's engagement with *Agamemnon* and *Hecuba* was shaped by and supplemented with the design and build of the space, other mythological sources such as Ovid's *Metamorphoses*, references to Greek religion, an embodied understanding of the movement vocabulary of the show in question and of Punchdrunk's immersive performance style in general, and the realities of performing for a mobile audience. When it came to the actual devising of *The Burnt City*, no one of these factors trumped the other; entire scenes were built around and removed due to any one of these components. The different nodes within the rehearsal process became individual threads within the braid of *The Burnt City*, creating a reinterpretation of Greek tragedy of unusual complexity in that it was not a reception of even a conglomeration of Trojan War tragedies, but of a far more disparate assemblage of sources of which this chapter had only scratched the surface.[35] The scale and scope of *The Burnt City* ultimately had less in common with contemporaneous adaptations of *Agamemnon* and *Hecuba* or the revisionist retellings of mythology that exist in wider popular culture, and more in common with the 'megatexts' we find in the fantasy worlds of Tolkien or C.S. Lewis, or in the Marvel and DC megaverses. These megatexts adhere to Tolkien's definition of secondary storyworlds, which exist in opposition to the primary world in which we live and are defined as credible, consistent, and coherent narrative universes with a distinct border separating them from reality.[36] Like other megatexts, *The Burnt City* featured numerous simultaneous narratives unfolding at tangents from one another, a sizeable cast of characters, and the ability to create its own community of superfans who engage in a form of fan fiction, which in Punchdrunk's case is known as extended audiencing.[37] If *The Burnt City* was more like the secondary storyworlds

---

[35] To summarise, the sources featured in this chapter include the two primary tragedies, *Agamemnon* and *Hecuba*, alongside Euripides' *Iphigenia at Aulis* and *Iphigenia among the Taurians*, material and literary evidence for the *arkteia*, and Ovid's *Metamorphoses*, alongside non-classical sources including Memling's *Last Judgement* and Bouts' *The Fall of the Damned*, Fritz Lang's *Metropolis*, Philip K. Dick's *Do Android's Dream of Electric Sheep*, and the dystopian science-fiction worlds referenced through Dobbie's sound design. Although I have only touched lightly upon the idea of collision sources in this chapter, the final production referenced, to differing degrees, *Metropolis*, *Blade Runner*, *Jacob's Ladder*, and *Bluebeard*; an interrogation of the role of these intertexts lies outside the remit of this book and my focus on the role of the classics in Punchdrunk's theatre.

[36] Tolkien (1947).

[37] On extended audiencing in Punchdrunk's *Sleep No More*, see the work of Ritter, including 2016 and 2020: 136–180. Ritter's theories can be applied to *The Burnt City*,

in the above-mentioned texts than it is like other twenty-first-century classical performance receptions, then it follows that its creation was an example of contemporary mythopoiesis.

A production is both an example of a classical performance reception and contemporary mythopoiesis when it is not simply a new version of one particular piece of mythology, or to use Sarah Iles Johnston's terminology another serial of the hyperserialised narrative that is the megatext of Greek mythology, but rather uses myth, as Neil Gaiman describes, as 'compost' to provide 'fertile ground' in which new stories grow.[38] Although the central spine of *The Burnt City* was a known narrative, even if we consider the classical content of the production in isolation we find that the production originates entirely new tales. For example, the *Bluebeard*-inspired storyline of the travelling characters Hades and Persephone, and the separate storylines involving the cast of resident characters were all innovations; there is no evidence, for example, of the resident characters such as Askalaphos ever interacting with the characters from the source tragedies in all extant ancient literature. Furthermore, the characterisation of the resident characters was often based upon a historical figure or a collision source, with the role of Kampe, for example, inspired by Weimar-era dancer Anita Berber and the role of Luba inspired by Luba Luft in *Do Androids Dream of Electric Sheep*. The blending of mythic figures with collision sources resulted in further originality. The end result of *The Burnt City* was thus an example of Iles Johnston's coherent and credible storyworld, which not only told multiple stories but also: involved the creation of paratextual materials by its fan base; facilitated spin-offs; was separated from the primary world by a distinct boundary (here the museum cross-fade experience and the donning of the mask); and had its own unique logic, which in *The Burnt City* included the masked audience, the relationship between the performers and the audience, and the looping, purgatorial narrative structure.[39]

An ungenerous reading of Punchdrunk's conglomeration of references to the ancient world in *The Burnt City* might position the assortment of classically-inflected sources as a kind of mythic soup rather than evidence

---

which received a similar form of audience engagement, as attested via the fan-art shared under #theburntcity on social media.

[38] Iles Johnston (2015) and Gaiman (2016: 64).

[39] Iles Johnston (2015).

of robust research. Granted, some of the company's classical references were somewhat randomised; the names of *The Burnt City*'s resident characters, for example, almost always referenced the Greek mythic Underworld but usually did not have any other dramaturgical connection to the world of the performance. However, understanding Punchdrunk's R&D and rehearsal period as equating to the form of mythmaking required to create a secondary storyworld clarifies that Punchdrunk's process did not simply involve combining an amalgamation of classical references but represented a formula for the creation of an independent narrative universe. Punchdrunk's excavation of Greek tragedy and inclusion of narrative from companion texts, material remains, and religious and cult activities shows that when the company worked on their core sources for narrative and character, they engaged in a close and critical engagement with classical antiquity where they mined, in a rhizomatic fashion, sources from the wider networks in which their core texts were suspended. Punchdrunk's engagement with the classics was in service of the wider project of creating the type of megatext that could immerse spectators into an experience and sustain countless visits to unpack a criss-crossing network of characters and a multiplicity of stories. In other words, Punchdrunk used the ancient world to support their own mythmaking.

Barrett and Doyle commented to the press in their pre-production publicity for *The Burnt City* that they understood their project as about mining the density and richness of Greek tragedy, which they saw as 'the bedrock of Western theatre'.[40] The rehearsal study contained in this chapter has demonstrated that in conceptualising their practice in such a way, the directors sold their project short. *The Burnt City* did mine 'the bedrock of Western theatre' (although positioning Greek tragedy in such a way is, it should be noted, at odds with the scholarly push towards decolonising the discipline and the move against positioning classical Greece as the exclusive origin of Western culture). However, by studying the processes involved in the R&D and rehearsal periods, we can see that *The Burnt City* also involved combining this material with a bespoke mix of additional ingredients to create a new narrative universe fit for original immersive performance.[41] Studying how process shaped product reveals that *The Burnt City* was created via a form of contemporary mythopoiesis.

---

[40] See, for example, Waite (2022) and James (2022).

[41] On the decolonisation of classics, see Umachandran and Ward (Forthcoming).

Works Cited

Bahr, Sarah. 2021. Andrew Lloyd Webber Delays 'Cinderella' Musical in West End. *The New York Times*, July 19. https://www.nytimes.com/2021/07/19/theater/andrew-lloyd-webber-cinderella-musical-delayed.html. Accessed 8 September 2022.

Gaiman, Neil. 2016. *The View from the Cheap Seats*. London: Headline.

Gardner, Lyn. 2021. Punchdrunk's The Burnt City. *Stagedoor*, September 5. https://stagedoorapp.com/lyn-gardner/punchdrunks-the-burnt-city?ia=1011. Accessed 6 March 2023.

Hamilton, Richard. 1989. Alkman and the Athenian Arkteia. *Hesperia: The Journal of the American School of Classical Studies at Athens* 58: 4: 449–472.

Hemming, Sarah. 2022. Punchdrunk's Immersive Theatre Returns with an Epic Tale of Troy. *Financial Times*, March 25. https://www.ft.com/content/b7407aa1-1157-4543-b05a-87f754b5a2c8. Accessed 19 August 2022.

Iles Johnston, Sarah. 2015. The Greek Mythic Story World. *Arethusa* 48: 283–311.

James, Anna. 2022. Punchdrunk's Felix Barrett and Maxine Doyle: "This Place is on a Scale that is Truly Mythic". *The Stage*, April 7. https://www.thestage.co.uk/long-reads/punchdrunks-felix-barrett-and-maxine-doyle-this-place-is-on-a-scale-that-is-truly-mythic-the-burnt-city. Accessed 12 May 2022.

Kahil, Lilly. 1983. Mythological Repertoire of Brauron. In *Ancient Greek Art and Iconography*, ed. Warren G. Moon, 231–244. Madison, Wisconsin: University of Wisconsin Press.

Lewis, Isobel. 2022. Andrew Lloyd Webber Jokingly Shares Covid Conspiracy in Speech to Audience at Cinderella Reopening. *The Independent*, February 4. https://www.independent.co.uk/arts-entertainment/theatre-dance/news/andrew-lloyd-webber-cinderella-reopening-covid-b2007658.html. Accessed 8 September 2022.

Machon, Josephine, and Punchdrunk. 2019. *The Punchdrunk Encyclopaedia*. London and New York: Routledge.

Maxwell, Dominic. 2022. Punchdrunk Creators: 'I Don't Like How Lots of Theatre Shuts Down Your Brain Activity'. *The Times*, March 22. https://www.thetimes.co.uk/article/punchdrunk-creators-the-burnt-city-interview-qsk0x5xxx. Accessed 6 March 2023.

McAuley, Gay. 2012. *Not magic but work: an ethnographic account of a rehearsal process*. Manchester and New York: Manchester University Press.

O'Mahony, Holly. 2022. Punchdrunk: The Burnt City, Woolwich Works. *Culture Whisper*, April 22. https://www.culturewhisper.com/r/theatre/punchdrunk_the_burnt_city_woolwich_works/16484. Accessed 6 March 2022.

Perlman, Paula. 1989. Acting the She-Bears for Artemis. *Arethusa* 22: 2: 111–133.

Punchdrunk. 2023. The Third Day. *Punchdrunk*. https://www.punchdrunk.com/project/the-third-day/. Accessed 6 March 2023.

Ritter, Julia M. 2016. In the Body of the Beholder: Insider Dynamics and Extended Audiencing Transform Dance Spectatorship in *Sleep No More*. In *Reframing Immersive Theatre: The Politics and Pragmatics of Participatory Performance*, ed. James Frieze, 43–62. London: Palgrave Macmillan.

———. 2020. *Tandem Dances: Choreographing Immersive Performance*. Oxford: Oxford University Press.

Segal, Charles. 1990. Violence and the other: Greek, Female and Barbarian in Euripides' *Hecuba*. *TAPA* 120: 109–131. https://doi.org/10.2307/283981.

Snow, Georgia. 2020. Andrew Lloyd Webber Delays Cinderella Opening Amid Coronavirus Fears. *The Stage*, March 5. https://www.thestage.co.uk/news/andrew-lloyd-webber-delays-cinderella-opening-amid-coronavirus-fears. Accessed 8 September 2022.

Soloski, Alexis. 2022. 'Sleep No More' Awakens After a Long Hibernation. *The New York Times*, February 9. https://www.nytimes.com/2022/02/09/theater/sleep-no-more-reopens.html. Accessed 6 March 2023.

Sourvinou-Inwood, Christiane. 1988. *Studies in Girls' Transitions: Aspects of the Arkteia and Age Representation in Attic Iconography*. Athens: Kardamista.

Tolkien, J. R. R. 1947. On Fairy-Stories. In *Essays Presented to Charles Williams*, ed. C. S. Lewis, 38–89. Oxford: Oxford University Press.

Umachandran, Mathura and Marchella Ward, eds. Forthcoming. *Forgetting Classics: The Case for Critical Ancient World Studies*. London: Routledge.

Virchow, Rudolf. 1880. Preface. In *Ilios: The City and Country of the Trojans: The Results of Researches and Discoveries on the Site of Troy and Throughout the Troad in the Years 1871-72-73-78-79. Including an Autobiography of the author*, ed. Heinrich Schliemann, ix–xvi. London: Murray.

Waite, Thom. 2022. Inside Punchdrunk's Radical Immersive Theatre Show, The Burnt City. *Dazed*, March 21. https://www.dazeddigital.com/life-culture/article/55727/1/inside-punchdrunks-monumental-immersive-theatre-show-the-burnt-city. Accessed 12 July 2022.

Zajko, Vanda. 2020. Contemporary Mythopoiesis: The Role of Herodotus in Neil Gaiman's *American Gods*. *Classical Receptions Journal* 12: 3: 299–322. https://doi.org/10.1093/crj/claa002.

CHAPTER 4

The Burnt City in Development: Abstracting Ancient Literature

On Tuesday 29 March 2022, *The Burnt City* cast, directors, stage management, and I gathered in the rehearsal room on the site of Punchdrunk's Woolwich home for the first day of week 10 of rehearsals. We sat together in a circle on the floor ready to discuss notes on the weekend's show. The company had now performed *The Burnt City* three times for paying audiences and were about to embark upon the second week of previews. The theatre had been dark for two consecutive days for the last time until the summer. The cast chatted animatedly while waiting for the notes to commence, being well rested thanks to the break and full of optimism and excitement thanks to the energy that audiences had brought to the show. Co-directors Felix Barrett and Maxine Doyle sat side by side as part of the circle, talking between themselves, before turning out to the group. As conversations hushed, Doyle commenced with the day's key piece of feedback: the performers needed to think about where human voice sat in the world. She continued:

> Sometimes, we need to find dialogue. Speak under the breath - this is not about declamation, the audience hearing what you are saying, but about the performance not being mime-y. If you want someone to come with you then don't gesture but say quietly "let's go". It is another layer of language that the work needs to evolve. In contrast, sometimes big vocalisations don't work in the space. For example, both Agamemnon and Polymestor

are doing naturalism and vocalisations during their violent ends, but this isn't working when it comes out of a passage with no vocals.

Vinicius Salles, who co-devised the role of Agamemnon, laughed as they copied the feedback down on their iPad with a stylus pen, recalling their performance of Agamemnon's death scene in the recent previews. In the initial previews of *The Burnt City*, Clytemnestra murdered Agamemnon in a walk-in shower in the Mycenaean Royal Palace, having rendered him defenceless by feeding him a lotus flower during a massage after his homecoming (the lotus flower represented a dangerous recreational drug within *The Burnt City*, in part inspired by Weimar dancer Anita Berber's penchant for eating rose petals dipped in chloroform and ether). Prior to his murder, Clytemnestra stripped Agamemnon naked and led him into the shower seductively, before revealing Aegisthus to Agamemnon and by association the bombshell that she was not the faithful wife pleased to see her returning husband which she had presented as earlier in the performance. Clytemnestra then slammed Agamemnon's head into the back wall of the shower, before holding him in a headlock and throttling him under the running water until he collapsed on the floor in front of her. The sequence came after ten minutes of abstracted performance and entirely wordless choreography. Agamemnon's shout as Clytemnestra landed her first blow, and then his gasping and choking as he died came in stark contrast to the silent backdrop which had preceded this moment of the performance and had rung out hollow in the space.

Doyle's request for the performers playing Agamemnon and Polymestor to remove language from the final moments of Scene Eleven was indicative of Punchdrunk's approach to ancient literature in *The Burnt City*, which involved transforming text into a visual and experiential dramaturgy not through a direct, movement-for-word form of translation but rather by abstracting select dramaturgical components from *Agamemnon* and *Hecuba*. The company's removal of spoken language throughout *The Burnt City* was not exhaustive; indeed, the performers who played Hecuba wove speech throughout their loop, including via prayers and incantations, and many one-on-one experiences also featured the spoken word. However, almost the entirety of Clytemnestra's loop was abstracted, and many of the narrative peaks from the two tragedies were told through choreographic language rather than verbal discourse, including the sacrifices of both Iphigenia and Polyxena and, after Doyle's note on 29 March, the death of Agamemnon and the blinding of Polymestor. Doyle's instruction for the performers to pare back vocalisations in favour of abstraction was illustrative of Punchdrunk's wider process of translating text into movement during the development of *The Burnt City*.

The presence of narrative in Punchdrunk's masked performances is sometimes deemed opaque and is a part of the company's work that divides critical opinion. When writing about *The Burnt City*, Duška Radosavljecić argued, for example, that it was 'not always entirely clear what it is the audience is watching—and if it has anything to do with the source materials drawn from Aeschylus and Euripides'.[1] This chapter addresses the critiques surrounding the presence of narrative in Punchdrunk's immersive worlds by documenting and showcasing Punchdrunk's approach to their source material. It also supplements the evidence presented in Chapter 3 to demonstrate further how examining the creative process underpinning a classical reception informs and enlightens our understanding of a final product. My examination of how Punchdrunk abstracted Greek tragedy during rehearsals reveals that the company's working practices can be thought of as a form of intersemiotic or intermedial translation, involving moving a text from a linguistic sign system, or the medium of literary text, into a choreographic sign system, or the medium of dance. Scholars of dance-based practice such as Jess McCormack have convincingly argued that the intermedial shift from text into movement can always be illuminated through a translation studies lens, even when there is no attempt at 'equivalence', as the boundaries between a free translation and an adaptation are porous during the shift from a written language into a movement language.[2] McCormack suggests that rather than looking for evidence of fidelity or equivalence, one should, for example, search for evidence of the choreographer or performer entering into dialogue with the source text to determine whether a translation studies approach might be applicable. Similarly, Madeleine Campbell and Ricarda Vidal argue that an intersemiotic transfer should be classified as a translation due to the process at play when reinventing a source text, rather than due to any explicit similarity between source and translation. They argue that a degree of kinship

---

[1] Radosavljecić (2022).
[2] McCormack (2018).

between source and translation is the requirement, rather than similarity, and that when it comes to intersemiotic translation we should reverse the traditional notion of the translator's invisibility and instead should focus on 'the translator's gaze [as] explicitly apparent or visible to the reader/viewer/audience/spectator as the "mottling", by becoming entangled in the translated artefact or event (as in dance or performance)'.[3] Although Punchdrunk's final product might not adhere to what scholars understand a translation of Greek tragedy to be, due to the extensive narrative alterations and the supplementary texts woven into Punchdrunk's mythic universe, when the company devised scenes which engaged with and responded to their tragic sources, they entered into a dialogue with their sources to transform text into movement, both to give shape to a scene and to determine minute beats of choreography.

This chapter showcases Punchdrunk's translatorial process during the development of four specific scenes, namely the sacrifice of Polyxena, the staging of the emerging relationship between Clytemnestra and Aegisthus, the production's finale, and the reunion between Clytemnestra and Agamemnon. It is not the aim of this chapter to rebut those critics who decry an absence of narrative within Punchdrunk's masked performances. Indeed, my continued use of Spectator-Participation-as-Research in Chapters 5 and 6 is predicated upon the centrality and equality of all audience experiences within Punchdrunk's work, rather than a hierarchy of experience which positions 'expert' audience members' experiences—whether in terms of being cognisant of Punchdrunk's performance style or well versed in the classical canon—as somehow more correct and valuable. Nevertheless, I here demonstrate that irrespective of how narrative is experienced at the point of reception, a close interrogation of text is integral to Punchdrunk's working practices. Just as an understanding of the processes of receiving antiquity can help one to understand a classical reception, so too does an understanding of how a source narrative is handled during rehearsals help one to comprehend the diversity of views regarding its role in the final performance.

---

[3] Campbell and Vidal (2019: 17).

Approaching *Agamemnon* and *Hecuba*

Doyle and Barrett approached their two source texts, Aeschylus' *Agamemnon* and Euripides' *Hecuba*, in different ways, which is in part reflected in the fact that they chose a specific translation of *Agamemnon* to respond to, namely Ted Hughes' translation, whereas they did not work with a specific translation of *Hecuba*.[4] The relationship between source text and target artefact in Hughes' *Oresteia* echoes some of the tensions surrounding the presence of the classics in Punchdrunk's work. Ted Hughes could not, to our knowledge, read ancient Greek. His translation method was, according to his friend and later scholar Keith Sagar, 'to procure from someone else, often a friend, a crib—that is a straightforward literal prose translation, from which Hughes would then produce his "version". He would also, of course, read all the other translations he could get hold of'.[5] Hughes' lack of Greek does not invalidate calling his text a translation; indeed, it is common practice within the theatre industry today to commission playwrights to create a 'performable' version from a literal translation, and there is substantial scholarly precedent for considering Hughes' text as a form of translation, too. Furthermore, Hughes himself used the term translation to describe his dramatic responses to Greek tragedy. Nevertheless, the relationship is indirect, mirroring the complexity between source and target in *The Burnt City*. Although an audience member might be hard pressed to find traces of Hughes' language within the minimal dialogue of *The Burnt City*, the company adhered relatively closely to the narrative of *Agamemnon* except for their treatment of Cassandra. The directors decided before the commencement of rehearsals that Cassandra's storyline, involving Agamemnon taking an enslaved Cassandra to Mycenae and then Clytemnestra murdering Cassandra alongside Agamemnon, was problematic from a feminist standpoint and revised her narrative so that she would not die and would instead go willingly to Greece, after receiving a prophecy which revealed that if Agamemnon made it

---

[4] On prior scholarship describing Hughes' *Oresteia* through the lens of translation, see, for example, Brown (2009) and Sagar (2009), and on Hughes' dramatic translations of the classics more generally (although with little reference to Hughes' *Oresteia*), see Hardwick (2009). On Hughes describing his work as a translation, see Sagar (2009: 9). On the practice of having a high-profile poet or playwright create a 'performable' translation from an expert's literal translation, see Brodie (2018: 6).

[5] Sagar (2001).

home to Greece then he would be killed. In contrast, when it came to reworking *Hecuba*, a close adherence to the narrative of the source tragedy was the exception, rather than the rule. The two key plot points of *Hecuba*, namely the sacrifice of Polyxena and the blinding of Polymestor, were both retained, but the circumstances surrounding both events were altered. Although Polyxena went 'willingly' to her sacrifice in *Hecuba*, in *The Burnt City* she not only went willingly but in fact died by her own hand. Furthermore, in *Hecuba* while it is Hecuba and her fellow female captives who blind Polymestor, they are only able to enact their revenge thanks to the assistance of Agamemnon. In contrast, in *The Burnt City* Hecuba achieved vengeance without male assistance.[6] The scale of Hecuba's revenge was also altered, with Hecuba no longer killing Polymestor's children in *The Burnt City* but only blinding Polymestor.[7] The timeline of Hecuba's story in *The Burnt City* was also much more elastic than in *Hecuba*. *Hecuba* has what we might consider an Aristotelian unity of time, taking place across one day and opening with the ghost of Polydorus explaining how Polymestor reneged on his guest friendship with the House of Priam and his promise to Hecuba to keep him safe, only to murder him for his gold. The play then stages subsequent events unfolding almost as if in real time. In contrast, the order of events was different in *The Burnt City*, with the story beginning prior to Polydorus being entrusted to Polymestor, which occurred in Scene Two (followed by Polymestor's murder of Polydorus in Scene Eight, after the sacrifice of Polyxena instead of before). Hecuba's narrative in *The Burnt City* thus encompassed months of story time, if not years.[8]

---

[6] On the Greek control of the stage space in *Hecuba* and the necessity that Hecuba gain Agamemnon's complicity to exact her revenge, see Battezzato (2018: 7).

[7] On Hecuba's revenge in Euripides, see Battezzato (2018: 14–18). Hecuba's revenge in *The Burnt City* follows the model set in Book 13 of Ovid's *Metamorphoses*, in which the murder of Polymestor's children is also absent. The *Metamorphoses* was not, however, a deliberate intertext here.

[8] If we take a literal view of time in *The Burnt City*, then we find that one loop of the performance (55 minutes) equated to over ten years of mythological action, with the timeline presenting the events from Agamemnon incurring Artemis' wrath (leading her to demand Iphigenia's sacrifice) through to Agamemnon's murder in chronological order. Barrett, however, described Punchdrunk's approach as 'trying to create a fever dream that's based on this material', and as such, it is perhaps unhelpful to think of time within *The Burnt City* in a linear and literal way. See Barrett, quotes in Hemming (2022).

It is too simplistic to say that Punchdrunk's approach to *Agamemnon* involved a close reading of and response to text, whereas their approach to *Hecuba* involved artistic licence. Nevertheless, there were distinctions in the company's conceptualisation of the two texts and in how they responded to the plays in rehearsal. What remained consistent was the company's push towards abstracting both source texts as much as possible, which is a trademark of Punchdrunk's process and involves distilling a text down to a core idea or essence and rendering it abstract through repetition in design or choreography. Abstracting the tragedies enabled echoes between the two texts, and in particular between the two female queens' experiences of war, to reverberate throughout *The Burnt City* and for a wider statement to land regarding the impact of war and the grief of bereaved mothers in particular.

Abstracting Narrative

Punchdrunk's handling of Euripides' *Hecuba* involved cutting back the components of the tragedy that did not exist within the world of *The Burnt City*, while simultaneously adding in the events which occur offstage in, or prior to, the action of *Hecuba*. The material created for the action that took place in the Trojan Town Square during Scene Five and Scene Six was indicative of this process and involved creating scenes that do not occur onstage within *Hecuba*, namely the arrival of the Greek army in Troy (representing the fall of the city) and the death of Polyxena. Both scenes are described, rather than staged, in *Hecuba*, with the army's infiltration of Troy sung in the chorus' analeptic third stasimon [905–952], while the death of Polyxena is described in Talthybius' messenger speech [518–582]. The rehearsals thus involved the company rendering this content as staged performance and reorienting the Euripidean narrative to suit the politics and tone of *The Burnt City*'s narrative universe.

The fall of Troy is not part of the narrative of either *Agamemnon* or *Hecuba*, with both plays set immediately after the Greeks have taken the city and focusing on the aftereffects of the war's conclusion in Mycenae and Troy respectively. Yet as the plot of *The Burnt City* commenced prior to the war, it was essential to represent Troy's fall within the loop structure. Directors Felix Barrett and Maxine Doyle consequently positioned the fall of Troy as Scene Five when creating the loop chart, immediately prior to Polyxena's sacrifice in Scene Six. They scheduled the scene to bring together four soldiers (Agamemnon, Neoptolemus, Patroclus, and the Watchman) and four Trojans (Hecuba, Polyxena, Cassandra, and Penthesilea, later renamed Macaria), meaning the scene would involve the largest collective of cast (almost half of all the travelling characters) of anywhere in the loop structure bar the finale.[9] The *précis* given to each character scheduled to participate in the scene prior to the commencement of rehearsals read:

> The city falls into darkness. The sirens sound. The search lights shift. A 'body' / a 'horse' a 'statue' [sic] is thrown from the mezzanine. Hecuba stands in the bistro square as ash begins to fall from the sky covering her shoulders. She stands as a fallen queen, her city smouldering around her. Troy is taken by the Greeks.

Although the only image from this brief that remained in the final performance was the (momentary) blackout as the Greeks entered the city, with the ash drop, for example, moving to the finale, the description is nevertheless indicative of how the company approached abstracting the destruction of Troy via distilled images. When rehearsals commenced in situ the directors quickly realised that aside from the practical difficulties surrounding their initial ideas, a good portion of the fall of Troy would need to be given over to the lead up to Polyxena's sacrifice. As such, the directors drew upon a third section of Euripides' text, namely the three-way dialogue between Odysseus, Hecuba, and Polyxena involving the Greek's demand for, and Polyxena's ultimate acceptance of, her sacrifice [216–443]. The rehearsals consequently focused not so much upon abstracting the fall of Troy, but rather on collapsing the invasion with the demand for Polyxena's sacrifice and turning the highly dialogue-based Euripidean plot into a visual dramaturgy.

---

[9] Mythologically, Macaria is not a Trojan but is named in the Suda as a daughter of Hades. Macaria is also the name given to a daughter of Herakles, who is sacrificed to Persephone to ensure the prosperity of Athens and the safety of Macaria's siblings. Like Polyxena, Macaria is represented in the extant tragic tradition as accepting the call for sacrifice willingly. See Gantz (1993: 464–465). In *The Burnt City* she was Polyxena's lover and one of a collection of resident characters who were named after Underworld figures from Greek mythology, including, for example, Askalaphos and Zagreus. The character was named Penthesilea in rehearsals due to the directors having an earlier interest in representing a female soldier within the world of *The Burnt City*.

Within *Hecuba* the Greek army's decision to sacrifice Polyxena at Achilles' tomb is communicated to Hecuba by the chorus and then reinforced by Odysseus, to whom Hecuba unsuccessfully supplicates to try to avert her daughter's death. As the directors conflated the roles of Achilles and Neoptolemus in *The Burnt City*, the narrative surrounding the ghost of Achilles demanding Polyxena's sacrifice was removed and she was instead killed on Agamemnon's command (although with Neoptolemus as executioner, as in *Hecuba*), in a form of warped retribution for the war costing Agamemnon Iphigenia. The recurrence of Neoptolemus in both Iphigenia's and Polyxena's sacrifices, due to Neoptolemus playing Achilles' role as the marriage ruse used to lure Iphigenia to her sacrifice in *The Burnt City*, furthered the twinning of the two deaths, which are not only emblematic virgin sacrifices in Greek literature but also involve close intertextual references, with Euripides alluding to the language that Aeschylus employs in the choral ode that describes Iphigenia's death in *Agamemnon*.[10] Within *Hecuba*, Polyxena grieves for her mother more than herself and informs Odysseus that she will not supplicate him for assistance in averting her sacrifice but will die willingly, seeing no hope of happiness in the alternative of a life of slavery. After Polyxena exits with Odysseus, Talthybius then describes the sacrifice in his messenger speech, which involves him narrating Polyxena's death in an eroticised manner.[11] Just as we must read Iphigenia's patriotic fervour at the moment of her sacrifice in Euripides' *Iphigenia at Aulis* through the lens of the extreme duress under which she is placed, so too must we recognise the highly problematic circumstances surrounding Talthybius' narration of Polyxena's 'willing' death, which on the surface might read as her defiantly grasping nobility and achieving the sacrificial equivalent of a military *aristeia*, but in practice is a desperate attempt to safeguard her body from

---

[10] See Battezzato (2018: 148–149) on Euripides' references to Aeschylus' language. For a more general discussion on virgin sacrifice in *Agamemnon* and *Hecuba*, see Loraux (1987: 31–48) and Scodel (1996). Although there is synergy between Iphigenia's sacrifice (in both Aeschylus' *Agamemnon* and Euripides' *Iphigenia at Aulis*) and Polyxena's sacrifice, there are also important distinctions between the circumstances under which the two women accept their sacrifice, with Papastamati drawing attention to the loss of a potential high-status marriage for Iphigenia, versus the loss of an undesirable alliance as concubine to a Greek general for Polyxena. See Papastamati (2017: 369).

[11] On the eroticisation of Polyxena in Talthybius' speech, see Segal (1990: 111–112). On the way Polyxena's speech anticipates the sexual connotations of her sacrifice, see p. 117.

further assault and humiliation.[12] Indeed, Talthybius' highly-charged description in *Hecuba*, which details how Polyxena stepped forward at the moment of her sacrifice, ripping her peplos, exposing her breasts, and appearing 'as glorious as a statue of a god' [560], on the one hand invites one to imagine the sacrifice through a male, heterosexual gaze, but on the other shows Polyxena using her body to create shock and awe in a paradoxical effort to safeguard her dignity after death.[13]

The narrative revolving around Polyxena's sacrifice in *Hecuba* is almost exclusively text based and involves a choral ode, a lyric exchange between Hecuba and Polyxena, a three-way dialogue (somewhat akin to a formal *agon* debate) between Polyxena, Hecuba, and Odysseus, and a messenger speech from Talthybius. The exchanges also involve what we might deem a problematic representation of female victimhood, which elides the brutality of Polyxena's murder and instead sensationalises its spectacle. The challenges facing *The Burnt City*'s cast and creative team were therefore twofold and involved representing a narrated scene visually and (almost) wordlessly and doing so in a way that did not replicate Euripides' problematic framing.

The first rehearsal of the fall of Troy took place on the morning of Monday 7 February 2022. Barrett, Doyle, the cast, and I met in the rehearsal room, rather than on set, as the unstructured, open space facilitated a series of improvisations through which the company could begin to find the scene. The group was particularly large, with the cast alone numbering thirteen and including the red and blue cast members playing the six travelling characters in the scene, except for one of the Hecubas who was absent, and the addition of Milton Lopes and Stephanie Nightingale, who were devising the resident roles of the Watchmen and Penthesilea, respectively. Doyle invited me to commence the session with an overview of sacrificial rituals in antiquity, to think through historical

---

[12] On the connection between Polyxena's sacrifice and death in battle, see Loraux (1987: 60) and Papastamati (2017).

[13] Polyxena's command 'let no-one touch my body' [548–549] is echoed by Hecuba, who later hopes that 'no one touches her' [605–606]. Scholars such as Battezzato (2018: 153) have posited that in both instances the suggestion is that the Greek touch is sexually inappropriate. Whether we find fears of necrophilia or mutilation within Polyxena and Hecuba's dialogue, or simply a desire for the recognition of and respect for Polyxena's personhood even when she has no autonomy and after death, we can be sure that Polyxena's request to die without being held down is also about dignity rather than only about nobility.

notes that the cast might embed within Polyxena's sacrifice. Rather than trying to implement small historical notes immediately, however, Doyle then moved on to workshop the initial interactions between the Greeks and the Trojans for when the army entered Troy. During the September workshops, a series of improvisions around Polyxena's sacrifice had taken place, and Doyle continued the rehearsal by playing a recording of the scene from September. In Punchdrunk's *Encyclopaedia*, Doyle stressed the importance of the 'concentrate' of the choreographic language that gets created during the pre-rehearsal studio workshops, with the process 'very much about equipping the performers to go into the building with the right material'.[14] In the recording of the studio session devoted to Polyxena's sacrifice, a few beats of narrative action around which to scaffold future rehearsals could be glimpsed, including: the Trojan women attempting to hold on to Polyxena for as long as possible while the Greek soldiers tried to extract her; a direct representation of the Euripidean description of Polyxena baring her breast and commanding Neoptolemus to look at her (here done wordlessly, by Polyxena opening her arms out wide and presenting herself to Neoptolemus, and then smacking her hands on her chest); and finally, Polyxena stabbing herself in the heart when Neoptolemus froze, seemingly unable to kill her. Doyle informed the cast that in today's rehearsal they were 'rediscovering, recreating, reinventing', using the recording as a springboard from which to choreograph the scene.

Although both Doyle and Barrett were present for the fall of Troy rehearsal, it was Doyle who led the initial improvisation around how the soldiers would extract Polyxena from the group of Trojan women, which Barrett observed and noted. Such a dynamic between the two directors was not uncommon, with Barrett spending much of rehearsals straddling the big-picture components of the production and moving between the performing company's rehearsals and the work of the set, lighting, and sound design teams, while Doyle, as choreographer as well as co-director, focused more closely on the performers. For the first improvisation, Doyle invited the full cast of thirteen to participate, with the Trojan women attempting to protect Miranda Mac Letten, who played Polyxena in the recording and who was now co-devising the role with Chihiro Kawasaki, from the advancing Greeks. The cast formed into two packs and began

---

[14] Doyle, quoted in Machon and Punchdrunk (2019: 53).

circling each other in the space, mirroring one another's movements as the women attempted not to break eye contact with the men or to turn their backs. The purpose of the improvisation was to explore the lead up to the family unit being surrounded; Doyle encouraged the cast to extend this process as much as possible, to 'enjoy the conflict of this because then it's more interesting'. She offered the guidance to 'notice where your focus is, where you are, who and what you see. The thickness in the air. Start to find your ally'. Although the company worked in the round, often framing tableaux so they could be viewed from 360 degrees, from where I was sitting the improvisation read as the women gradually becoming clustered upstage right, while the men pushed them towards the corner from downstage left, spreading themselves out and physically elongating their line of attack. The improvisation became deeply uncomfortable to witness, with the seven men cornering the six women, until Doyle intervened and flipped the gender divide 'just for process' and made the Greek soldiers embody the family unit and the women the invading army. When the performers reached the endpoint of the exercise, Doyle commented 'magical, brutal'.

The group then came together and shared their discomfort at the gender dynamics of the scene, with Doyle explaining 'that's why I had to flip it'. Doyle shared her perceived solution to the brutality of the exchange as being about delving into the psychology of the scene, to make sure it was not just 'the victims and the aggressors, but about how to find the conflict, the shame'. Luke Murphy, who co-devised the role of Neoptolemus and was, like Mac Letten, a long-time Punchdrunk performer, offered the suggestion that they bring in a no-touch policy for when the soldiers corral the women to avoid the image of male violence against women being quite so dominant; Murphy suggested that they consider using the chairs from the bistro set dressing as the language of the scene, for example for barricading and/or climbing upon. Even in such an early, exploratory improvisation, Doyle gave individual notes, turning to Mac Letten and noting that 'the less you did the more powerful. [Your sacrifice is] an invitation you choose to accept and then you start to initiate'. Mac Letten then added, looking back to the September workshops, that 'there's a beat we've found in some improvs, but not in others, about opening the sacrifice up to the audience'. Although the specifics of the blocking and choreography were still entirely unknown, the emotional dynamics of the scene quickly became solidified. The cast knew what narrative and emotional beats they needed to communicate; future rehearsals would help them unpack how to do so.

Whereas the morning's rehearsal involved improvising choreography to give clarity to the cast regarding the psychology and emotions that Scene Five would communicate, the afternoon's rehearsal was all about fixing the precise blocking for the aftermath of Polyxena's sacrifice. The directors had predetermined that Polyxena's sacrifice would take place in Scene Six and be a rigged sequence involving Polyxena hanging suspended from the roof by her feet. The treatment of Polyxena's corpse was in stark contrast to the image Talthybius creates in *Hecuba* of Polyxena's dying act, which he describes through the lens of the male gaze by detailing how Polyxena 'took great care to fall in a seemly fashion to the ground, concealing from male eyes what should be concealed' [569–570].[15] Although the level of nudity surrounding Polyxena's sacrifice was still to be determined, there was a want within the company for the scene not to be built around the male gaze, and the early scene *précis* described the soldiers as bowing their heads and averting their eyes. The image of Polyxena's corpse within *The Burnt City* therefore would aim— even if it encompassed nudity—not to objectify and sexualise Polyxena, nor to valorise her 'willingness' as the Greek text does by describing the soldiers throwing leaves and flowers upon her corpse in a *phyllobolia* usually reserved for (male) athletic victors.[16] The hoisting of her corpse into the air instead stripped the scene back to the essence of the brutality inflicted upon women's bodies during war and dived in to the shame that Doyle mentioned in the morning's rehearsal as key to the complexity of the scene.

To find the blocking surrounding the suspension of Polyxena's corpse, the cast worked in the performance space with an aerial expert who assessed the safety considerations of the proposed action, with the rigged sequence including Polyxena hanging suspended upside down above a concrete floor (although a crash mat provided some protection). Almost everyone involved in the scene played an integral role in creating the image of Polyxena's death, from monitoring the safety cues through to

---

[15] Translation adapted from Kovacs (2005).

[16] Papastamati notes that the *phyllobolia* is not only reserved for athletic victors but is also part of the *makarismos* ritual for newlyweds. The action thus furthers the ritual twinning of marriage and death during the virgin sacrifice, as well as alluding to the heroism of Polyxena. See Papastamati (2017: 375).

working the rig to hoist her body up in the centre of the Town Square. The company talked through a number of safety precautions and checks, ranging from how the cast would confirm the locking of the carabiner that attached the strop around Polyxena's feet to the aerial rig, how Neoptolemus would cradle Polyxena's head as she was hoisted into the air, how Polyxena would signal whether she needed to be lowered, how the cast (particularly Neoptolemus and Hecuba) would monitor Polyxena for signs of struggle or unconsciousness, and how Polyxena's 'corpse' should be positioned once she was lowered to the floor at the end of the scene to aid blood flow. Both verbal and visual cues were used while the cast worked in the noisy rehearsal environment amidst the still-continuing set construction. When the performers were satisfied with the clarity of their cues, they then commenced practising the aerial sequence to set the timings of the scene. Going into the rehearsal, the company estimated that Polyxena would be suspended for two-and-a-half minutes, but as soon as Mac Letten was hoisted into the air and fed back about the pressure of the strop on her ankles, the total time for which Polyxena was suspended was reduced to ninety seconds. Both casts then continued to practise the sequence for the remainder of the session, rehearsing the safety cues and consolidating the timings.[17]

After a full day of rehearsing the fall of Troy and the sacrifice of Polyxena, the directors and cast appeared to have a clear understanding of the emotional and psychological dramaturgy surrounding the call for Polyxena's sacrifice, as well as the mechanics of the aftermath of Polyxena's sacrifice. Unlike the rehearsal of Iphigenia's sacrifice (discussed in Chapter 3), Polyxena's sacrifice did not come together in just one day, with the eroticisation of Polyxena's death within the source material, and the optics of the Greek army extracting her from the Trojan women proving more difficult to abstract and reorient. The process of abstraction thus continued when the company gathered again at the end of the week, on Thursday 10 February 2022, to continue devising the scene, this time in the performance space rather than the rehearsal room.

The rehearsals on 10 February were in preparation for the company's first run through of Scenes One to Five, which was scheduled to take place between 3 and 6 pm. Prior to the run, the cast continued devising Scene Five, with Barrett and rehearsal director Carl Harrison leading a rehearsal

---

[17] A pre-show aerial call ensured these safety cues were constantly revised ahead of every single performance of *The Burnt City*.

in the Town Square. There were two priorities for rehearsal ahead of this run, namely to try and pin down some blocking for firstly the extraction of Polyxena, and secondly for the Greek soldiers' preparation for the sacrifice. The cast commenced with what they were then terming the 'chair pile sequence', which was how they translated Monday's corralling improvisation into the performance space. The scene involved the soldiers pushing the Trojan women up onto the pile of cascading Art Deco theatre seats that spilled down to the floor from the upper window of a building (intended as an opera house) called the Palladium.[18] The cast commenced a first attempt of situating the sequence within the space, concluding the improvisation when the women were cornered on the chairs in a position that Harrison joked looked akin to a 'Christmas window at Selfridges'. Barrett noted that the current sequence was 'very, very fiddly', confirming that the beats of the scene should be [for the Greeks] searching, finding, and corralling, and that Agamemnon as leader should not be involved in the corralling but should be static. Murphy then suggested that the drive towards the chair pile should be one straight line, rather than the cast circling and moving about the square. Even with the added direction and consequent simplification of the scene, the action still proved a challenge, as the female performers struggled to run backwards and climb upon the precarious chair structure; the evening's rehearsal notes requested that construction add in additional, reinforced steps within the chairs to aid the action.

With limited time left during the afternoon's rehearsal, the cast then split into two groups, with the soldiers rehearsing how they would set up the ritual with Barrett, and the women rehearsing how Polyxena would journey from the chair pile into the centre of the Town Square with Harrison. For the ritual set up, Barrett noted to the cast that from the audience's perspective the scene should 'feel experiential. [Think about] eye contact, touch, so they feel like they are there with you'. He then noted that 'the circle is the image, the shape of the show, anything to do with rituals, the finale, will make that shape', stressing that the cast should

---

[18] The name 'Palladium' appeared in neon writing on the top of the building's facade. Around the back of the building, there was an entrance sign indicating the 'stage door', which Polymestor and Persephone both used for one-on-ones. Posters for fictionalised performances at the Palladium were plastered onto the lower walls of the building to indicate its intended function.

find a way to push the audience out into a circle to watch Polyxena's sacrifice. Following my overview of sacrificial ritual at the start of the week (which largely drew upon the step-by-step account in *Odyssey* 3.430–463), Barrett had an interest in playing with some of the tactile elements used to prepare sacrificial animals and to purify the space and the participants in antiquity. Barrett floated the possibility of, for example, draping a ribbon across the audience's hands to demarcate a boundary between a front row of audience members and the performers, or scatting barley oats on the ground to create the outline of the circle and an implied barrier between the audience and the action, or perhaps even cleansing the front row of the audience's hands with water. Meanwhile, Kawasaki rehearsed her descent from the chair pile, with Harrison offering the direction that 'you have one job, which is choosing to accept your sacrifice with your chest. Everyone else's job is to facilitate you'. Kawasaki rehearsed a slow-motion descent down the chairs. She led with her heart with her arms outstretched behind her as her family attempted to hold on to her hands and create a 'Sistine chapel' goodbye between Polyxena and Hecuba. The action of leading with her heart meant that Kawasaki had to look straight ahead, rather than down at her feet, which proved difficult on the unfamiliar structure; upon noticing the challenge Harrison reassured the cast that for today, 'let's keep doing it practically and technically. The drama will come'.

By the afternoon's run, Scene Five and Scene Six had come far in comparison with where the scenes were at the start of the week when doing exploratory improvisations in the rehearsal room. Yet almost everything rehearsed on 10 February, including the tactile inclusion of the audience within the sacrifice scene and the use of the chair pile for the corralling sequence, would not make it into the final performance. The process of abstracting a scene involving so much narrative involved two steps forwards, one step backwards, and when I next witnessed the scene, on 24 February 2022, I encountered it almost entirely anew.

Friday 25 February was earmarked on the rehearsal schedule as the first run of a full loop of *The Burnt City*, and on Thursday 24 February, the cast came together to recap the eleven scenes of the show. In preparation for the full loop, the cast were given twenty minutes of rehearsal time per scene; I positioned myself in the Town Square for the time devoted to Scenes Five and Six, where I witnessed both the red and the blue cast running through the scenes. The lead up to Polyxena's death had become more abstracted than it was on 10 February, with the corralling onto the chair pile scrapped. Instead, when the Greek soldiers entered through the double doors of the Palladium (Fig. 4.1), they stood face to face with the Trojan women, who slowly leant towards their left, with the Greeks mirroring the women's tilt and creating the sensation that the world was spinning off its axis. The two groups mirrored one another, maintaining negative space as they slowly circled the Town Square, while the Watchman poured grains from a hessian bag onto the floor in the outline of a circle around the performers. Hecuba then stopped the circling, positioning herself between the Trojan women and the soldiers, and rhythmically beat her breast in a foreshadowing of the language of the finale. The other Trojan women joined in the breast beating, beginning to run in a circle around the Greek soldiers, before Polyxena launched herself at Agamemnon by jumping onto his shoulder, lifting her arms up to the sky in an image that recalled Iphigenia's physicality in the Pompeiian wall fresco of her sacrifice from the House of the Tragic Poet. When the soldiers lowered Polyxena to the ground and placed her in front of Agamemnon, she then pulled her hair up to the ceiling, which the other Trojan women, who were clustered on Polyxena's diagonal, mimicked. Polyxena then draped her hair down Agamemnon's head and torso, before proceeding to throw her head back and forth, flicking her hair on his face defiantly and insultingly while the other Trojan women spun around, corkscrewing themselves in a wide circle around the central action while tearing their hair. When Agamemnon forced Polyxena to stop she continued her defiance, staring him down while removing her dress, with Agamemnon only breaking eye contact to indicate to Neoptolemus to step forward. Polyxena then advanced on Neoptolemus, seizing his hand and driving it into her heart. The scene was rehearsed to Stephen Dobbie's sound design, which in the lead up to Polyxena's sacrifice featured a series of low, sustained bass notes, which created a dark and foreboding atmosphere, before transitioning to a sample of the song 'All the Earth' from the video game *Everybody's Gone to the Rapture* as Polyxena's body was hoisted up above the square. The music was operatic and classical in tone and featured a soaring, melancholic soprano.[19] The music worked to heighten the pathos surrounding what until now had been mechanical action, driving home for me the sense of the futility of

---

[19] On the music composition for *Everybody's Gone to the Rapture*, a game which shares qualities with the dystopian science-fiction intertexts employed throughout *The Burnt City*, see Stuart (2015).

war and the pointlessness of Polyxena's sacrifice. At the end of the scene's rehearsal, Doyle gave some encouragement, checking in that everyone was happy to perform the scene as it was for the upcoming run even though 'we haven't solved the scene'. Although the scenes were not finished, the company had edged closer towards finding a solution to the problematic representation of male on female violence in the original text, abstracting the encounter and finding a language for Polyxena's sacrifice which captured the emotional tug of her death, Polyxena's defiance, and her wish to write her own ending, all without sexualising her sacrifice.

Over the coming weeks, the scenes were rehearsed and re-rehearsed to tighten the narrative beats in the lead up to Polyxena's sacrifice and to clarify the emotional journeys of the characters within the scene. Small adjustments to the tempo and to the staging helped communicate the narrative as efficiently as possible. By previews, for example, the positioning of Hecuba and Agamemnon was fixed so that Hecuba was immediately behind Neoptolemus during Polyxena's death. The proxemics enabled a moment of eye contact between mother and daughter

Fig. 4.1 The Greek army enters Troy in Scene Five ('Fall of Troy') of *The Burnt City*. Image credit: Julian Abrams. Courtesy of Punchdrunk

and for both Neoptolemus and Hecuba to see, as per one of Barrett's notes, the 'life fade away from her eyes', and for audiences then to witness the impact of the characters experiencing such a moment throughout the rest of their loop. Agamemnon was positioned on the other side of the circle (which was now created by the Watchman tracing a chalk circle on the ground, rather than pouring barley onto the floor), looking out into the crowd; when Robert McNeill performed the role, I noticed a muscle in his cheek spasming during the sacrifice, with the indication of gritted teeth capturing the sense of shame Doyle had asked for in the first rehearsal. I found observing the tragic sadness of Hecuba watching on and Agamemnon looking away as arresting as the actual sacrifice, which was, like in Iphigenia's sacrifice, done without a weapon, with the violence abstracted and the fatal blow represented purely through blood. The busyness of the stage action during the early improvisations and rehearsals belied the simplicity of the final scene, which landed narrative and emotional poignancy through eye contact and stillness as much as through the physical corralling of the women and the extraction of Polyxena. The rehearsal process thus involved the directors entering into a dialogue with multiple specific pieces of Euripides' *Hecuba* to create the scenes, filtering narrative beats and reorienting character relationships before facilitating the performers' process of transforming Euripides' version of the story into something that fitted organically into *The Burnt City*'s universe.

Abstracting Emotion and Psychology

Creating both the fall of Troy and the death of Polyxena sequences involved distilling the narrative of *Hecuba* down to the simplest, most essential beats of action and abstracting it so that the scenes encompassed the same end goal as the source text, but in a way that aligned with the ideological principles underpinning Punchdrunk's production. When it came to creating the action that occurred in Greek Mycenae at the same point in time, Punchdrunk was faced with a different challenge, which was to invent specific moments of the relationship between Clytemnestra and Aegisthus for when Agamemnon was at war in Troy. To do so, the company had to abstract not narrative but the concept of a corrupted union spawned from a bereaved mother's grief.

The relationship between Aegisthus and Clytemnestra is tangentially alluded to throughout *Agamemnon*.[20] The allusions start in Aeschylus' prologue, when the Watchmen informs the audience that the goings-on within Agamemnon's *oikos* (household) will remain—for now—secret, announcing (in Hughes' version) that 'Those who know too much, as I do, about this house, / Let their tongue lie still-squashed flat' [76–77]. Cassandra later makes explicit reference to the relationship in her prophetic monologues during the fourth episode, referring (again in Hughes) to revenge being planned by 'a lion in this Palace, / A cowardly lion / Plotting the death of the great King' [1730–1732] and to 'This lion-woman who coupled with a wolf / In her lord's absence' [1781–1782]. The two characters, however, only appear together for the final minutes of the tragedy, when Aegisthus enters the stage for the exodus and joins Clytemnestra, who is already on stage having re-entered in the fifth episode with the corpses of Agamemnon and Cassandra. The absence of Aegisthus for the majority of the play reinforces Cassandra's characterisation of him as *analkin*, translated above as cowardly but literally meaning without strength, impotent, or feeble. His absence means that the audience receives little insight into the emotional dynamics between Aegisthus and Clytemnestra outside of the Watchman and Cassandra's judgement of its adulterous nature.[21]

The opacity surrounding Aegisthus' character and the specifics of his relationship with Clytemnestra during Agamemnon's ten-year absence made Aegisthus a trademark case study for the type of character-building that Punchdrunk are renowned for in their masked performances. The degree of poetic licence that Punchdrunk had when building Aegisthus' loop was furthered due to the narrative in *The Burnt City* ending immediately after Agamemnon's murder, which equated to before Aegisthus' onstage appearance in *Agamemnon*. The fact that none of Aegisthus' scenes were based directly upon scenes from *Agamemnon* was both a

---

[20] Allusions to Clytemnestra's adultery with Aegisthus can be found in *Agamemnon* in the Watchman's speech [19–21, 36–39], in Clytemnestra's speech in the second episode [611–612], in the chorus' second stasimon [807–809], and then most clearly in Cassandra's second and third *rhesis* within the fourth episode [1223–1225, 1258–1259]. The Watchman's allusion is an infamous line, translated by Sommerstein 2008 as 'a great ox has stepped upon my tongue' [36–37]. Hughes' translation of the other allusions bears closer resemblance to the imagery of the Greek.

[21] On Aegisthus' absence prior to the exodos of *Agamemnon*, see Raeburn and Thomas (2011: 232).

blessing and a curse; during the September 2021 workshop phase Andrea Carrucciu, who co-devised the role of Aegisthus, expressed alarm that I could not give him a greater number of primary sources to draw upon when building the character.[22] Out of this blank slate, Barrett and Doyle predetermined that in Greek Mycenae during Scenes Five and Six the action would document the beginnings of the union and conspiracy between Clytemnestra and Aegisthus. Both scenes were intended to be abstract, choreographically rich sequences revolving around the twenty-metre-long concrete plinth table that was the centrepiece of the Mycenaean Royal Palace. The first of these scenes, 'Grief', involved an embodied representation of Clytemnestra's pain after witnessing Iphigenia's wedding-come-sacrifice from the mezzanine above the tank traps in No Man's Land, with Aegisthus arriving to catch Clytemnestra in the throes of grief and to offer her comfort. Throughout their duet, the characters grew increasingly co-dependent, finishing the scene not as the distant relatives they appeared to be during Scene Three ('Wedding Breakfast'), but as lovers (Fig. 4.2).

Scene Six, 'Dinner', represented the corruption of Aegisthus and Clytemnestra's union and the nightmarish curse that envelops the House of Atreus. In preparation for the first rehearsal of Scene Six, Doyle asked me to supply the directors and rehearsal directors with all extant ancient literary descriptions of the murder of Agamemnon (which include, alongside *Agamemnon*, parts of Homer's *Odyssey* and Pindar's *Pythian 11*), as well as the concluding scenes from Seneca's *Thyestes*. *Thyestes* does not feature (or reference) the murder of Agamemnon but rather tells the story of the House of Atreus' previous generation, namely the brothers Atreus and Thyestes, Agamemnon's father and Aegisthus' father, respectively. Doyle was interested in the language surrounding the banquet scene in *Thyestes*, where Atreus serves his murdered nephews to their father Thyestes in a horrific scene of vengeance. The dialogue in question included Atreus' final soliloquy [885–919], Thyestes' *canticum* [920–969], which contains a partial description of the banquet that Atreus has served, and the subsequent dialogue between Atreus and Thyestes which reveals the horrific contents of the cannibalistic meal [970–1051]. The text provided inspiration for the disturbing qualities of Clytemnestra and

---

[22] Aside from Aeschylus' *Agamemnon* and *Libation Bearers*, Aegisthus only appears in a small number of extant ancient sources. He appears or is mentioned in, for example, Homer's *Odyssey*, Sophocles' *Electra*, and Euripides' *Electra*.

Fig. 4.2 Andrea Carrucciu and Dafni Krazoudi as Aegisthus and Iphigenia in Scene Three ('Wedding Breakfast') of *The Burnt City*. Image credit: Julian Abrams. Courtesy of Punchdrunk

Aegisthus' banquet, which did not involve one party tricking the other into cannibalism but still worked to show corruption embedding itself within the Royal Palace. Key sources of inspiration for devising choreography included the language of Atreus' ekphrastic description of the unwitting Thyestes eating his own children [908–919], which details Thyestes gorging himself on food and wine in an unrefined manner, as well as the tension between wanting to celebrate versus feeling pain and sorrow which is evidenced in Thyestes' *canticum* [938–969]. The imagery of pregnancy and childbirth found throughout the episode was a final point of reference.[23]

At midday on 11 February 2022, the blue and red cast members playing Aegisthus, Clytemnestra, and the Oracle, plus Harry Price, a swing who was learning the role of Aegisthus, two members of stage

---

[23] On the potential references to pregnancy and childbirth in *Thyestes*, see Poe (1969: 372) and Littlewood (2008: 251–253).

management, and I gathered in the Royal Palace to begin devising Scene Six. The *précis* that the performers received for Scene Six in advance of the rehearsal read:

> Seated opposite Clytemnestra at the 20 metre table - a 'lavish' dinner is served. This is the Greek specialty of stuffed horse. The dinner morphs into something nightmarish as Aegisthus begins to pull entrails from the horse smearing them along the table. This then shifts into a dance of desire, their relationship is consummated - and a shared plan to murder Agamemnon evolves.

Rehearsal director Emily Terndrup, who co-devised the role of Clytemnestra and had worked with Punchdrunk for a decade, led the process of turning this *précis* into a scene, commencing the rehearsal by noting that the order of the action would change to lead with Clytemnestra and Aegisthus consummating their relationship and then plotting Agamemnon's murder at the end of Scene Five, 'Grief', before transitioning into the dinner scene.[24] At today's rehearsal, Terndrup detailed, the cast was to focus on the practical considerations surrounding the dinner sequence, which was to be a 'big movement piece' as the couple gorged themselves on entrails and blood. The focus of this session was on how the entrails would be handled and how stage blood might feature.

The rehearsal commenced with the company talking through the overarching blocking of the scene. The meal would begin with the Oracle delivering Aegisthus and Clytemnestra's entre to the table, which was to be followed by a main course centrepiece of a horse's skull and entrails, which stage management had brought into the Palace for the rehearsal. Two immediate questions arose, including where Aegisthus and Clytemnestra would sit (together, or at either end of the table) and where the dinner would be brought from, with Jane Leaney, who was co-devising the role of the Oracle, suggesting to stage management that they include a request in the rehearsal notes for a purpose-built cabinet to be created and set behind the long wooden pews on the external wall of the warehouse (such a structure was indeed built over the coming

---

[24] Decisions regarding changing the order of material or the essence of a scene were often communicated through the rehearsal directors for efficiency, with Barrett, Doyle, and Duggan sharing such information at their morning meeting for circulation that day.

weeks). The company then continued to talk and walk through the scene, practising handling both the giant milky white, semi-translucent plastic tablecloth, which protected the concrete table from the stage blood, and the long plastic gowns that Clytemnestra and Aegisthus would wear for the scene to protect their costumes. The cast began exploring how much plastic they needed for the table, and how they might incorporate covering the table into the performance.

Having touched upon the initial practicalities governing the scene, Terndrup pushed the cast to move on, commenting 'let's think about where we want to end up, then how we want to get there. Working backwards. Don't get bogged down in logistics. What images do we want to see, in what order, and what do they mean?'. Terndrup's comment reminded me of Doyle's note during rehearsals on 3 February, when she turned to me and mentioned that 'the temptation with this work is to spend too much time discussing things'; clearly, effective direction meant never losing sight of the rehearsal schedule and the necessity for all the scenes to be devised in the limited time available. The cast quickly came to an agreement that the first image, once Clytemnestra and Aegisthus commenced their dinner, would be one of civility. Terndrup, sat at the end of the table, mimed dabbing her mouth with a napkin as she improvised what this might look like.

Both the red and blue casts then filmed, in turn, an improvisation of the scene, commencing with the Oracle setting the tablecloth and running through to the moment when Aegisthus and Clytemnestra came together around the horse's skull. There was no music or sound design yet, so the cast performed in silence, with the intermittent sound of drills from the still-continuing set construction punctuating the rehearsal. Leaney set the tablecloth by walking down the plinth like it was a catwalk, holding the corners of the plastic behind her shoulders. Terndrup and Paul Zivkovich, as Clytemnestra and Aegisthus, marked out the final pieces of choreography from Scene Five, rolling towards the centre of the plinth before standing side by side at the mid-point of the table. Leaney presented them with the translucent plastic robes, through which they each slipped their arms before Leaney fastened each robe at the back of the neck. Terndrup and Zivkovich then stood at either end of the table, each in front of a plate and a champagne glass. They paused for a moment, before climbing onto the table and crawling slinkily, akin to a lion stalking its prey, towards one another, where they bowed heads and marked out sniffing a centrepiece.

After a lunch break, the company returned to the Palace to commence work with the entrails and blood. There was, by now, an understanding that the remainder of the scene would involve a dark and disturbing duet with the entrails. The performers jumped straight in to improvising with their new props, which included large intestine-like lengths of entrails alongside smaller, more ambiguous-looking pieces of offal. Carrucciu and Omagbitse Omagbemi, the blue cast Aegisthus and Clytemnestra, did an initial improvisation using the dry entrails and wearing the plastic robes. They commenced the scene from either end of the table, crawling towards each other and meeting at the centre where the horse's skull and the dry entrails had been placed. Their movements were animalistic, not only in their approach to one another but also in how they touched heads and arched their backs to bend down and sniff the entrails. Omagbemi then picked up some of the entrails, while Carrucciu grasped (then bit) the other end, creating a momentary tug-of-war effect. They experimented with throwing the entrails to create a smacking sound on the plinth, and then with wrapping the entrails around one another's necks, with Carrucciu using the entrails like a leashed collar around Omagbemi's neck to pull her towards him. There was fluidity in their movements, punctuated by occasional clarifications and requests to one another (Omagbemi repeatedly asking Carrucciu to 'drop it, drop it' when he held the entrails in his mouth prompted a laugh from those observing). The focus was on finding one or two images with the entrails that the cast could then build choreography from, rather than on attempting to create the full shape of the scene immediately.

As the performers prepared for a second improvisation, Senior Stage Manager Hetti Curtis arrived with a black laundry bucket containing stage blood, into which Carrucciu and Omagbemi submerged the entrails before commencing the scene again. The blood immediately changed the focus of the rehearsal to become more about the practicalities of the props and the ideal viscosity of the stage blood. Once a workable blood-to-water ratio was found, the improvisations recommenced, with both red and blue casts taking turns with the bloodied entrails, and even the two Aegisthuses, Zivkovich and Carrucciu, working together as they continued to learn how the entrails behaved when thrown, whipped, pushed, and pulled. Associate Director Kath Duggan arrived to watch the improvisations, giving verbal feedback and encouraging the performers to embrace 'big motions, tussle'. Her questions spurred on additional improvisations; she prompted the performers 'When you get the blood, how far can you slide it? A first task—how do you paint the table with blood using the entrails? If you get a bit on you what does that mean? How do you get more?'. Duggan followed the performers up and down the table, encouraging them to slide the entrails back and forth and offering specific prompts such as 'after the next slide can you scoop them up and make an image'. As we reached the end of the rehearsal, the performers had set little concrete choreography, but had gained an embodied understanding of how the blood and entrails behaved, including how the blood splattered on the table and how much tension they could place the entrails under. With this knowledge, the cast and creative team could then dive deeper into the scene's psychology in subsequent rehearsals.

I next saw the company working on Scene Six a week and a half later, on Monday 21 February 2022. The performers had, however, worked together with Doyle and Barrett on the scene prior to this rehearsal, on 14 February, to begin to set the timings for eating the dinner and tussling with the entrails to the chosen Elisabeth Welch backing track 'Drop in next time you're passing'. On 21 February, the cast had two hours to continue devising the scene ahead of the company's first run of a full loop at the end of the week. Both the red and blue cast members playing Clytemnestra, Aegisthus, and the Oracle gathered back in the Palace to begin fine tuning the scene's choreography. Terndrup once again provided an initial prompt to the group, asking 'did we earn the blood, did we earn the plastic'; Terndrup's comment implied an awareness of the level of spectacle that the scene embodied, and the need for the emotional complexity between Aegisthus and Clytemnestra to match the opulence of the abstraction.

The action of the rehearsal commenced when Barrett and Stephen Dobbie arrived. The cast then ran Scene Five and Scene Six together to see for how long the current action lasted, and to allow Dobbie to continue to build the sound design and ensure audio cues were added in where required. Despite the minimal amount of time spent on Scene Six since I last saw it, the cast had solidified a great deal more action. Some of this was thanks to set dressing; stools were now at either end of the table, and each place setting had additional cutlery and crockery which facilitated beats of action as the cast took a sip from the cups and cut up and ate several small bites of food. Clytemnestra and Aegisthus now set the tablecloth themselves, rather than the Oracle doing it, and were now walking along the ground by the table instead of crawling along it to the horse's head. The first beat of action once the centrepiece arrived was now to hook the eyes out of the skull and feed them to one another as the dinner descended into its disturbing second half. The performers had adopted Duggan's suggestion to work on finding a series of images during the action with the entrails, with three specific images now visible, namely: Clytemnestra and Aegisthus painting the table with the entrails as they slid them from the centre of the table to its far end; Clytemnestra and Aegisthus pressing the entrails between their bodies and dancing slowly with one another; and Clytemnestra scooping the entrails up and clutching them to her stomach, with the image adjusting to be akin to a mother cradling her baby and providing a poignant final note to the scene when Clytemnestra came to a stop, standing atop the table and facing Iphigenia's bedroom. The run was timed at 12 minutes, two minutes longer than the two scenes were scheduled to last.

When *The Burnt City* opened, the choreography involving the entrails looked quite different to what was initially workshopped during February 2022. As the cast learnt more about how the entrails looked in show lighting conditions, and how the blood splattered as the entrails moved about the space, they began working more with the stage blood than the entrails, pouring the blood from a gravy boat onto the tablecloth, dipping their hands in the blood, and then wiping their hands on their robes. Instead of dancing together, with the entrails pressed between their bodies, at the time of opening Clytemnestra danced on top of the table and Aegisthus by the side of the table. The two characters individually appeared crazed and enraptured as they danced with their hands and wrists soaked in blood, creating a literal representation of 'getting your hands dirty' and a prolepsis of their role in Agamemnon's death. Clytemnestra then scooped up the entrails and put them as a crown on Aegisthus' head, in a nod to the deluded pleasure he took in illegitimately occupying the throne in Mycenae during Agamemnon's absence. Clytemnestra's final image remained that of cradling the entrails like a baby. The scene was performed in near silence, with the Elisabeth Welch track ceasing after the more refined part of the dinner. Like the creation of the fall of Troy, the journey to devising the dinner scene was not linear. Nevertheless, traces of the research conducted prior to rehearsals, and of the action created but then abandoned during the February rehearsals, were evident in the final product, revealing the necessity of the full process to the final scene's creation. While on the one hand Clytemnestra's handling of the entrails as akin to a baby allowed her to recollect Iphigenia, on the other it nodded almost imperceptibly to the blending of a horrific banquet with imagery of pregnancy and childbirth in Seneca's *Thyestes*. The idea of making a series of images with the entrails carried through to the final performance, as did the idea of 'earning' the blood through ensuring that the scene furthered the characterisation of Clytemnestra and Aegisthus and the psychology of their relationship. Whereas the abstraction in the fall of Troy involved concentrating Euripides' narrative down to its essence, here the abstraction was geared around distilling down to the idea of a cursed family and an illegitimate, shameful relationship between a couple who were emboldening one another on a dark and disturbing journey.

The rehearsals of the dinner banquet reinforce how it is too simplistic to say that the company's representation of *Agamemnon* and *Hecuba* was one of close adherence verses freedom. On the one hand, the dinner sequence involved enormous artistic licence, as the scene was Punchdrunk's original invention and had no reference point from within *Agamemnon*. However, in terms of narrative linearity, the scene did not change the plot points contained within *Agamemnon* like the company's alterations to *Hecuba* did, but rather filled in the blanks surrounding what the couple were doing before they appear onstage together in *Agamemnon*. The scene arose from the directors' interrogation of the glimpses into the relationship that are included in Aeschylus' text. It is consequently an illuminating example of the intermedial form of translation that Campbell and Vidal highlight, where we can see the process of reinvention entangled up within the translated artefact and the final product existing in kinship with, rather than as an equivalent to, the source material. It is consequently more helpful to think of Punchdrunk's responses to *Agamemnon* and *Hecuba* not in terms of closeness or faithfulness, but rather in terms of the different, dynamic processes of reception, which involved reorienting and then abstracting the narrative of *Hecuba*, and spring-boarding from and inventing backstories and missing moments within *Agamemnon*. When it came to abstracting the ancient plays for other purposes, the process of transformation pivoted again.

ABSTRACTING LANGUAGE

The rehearsals that ran on 15 and 16 February 2022 were part of the first tranche of rehearsals, where the cast and creative team worked through the loop chart and devoted one full day to each consecutive scene. 15 February was devoted to Scene Eight, and 16 February to Scene Nine, with some time put aside to work on the finale at the end of each day. A broad range of material was workshopped across the two days, which included a close interrogation of Ted Hughes' translation of *Agamemnon* on two occasions. In these instances, which took place during a rehearsal of the Greece finale on 15 February and a rehearsal of Scene Nine, 'Robe', on 16 February, the company proceeded to abstract not narrative or concept but rather the specific linguistic choices and colour of Hughes' text. In these engagements with ancient literature, the company took two contrasting approaches. In the first instance, Punchdrunk took imagery from Hughes' translation and infused it into another scene, at a different point to where it lay in *Agamemnon*, while in the second instance, the company attempted to respond to and directly embody a specific piece of Hughes' dialogue in an equivalent scene within *The Burnt City*, by translating language into a visual and experiential dramaturgy. My analysis of the two rehearsals progresses closer towards demonstrating how Punchdrunk directly represented ancient literature in *The Burnt City*. Discussing them in turn reveals how the two instances were a continuum of one another. Both examples, as well as the examples discussed earlier in this chapter, can be considered through the lens of translation to unpack how Punchdrunk conceptualised and responded to ancient Greek literature in their immersive experience.

On 15 February, Doyle, Harrison, the red cast, select swings, and I gathered in downstairs Greek Mycenae at 5 pm to spend an hour on the finale.[25] The focus for the hour, Doyle detailed, was to work on the final

[25] The rehearsal of the Greece finale on 15 February was an initially unscheduled part of the day's work, with the original schedule amended during the company's warm up. Punchdrunk's rehearsal schedule was released each evening for the following day. Occasionally, however, the schedule would change in response to priorities raised during the morning meeting between Barrett, Doyle, Duggan, and the rehearsal directors, in which case an announcement was made to the cast during warm-up and a revised call (often simply the original printed call with pencilled-in corrections) placed in the rehearsal room. An electronic archive of rehearsal schedules can fail to keep up with the dynamic changes necessitated during a period of creative work, and as such can only be thought of as a trace of and template for creative process. The distinctions between the written

image of the show, after the stair descent sequence discussed in Chapter 3. The final image was to be created using twelve bodies and was inspired by Clytemnestra's final monologue in the first episode of Ted Hughes' translation of *Agamemnon*, in which she vividly describes the immediate aftermath of the Greeks entering Troy. On the one hand, the rehearsal was a rare instance of the broader performing company engaging with a specific piece of text. On the other hand, however, the engagement was still channelled through the directors' (and particularly Doyle's) interpretation; the performers did not work with the text in front of them and indeed each individual's level of engagement beyond reading the core texts was at their own discretion. Hughes' language for Clytemnestra's monologue is graphic and brutal and is a trademark example of what Vanda Zajko terms Hughes breathing life into and extending Aeschylus' imagery.[26] Clytemnestra's speech is just thirty lines in the Greek [320–350], and although the monologue is noteworthy for the ominous tone it strikes when describing the Greeks sacking Troy, with the precariousness of the Greeks' prosperity stressed, the visceral gore of Hughes' description is absent. Hughes interpolates a dense and disturbing description of the city being sacked and its inhabitants being murdered, which takes the place of Aeschylus' use of the metaphor of mixing oil and vinegar to juxtapose the auditory cacophony of the Greek's victory shouts and the Trojan's anguished cries. Instead of the detached perspective from which Aeschylus invites us to imagine the scene, Hughes' poetry immerses one into the scene through arresting, emotional imagery. The Trojan women become 'a population of mourners' [558] and the men 'a litter of corpses, / Rubbish-heaps of corpses' [559–560], while the city itself is, in Hughes' translation, seething 'with tossing bodies, / severed limbs, heads, chunks, gobbets' [548–549] and 'as under a downpour / of bodies from the heavens, / shattered and entangled with each other' [561–563]. The richness of Hughes' poetry, and particularly the language used to describe the Trojans, supplemented the Dirk Bouts painting *The Fall of the Damned* and Cherubini's 'Requiem in C Minor' as a third intertext used to create the sense of a war requiem within the finale.

documentation of rehearsals and the processes that I experienced shows the value of an autoethnographic study of rehearsal, and the limitations of pure archival research into creative process.

[26] Zajko (2011: 117).

The rehearsal was focused on trying to make an image with the cast's bodies on the tank traps. The two custom-built traps dominated the downstairs No Man's Land area of Greece and consisted of two shorter steel beams which made a saltire diagonal cross and supported a third, longer beam which rested upon the centre of the 'X' and rose to a high apex where the sacrifices of Iphigenia and Patroclus took place. Patroclus' sacrifice was a *Burnt City* invention, inspired by Iphigenia's role sacrificing foreigners in Euripides' *Iphigenia among the Taurians*. Although the cast members involved in the sacrifice of Iphigenia were used to walking upon, climbing up, and sliding off the tank traps (the company had not yet rehearsed the sacrifice of Patroclus), other cast members had not yet worked on the structure, and I saw Ali Goldsmith, a swing rehearsing the role of, among other parts, Agamemnon, reassure his castmates that walking on the construction was 'not as scary as it looks'. The performers commenced climbing up and laying upon the three sides of the tank traps to create the tableau, with Harrison adjusting their positioning and offering the direction that 'we want the energy going up the trap, like you were trying to get up there when you died'. Harrison and Doyle walked around the space, viewing the image from different angles and conversing with one another, before announcing that the image was stronger without the bodies on the smaller two beams. Doyle also proposed that they explore the image with the two queens, Clytemnestra and Hecuba, standing opposite one another, either side of the trap.[27] Still not satisfied with how the image read, Doyle and Harrison then directed a handful of cast members to climb off the tank trap and reassemble underneath it, with a series of bodies now both within and spilling out from the sandbags at the base of the structure. Harrison and Doyle continued to inspect the imagery, but were still dissatisfied, and in the final moments of rehearsal the image of the collapsed bodies upon the tank trap was abandoned, with the cast instead instructed to experiment with running in a circle and collapsing upon the floor while the Cherubini finale music played on a portable speaker. The scene was not intended as a movement-based equivalent of a word-for-word translation of Hughes' text, but rather, to continue with translation terminology, as a sense-for-sense translation of key images, with an abstract rendering

---

[27] Ultimately, as discussed in Chapter 3, the two queens were split across the two finales, with Clytemnestra remaining in Greek Mycenae and Hecuba moving to the Trojan finale in the other warehouse.

of Hughes' 'tossing bodies' [548], 'litter of corpses, / rubbish-heaps of corpses' [559–560], 'shattered and entangled with one another' [563] beginning to emerge (Fig. 4.3).

In contrast to the rehearsal on 15 February, which involved creating images in response to specific lines from Hughes' translation, the rehearsal on 16 February instead responded to a broader piece of dialogue from Hughes' script, namely Clytemnestra's hyperbolic speech upon Agamemnon's return to Mycenae and the couple's debate regarding whether Agamemnon will acquiesce to Clytemnestra's demands and enter the Palace by treading upon the opulent carpet she had laid out for him [855–957].[28] Although Agamemnon and Clytemnestra interact from Scene Nine through to Scene Eleven in *The Burnt City*, in *Agamemnon*

Fig. 4.3 Omagbitse Omagbemi as Clytemnestra in the final image of the 'Greece' finale in *The Burnt City*. Image credit: Julian Abrams. Courtesy of Punchdrunk

[28] An analysis of Hughes' translation of this passage, and Katie Mitchell's staging of it in her 1999 production for the National Theatre in London, can be found in Hardwick (2005: 217–221).

the exchange represents the only time that Clytemnestra and (an alive) Agamemnon appear onstage together. Doyle, who led the rehearsal, invited me to give an initial overview of the scene to underline the narrative beats of the exchange and the stakes for all the characters involved, particularly regarding how Clytemnestra's victory over Agamemnon during the exchange was representative of her continuing role as head of the household, and how it foreshadowed her ultimate defeat of Agamemnon through his murder. Extracts of the scene in question were then distributed to the cast members present, which included those playing Agamemnon, Clytemnestra, Cassandra, Apollo, and Artemis.

There are two central parts to the third episode in Aeschylus' *Agamemnon*, namely Clytemnestra's *rhesis* (and Agamemnon's reply), where she presents the carpet to Agamemnon and asks him to walk upon it, and the stichomythic exchange between the two characters which ends with Agamemnon agreeing and then entering the Palace. The directors predetermined that the first half of the scene would take place with Clytemnestra standing at the mid-point of the tank trap at the far side of No Man's Land, elevated to welcome Agamemnon home from war. Emily Terndrup and Folu Odimayo, the latter one of the swings for the part of Agamemnon, commenced the first improvisation of the initial interactions between Clytemnestra and Agamemnon, with Clytemnestra standing slightly higher up the tank trap, looking down on Agamemnon who had to climb up to greet her. Terndrup's approach involved channelling individual lines from Hughes' translation, and at this first rehearsal, she even muttered some of the lines under her breath. The process the cast went through involved reducing the dialogue down to the most essential beats or intentions, and then later building in the broader emotional and psychological resonances created through the remainder of Hughes' language. For example, Terndrup experimented with playing just a few of the lines as movement beats, including Clytemnestra's opening line 'Why should I be ashamed / to let the world hear my love for my husband?' [1212–1213], for which she channelled 'I love you' and lifted her arms up to the sky. For her later statement 'I have wept myself dry / as a lump of rubble' [1235–1236], she channelled 'I have cried for you' and held Agamemnon's shoulders and bowed her head. When Vinicius Salles arrived to work with Terndrup, they responded to Clytemnestra's display by finding a visual way of channelling the line 'Greet me as a man'

[1285], with Agamemnon forcing Terndrup to stand upright and stop bowing.

Rehearsing the first half of Scene Nine involved responding to specific lines of dialogue from Hughes' translation. The second half contrastingly involved channelling the text's broader narrative and the beats of persuasion and resistance, in what is known in scholarship as the 'carpet' or 'tapestry' scene. Hughes' translation of the carpet scene contains many examples of his trademark (and controversial) interventions into *Agamemnon*. Bernard Knox, for example, accused Hughes of 'vulgar sensationalism' and the 'trashing of a poetic masterpiece', while Michael Silk declared it to be 'at its best [...] far and away the most compelling impression of Greek tragedy in English'.[29] The scene once again features arresting, original imagery, with Agamemnon flipping 'his life like a coin, heads or tails, in the dust of / a far-off battle' [1218] as well as an expansion of Aeschylus' own text, in terms of both the scope of imagery and the duration of dialogue. While Aeschylus' Clytemnestra claims that Agamemnon needed three bodies to survive the death reports she had received during the war, Hughes' Clytemnestra claims 'The wounds they gave my husband would have drained the whole army / The deaths they dealt him in their tales would have made a mountain of ashes' [1221-1222]. Hughes also moved Aeschylus' stichomythic exchange from a quick-fire, thirteen-line back and forth into a passage three times as long, with the additional material belonging almost exclusively to Clytemnestra.[30] One can argue that Clytemnestra's verbosity comes at the cost of the sense of a confrontation between near equals that is captured in the form of the stichomythic exchange in the original. What is gained is additional—or altered—characterisation. Hughes' translation gives greater prominence to Clytemnestra than Aeschylus does; in

---

[29] Knox (2000: 82) and Silk (2009: 253).

[30] Although much of the dialogue that Hughes gives Clytemnestra is Hughes' own interpolation, one speech within the exchange is not original material but rather was pulled from later in the play, when Agamemnon exits the stage to the Palace. Taplin (2002: 3) notes that Hughes likely adopted this ordering from the Philip Vellacott Penguin translation of 1956, given that Vellacott positions the speech here despite the ordering not being found in any standard edition of the play. If Hughes was working from Vellacott's translation, then Clytemnestra's heightened prominence in this exchange is somewhat less interventionist, although Clytemnestra still has more than double the dialogue of Agamemnon during their subsequent exchange. For a comparative analysis of Hughes' translation and other translations of this passage, see Walton (2005: 199-201).

Hughes's text, Clytemnestra has six long responses, and only one single line response, during what was the stichomythic exchange, contrasting against an Agamemnon who speaks *only* in single-line responses on all but one occasion. The overall effect of Hughes' text is of Clytemnestra outmanoeuvring Agamemnon through her verbal dexterity, to which Agamemnon puts up only the feeblest defence. The challenge facing the cast was therefore to capture both the tension between Clytemnestra and Agamemnon during the exchange, and the alterations that Hughes presents to the status of Clytemnestra.

The rehearsal of the second section of Scene Nine commenced with a discussion of the practicalities surrounding the scene. In addition to the cast from this morning, Jane Leaney was now present as the Oracle took the role of the attendants in *Agamemnon* and procured the fabric for Clytemnestra. In *The Burnt City*, the purple carpet was abstracted into a billowing silk cloak, which Clytemnestra would convince Agamemnon to wear while ascending the stairs to the Palace. The immediate practicalities were rehearsed including the mechanics surrounding how the cloak would be produced and where its storage box would be positioned. The cast then began rehearsing the beats of the status struggle between Agamemnon and Clytemnestra. Salles and Terndrup talked through the moments of resistance, posing a series of questions to one another: how does he get the robe on? Does it get pushed off? Do the Oracle and Cassandra assist Clytemnestra in pulling it over his shoulders? Although Hughes' exchange between Agamemnon and Clytemnestra involves several refusals, the cast experimented with distilling the struggle down to just two or three moments of tension, playing with positioning these moments when the cloak was produced and Clytemnestra indicated that Agamemnon should wear it, when it was initially placed upon Agamemnon's shoulders, and when the thumbholes were slipped over his thumbs. The cast blocked the scene with Clytemnestra standing upon one of the lower stairs, raised above Agamemnon who remained standing on the floor of No Man's Land, with the Oracle and Cassandra on either side and slightly behind him. The stagecraft visually captured the sense of Aeschylus' tragedy, where Clytemnestra stage manages Agamemnon's entrance into the Palace by directing her attendants to spread out the fabric. Clytemnestra's elevation also reflected the superior status that Hughes grants to Clytemnestra and meant that although the tension between the characters during their reunion was palpable, Clytemnestra remained in a position of authority throughout.[31]

The two mid-February rehearsals demonstrated how Punchdrunk abstracted a third and final component of ancient literature, building upon their abstraction of narrative and the emotional and psychological dynamics of their sources to include Ted Hughes' specific linguistic choices in his *Agamemnon* translation. The company's process involved taking imagery from throughout Hughes' text, which was not found in Aeschylus' original play, and attempting to speak to the sense of this imagery, and even recreate it, during their finale. Their process also involved channelling individual pieces of dialogue and finding an embodied and visual mode through which the lines could be expressed.

Despite the different ways that Punchdrunk approached Hughes' text, there were common features throughout their process, which consistently involved selecting what both the directors and the company deemed to be the core, most essential lines of dialogue and finding ways of abstracting these lines through the performers' bodies. The process was evident in both the more director-led rehearsal of the finale and the more performer-led rehearsal of Agamemnon's homecoming (although both Salles and Terndrup were rehearsal directors as well as performers). Punchdrunk's choreographic process had synergy with Hughes' own approach to translation, which involved not a word-for-word approach but a sense-for-sense one, or as Hughes himself put it as trying 'to release the howl in every line'.[32] Having released the 'howl in every line', Hughes then combined Aeschylus' text with his own poetry; Lorna Hardwick, for example, describes how Hughes 'excavated the ancient theatre texts to lay bare the mythology in ways that allowed his own poetry to be an intertext'.[33] The dramaturgical language of Punchdrunk's masked performances worked as a similar intertext which bound together the

---

[31] On Clytemnestra's 'stage-managing', see Raeburn and Thomas (2011: 162).

[32] Hughes, quoted in Sagar (2009: 21). Michael Silk uses Dryden's translation terminology to describe Hughes' text, noting that it operates in the 'range between paraphrase and imitation: a range that leaves open how far, or whether, the idiom of the new version will seek to convey the idiom of its original—which, in the present case, it both does and does not'. See Silk (2009: 241).

[33] Hardwick (2009: 55). Susan Bassnett also notes how Hughes used archaeological metaphors to describe his approach to translating the classics, via 'digging something out from the language of the original' to get to the 'real core of the play'. See Bassnett (2020: 89).

excavated components of Hughes' language. The similarities between Hughes' approach and Punchdrunk's, as well as the insights contained in the rehearsal study featured in this chapter, demonstrate how considering Punchdrunk's creative process through the lens of translation can help clarify the company's method of abstracting ancient literature.

* * *

Scholars often speak not only of the interlingual shift from one language to another as translation, but also of the intermedial shift from page to stage when a company brings to life and verbalises a script. Indeed, Duška Radosavljević argues that 'any process of page-to-stage transition involves a certain level of translation or adaptation, even if no translation from another language is involved' because 'theatre language should be understood to be distinct from the language of literature'.[34] Within choreographic discourse, the term translation is also used when a script is not verbalised, but is borrowed from and reappropriated within dance-based practice.[35] In her study of the practices of, for example, choreographer and director Pete Shenton and physical theatre company DV8, McCormack demonstrates how contemporary choreographers aim to 'avoid the trap of aiming for a "literal" translation and instead focus on creating "other" or new meanings'.[36] Choreographers are, McCormack argues, not 'confined by the concepts of fidelity or equivalence' but rather engage in a form of creative translation through 'entering into a dialogue with the source text'.[37] In each rehearsal process studied in this chapter, Punchdrunk entered into such a dialogue with their texts, on occasion working closely with their sources and interpreting specific imagery or dialogue beat for beat, movement for word, while on other occasions creating new meanings in response to the texts. Within choreographic practice, both approaches exist in the continuum of translation.

Punchdrunk's engagements with Greek tragedy ranged from their close engagement with Ted Hughes in the finale and 'Robe', through to their much more distant engagement with the source texts during

---

[34] Radosavljević (2007: 65).
[35] McCormack (2018: 1–2).
[36] McCormack (2018: 12).
[37] McCormack (2018: 21).

'Dinner', with their response to *Hecuba* during 'fall of Troy' and 'Polyxena's death' falling somewhere in between. Without having access to Punchdrunk's creative development process, one could be tempted to dismiss the directors' claims that a close textual engagement underpinned *The Burnt City* due to how distant certain scenes appear from their source texts.[38] My rehearsal study, however, has shown that irrespective of how Punchdrunk's work is understood at the point of reception, their creative process consistently involved close textual engagement. When working on Polyxena's sacrifice, this engagement did not involve responding to the specific linguistic choices of a particular translation, but rather involved the directors entering into a dialogue with the source text and reorienting it to ensure that the essential narrative beats adhered to the ideological principles underpinning the production. When working on Clytemnestra and Aegisthus' banquet scene, the company imaginatively reconstructed a 360-degree understanding of the actions and behaviours of the dramatis personae from *Agamemnon*, to fill in the blanks regarding the 'offstage' behaviours of the couple during the opening moments of the tragedy. The newly-created content combined the company's choreographic language with distinct imagery from supplementary pieces of ancient literature involving other generations of the same family. Finally, when building the finale and 'Robe', the company communed with Hughes' language, finding choreographic responses to Hughes' unique imagery and his adjustments to Aeschylus' dramaturgical dynamics. Examining the company's rehearsal process throughout the development of *The Burnt City* reveals the directors and the cast created their immersive world by translating their literary sources, including their narrative, emotion, psychology, and specific linguistic qualities, into physical performance and dance.

The rehearsal study in this chapter has highlighted how Punchdrunk responded to Aeschylus' *Agamemnon* and Euripides' *Hecuba* during the creative development of *The Burnt City*. The chapter exists in partnership with the rehearsal study contained in Chapter 3. Together, the chapters illuminate how Punchdrunk interrogated Greek literature

---

[38] See, for example, Doyle in Higgins (2022), where she claimed that 'We adhere very closely to the text, but we use it as a stimulus or a starting point to create an abstract language of dance and movement, and prop and gesture and action, and we take away the spoken word. And we focus much more on the sort of emotional and subtexts of pieces'.

to create *The Burnt City*, blending big-picture insights into the practicalities of constructing a Punchdrunk performance, the dynamics of collaboration and community within the company, and the continuing evolution of the entire performance right up until preview performances, with specific glimpses into how the company developed *The Burnt City* during individual moments of rehearsal. Although the chapters showcase how Punchdrunk made meaning during the rehearsing of theatre, my representation is neither exhaustive nor objective, as I was inevitably an invested observer due to my contributing role within *The Burnt City*. As such, I utilised a Spectator-Participation-as-Research methodology to embrace my dual position as observer and co-creator, and to accept the partiality of my rehearsal observations as a pre-condition of my analysis. Even without my creative involvement within *The Burnt City*, a totalising rehearsal study would be a pipe dream, as not only was it impossible to observe the creation of a multi-stranded, fragmented rehearsal process, but the boundaries of rehearsal were more porous in Punchdrunk's theatre than perhaps in other contexts. Indeed, even after opening night and the conclusion of the designated rehearsal period, development continued. Additional one-on-one spaces were built, and performances devised, well into the summer of 2022; around a similar point in time the bar and audience entrance was reconfigured too.[39] Developments were not purely cosmetic or related to one-on-one experiences, but even included alterations to the loop structure of both travelling characters (especially Hades) and resident characters, resulting in larger shifts in the performance's content.[40] Furthermore, in January 2023, one year after rehearsals had commenced, a large swathe of new performers joined the company, taking over from members of the Contract One cast and putting their own subtle spin on each role. Due to the ever-evolving cast, the company were often in and out of rehearsals; my rehearsal study thus examined only the distinct section prior to opening night during the initial devising of the show. It is a truism to say that in interactive, immersive theatre, where the audience is always a somewhat

---

[39] See Gayet (2022).

[40] During a pre-show talk ahead of a performance of Punchdrunk's 2013–14 *The Drowned Man*, Barrett and Doyle addressed the difficulties of knowing when a Punchdrunk performance had finished evolving, with Doyle noting that they get 'to the point where we sort of know 80% of it', and then battle with the desire 'to keep chipping away at it'. See Price (2014).

unknown entity, a performance will always be in flux, but in *The Burnt City*'s case even formal development continued beyond the boundaries of rehearsal. By examining even this specific window of rehearsals, however, the mythopoetic process of creating the megatext of *The Burnt City*, and the company's translatorial engagement with *Agamemnon* and *Hecuba*, is clear, with my insights highlighting Punchdrunk's unique processes of transforming the classics into immersive experience.

WORKS CITED

Bassnett, Susan. 2020. *Ted Hughes*. Cambridge: Cambridge University Press.
Battezzato, Luigi, ed. 2018. *Euripides: Hecuba*. Cambridge: Cambridge University Press.
Brodie, Geraldine. 2018. *The Translator on Stage*. Bloomsbury: New York and London.
Brown, Sarah Annes. 2009. Classics Reanimated: Ted Hughes and Reflexive Translation. In *Ted Hughes and the Classics*, ed. Roger Rees, 282–299. Oxford: Oxford University Press.
Campbell, Madeleine and Ricarda Vidal. 2019. The Translator's Gaze: Intersemiotic Translation as Transactional Process. In *Translating Across Sensory and Linguistic Borders: Intersemiotic Journeys between Media*, ed. Madeleine Campbell and Ricarda Vidal, 1–36. Cham: Palgrave Macmillan.
Gantz, Timothy. 1993. *Early Greek Myth: A Guide to Literary and Artistic Sources*. Baltimore, London: The Johns Hopkins University Press.
Gayet, Mathieu. 2022. 'A Modern Contemporary Audience Needs to Have Agency and Empowerment'—Felix Barrett, Maxine Doyle (Punchdrunk). *XR Must*, November 8. https://www.xrmust.com/xrmagazine/felix-barrett-maxine-doyle-punchdrunk/. Accessed 25 January 2023.
Hardwick, Lorna. 2005. Staging *Agamemnon*: The Languages of Translation. In *Agamemnon in Performance: 458 BC to AD 2004*, eds. Fiona Macintosh, Pantelis Michelakis, Edith Hall, and Oliver Taplin, 207–221. Oxford: Oxford University Press.
———. 2009. Can (Modern) Poets Do Classical Drama? The Case of Ted Hughes. In *Ted Hughes and the Classics*, ed. Roger Rees, 39–61. Oxford: Oxford University Press.
Hemming, Sarah. 2022. Punchdrunk's Immersive Theatre Returns with an Epic Tale of Troy. *Financial Times*, March 25. https://www.ft.com/content/b7407aa1-1157-4543-b05a-87f754b5a2c8. Accessed 19 August 2022.

Higgins, Charlotte. 2022. "Adrenaline-fuelled": Punchdrunk Return with the Horrifically Timely Siege of Troy. *The Guardian*, March 21. https://www.theguardian.com/stage/2022/mar/21/adrenaline-fuelled-punchdrunk-horrifically-timely-siege-troy. Accessed 31 October 2022.

Knox, Bernard. 2000. Uglification. In *The New Republic*, April 17–24, Issue 16/17: 79–85.

Kovacs, David. 2005. Hecuba. In *Euripides II*, ed. David Kovacs, 393–519. Cambridge, Massachusetts, and London: Harvard University Press.

Littlewood, Cedric. 2008. Gender and Power in Seneca's *Thyestes*. In *Oxford Readings in Classical Studies: Seneca*, ed. John G. Fitch, 244–263. Oxford: Oxford University Press.

Loraux, Nicole. 1987. *Tragic Ways of Killing a Woman*. Trans. Anthony Forster. Cambridge, MA: Harvard University Press.

Machon, Josephine and Punchdrunk. 2019. *The Punchdrunk Encyclopaedia*. London and New York: Routledge.

McCormack, Jess. 2018. *Choreography and Verbatim Theatre: Dancing Words*. Cham: Springer International Publishing.

Papastamati, Styliani. 2017. The Poetics of *kalos thanatos* in Euripides' *Hecuba*: Masculine and Feminine Motifs in Polyxena's Death. *Mnemosyne* 70: 361–385.

Poe, Joe Park. 1969. An Analysis of Seneca's Thyestes. *Transactions and Proceedings of the American Philological Association* 100: 355–376. https://doi.org/10.2307/2935921.

Price, Ludi. 2014. Excerpts from "The Drowned Man" Pre-show talk, December 1st 2013: Meet the Directors. *The Fan LIS Scholar*. https://blogs.city.ac.uk/ludiprice/2014/04/25/excerpts-from-the-drowned-man-pre-show-talk-december-1st-2013-meet-the-directors/. Accessed 2 March 2023.

Radosavljećić, Duška. 2007. Translating the City: A Community Theatre Version of Wim Wenders' Wings of Desire in Newcastle-upon-Tyne. *Journal of Adaptation in Film & Performance* 1: 1: 57–70. https://doi.org/10.1386/jafp.1.1.57_7.

———. 2022. "The Burnt City", One Cartridge Place. *The Theatre Times*, May 24. https://thetheatretimes.com/the-burnt-city-one-cartridge-place/. Accessed 19 August 2022.

Raeburn, David and Oliver Thomas. 2011. *The Agamemnon of Aeschylus: A Commentary for Students*. Oxford: Oxford University Press.

Sagar, Keith. 2001. *Alcestis*. http://keithsagar.co.uk/Downloads/Alcestis2.pdf. Accessed 17 August 2022.

———. 2009. Ted Hughes and the Classics. In *Ted Hughes and the Classics*, ed. Roger Rees, 1–24. Oxford: Oxford University Press.

Scodel, Ruth. 1996. Δόμων ἄγαλμα: Virgin Sacrifice and Aesthetic Object. *Transactions of the American Philological Association (1974–2014)* 126: 111–128. https://doi.org/10.2307/370174.

Segal, Charles. 1990. Violence and the Other: Greek, Female, and Barbarian in Euripides' *Hecuba*. *Transactions of the American Philological Association (1974–2014)* 120: 109–131. https://doi.org/10.2307/283981.

Silk, Michael. 2009. Ted Hughes: Allusion and Poetic Language. In *Ted Hughes and the Classics*, ed. Roger Rees, 233–262. Oxford: Oxford University Press.

Sommerstein, Alan. 2008. *Aeschylus: Oresteia*. Cambridge, MA, and London: Harvard University Press.

Stuart, Keith. 2015. Everybody's Gone to the Rapture: Writing a Score for the End of the World. *The Guardian*, July 30. https://www.theguardian.com/technology/2015/jul/30/everybodys-gone-to-the-rapture-video-game-sound-music. Accessed 3 August 2022.

Taplin, Oliver. 2002. Contemporary Poetry and Classics. In *Classics in Progress: Essays on Greece and Rome*, ed. T. P. Wiseman, 1–19. Oxford: Oxford University Press.

Walton, J. Michael. 2005. Translation or Transubstantiation. In *Agamemnon in Performance: 458 BC to AD 2004*, ed. Fiona Macintosh, Pantelis Michelakis, Edith Hall, and Oliver Taplin, 189–206. Oxford: Oxford University Press.

Zajko, Vanda. 2011. Hughes and the Classics. In *The Cambridge Companion to Ted Hughes*, ed. Terry Gifford, 107–120. Cambridge: Cambridge University Press.

CHAPTER 5

The Burnt City in Performance: Place, Space, and Experience

Earlier in this book, I argued that Punchdrunk's process of creating *The Burnt City* could be likened to a form of mythopoiesis, involving the artists braiding together a plethora of sources and original ideas to create their own megatext. The resulting production facilitated immersion through the complexity and self-sufficiency of its mythic universe. In this and the following chapter, I drill down into what I mean by 'facilitated immersion' to explore the audience experience in *The Burnt City*, and how *The Burnt City* might change our understanding of the history of immersivity. I define an immersive experience as one that holds four characteristics. An experience is immersive when it: (1) displaces one from their present reality; (2) engulfs one's senses; (3) encourages one to feel differently; and (4) encourages one to think differently. These four qualities are labile; although all four will be present in each of my examples, different qualities come to the fore in different experiences. The displacement of reality does not need to be totalising but can be an augmentation of reality that shifts the dramaturgy of the everyday, as occurred in, for example, Punchdrunk's *Kabeiroi*. Although qualities three and four, related to the phenomenological and cognitive power of immersive experiences respectively, are interlinked and co-dependent, I separate them out to ensure that, for example, embodied performance techniques within literary forms of immersion are given due attention and are not subsumed under the other features of immersivity. An immersive

© The Author(s), under exclusive license to Springer Nature Switzerland AG 2024
E. Cole, *Punchdrunk on the Classics*,
https://doi.org/10.1007/978-3-031-43067-1_5

experience is, as Rose Biggin argues, not necessarily an either/or state; rather, an immersive experience is a graded, fleeting, intense, and necessarily temporary state defined by an awareness of its temporal and spatial boundaries.[1]

This chapter explores how the components of *The Burnt City* relating to place, space, and experience coexisted in performance and helped facilitate an immersive experience. I consider how Punchdrunk's construction of space and place helped the audience to engage with the first feature of an immersive experience, namely the displacement of the audience from their present reality. Marie-Laure Ryan summarises the distinction between place and space as an opposition between a concrete environment versus abstraction, between containment and security versus movement, freedom, danger, and adventure, and finally between history, memory, and community versus timelessness and anonymity.[2] In *The Burnt City*, I separate these categories out as relating to, on the one hand, geographic and architectural place and, on the other hand, designed and dramaturgical space. When it comes to analysing the strands of meaning relating to place, space, and experience within *The Burnt City*, I borrow from Mike Pearson and Michael Shanks' use of archaeological metaphors for the analysis of performance and argue that the individual components are akin to different strata.[3] The archaeological language helps distinguish my discussion of potential audience experiences from the practitioners' mythopoetic process of braiding together the texts that constitute *The Burnt City*. Throughout my analysis, I demonstrate how *The Burnt City*'s status as a classical reception expedited the process of enfolding the audience into the world of the performance and gave added logic to their positionality within the production's multiple spatial worlds.

Archaeological metaphors can be problematic as they encourage one to think in vertical, disconnected terms. A language of layers and strata can fail to attend to how a performance's components are co-dependent, mutually illuminating, and only fully understood when comprehended collectively. Indeed, when it came to experiencing the layers of place within *The Burnt City*, one could engage with any, all, or none of the layers, which included the geographic location of the south-east London

---

[1] Biggin (2017: 1).
[2] Ryan (2015: 86).
[3] See Pearson and Shanks (2001).

suburb of Woolwich, the historical connotations of the Royal Arsenal, and the architecture of the performance's venue. Although engaging with any one of these layers might have added meaning to, or sharpened the resonances of, *The Burnt City*, they existed separate to the level of one's immersion within the world of the performance. These different levels were thus not distinct layers which must be experienced in a particular order and to a specific depth. In contrast, when it came to experiencing the designed and dramaturgical spaces of the performance, the layers did work together to facilitate immersion. The separate spatial layers included the mock museum housed in One Cartridge Place, which was used for the original cross-fade entrance to lead spectators into the world of the performance, alongside three inner spaces within *The Burnt City*, namely the co-dependent Greek Mycenae and Troy, and the mythological Underworld which acted as a conceptual lynchpin for the entire performance. Accessing and comprehending the coexistence of spatial layers in *The Burnt City* worked akin to dream layering in the film *Inception*. An understanding of each spatiality equated to going one step deeper into one's subconscious. Feeling immersed not only in the Trojan War, but also in the sense of the Trojan War being replayed, on a loop, in Hades' realm, represented a particularly deep, layered form of immersion. As such, although I remain cognisant of the limitations of an archaeological framing metaphor, I mitigate these by showcasing how the distinct layers of experience built upon one another to add up to more than the sum of its parts. Although one could experience the layers of *The Burnt City* relating to place separately, when the spatial layers were experienced collectively, then the audience was displaced from their present reality to a greater extent and the potential immersivity of the experience was greater.

Alongside exploring place and space in isolation, this chapter also considers the audience's encoded experience in relation to both. Punchdrunk's production utilised participatory strategies to enable individuals to occupy space within a reception of ancient tragedy. Here, I consider not only my own spectatorial experience and occupation of space within *The Burnt City*, via the continued employment of a Spectator-Participation-as-Research methodology, but I also explore how others have theorised the audience's role within a Punchdrunk performance, to question how the audience's position did or did not facilitate immersion. A mobile audience, as is well-documented in scholarship, does not necessarily equate to an active audience, and nor does it guarantee the experience of immersion. However, Punchdrunk's audience were not only mobile, but were charged with holding a specific identity, which according to Punchdrunk can be likened to a chorus of furies or a collective of shades, and according to theatre scholar David Bullen can be likened to initiands in ancient ritual experiences. I tease out how these different conceptual framings of spectatorial experience intersect with and augment one's understanding of place and space within *The Burnt City*. Having an audience physically occupy space within a tragic reception changes how one is invited to relate to the performance in ways distinct from what would be the case if the work was created for a different theatrical form, or if the work in question was a Punchdrunk production that was not based upon classical literature. I consequently argue that the coexistence of place, space, and experience, and the centrality of antiquity to these dimensions, played a decisive role in facilitating the potential immersivity of *The Burnt City*.

Place

As I walked from Woolwich's DLR station towards the home of *The Burnt City* at One Cartridge Place, in April 2022, I crossed Beresford Street, a main road which separated the diversity, vibrancy, and grit that many might have identified with the south-east London suburb of Woolwich, and the new, swish developments housed in Woolwich's former Royal Arsenal, where apartments retailed for up to and over one million pounds and the 'sell' of the area was not Woolwich's historic identity but that of more generic riverside living. For now, until the new Elizabeth Crossrail line opened complete with a station inside the Arsenal, visiting *The Burnt City* started with a walk through what felt like two distinctly different cities. Having emerged from the station among a throng of people to the shouts of newspaper hawkers and the sermonising of a preacher, I found myself suddenly surrounded by quiet. I walked down the wide, partially pedestrianised Major Draper Street within the Arsenal, taking in my surroundings, and after just a few steps came face-to-face with a 'Next of Kin Memorial Plaque' which recorded the over one million bronze plaques made in the Royal Arsenal and sent to the next of kin of the British and Empire service personnel who died as a direct result of the First World War. I stopped to inspect the replica plaque, which was a magnified, specially designed penny, before panning my gaze across to the green square on my left, taking in the three black cannons which further attested to the region's military history. These cannons were the first of many now-decorative weapons that I encountered scattered across the Arsenal. A place of two identities, littered with the detritus of war—what could be a more apt location for Punchdrunk's tale of two warring cities?

Place, which I take to mean either geographic or architectural location and as something distinct from designed space, has always been significant to Punchdrunk's practice, as seen in my overview in Chapter 2 of the company's outdoor *House of Oedipus* at Poltimore House and their geo-locative, London-based *Kabeiroi*. Indeed, during the pre-publicity for *The Burnt City*, Felix Barrett commented to journalist Alice Saville that 'we've always said we're site-sympathetic'.[4] The company defines site-sympathetic as 'the activity of responding to the *feeling* as much as the aesthetic of an uninhabited found space'; Barrett further explained that it 'is an impressionistic response; drawing on similar impulses [to site-specific theatre] but creating a dream world within the space rather than a practical, literal retelling of the building'.[5] He has cited Romanian director Silviu Purcărte's rehearsal technique for his 1996 *Les Danaïdes* as one of the inspirations for the development of his theatrical practice, which, like Punchdrunk's masked shows, combined a site-sympathetic location with a classic text. For the rehearsal of *Les Danaïdes* this involved an aircraft hangar in which a durational improvisation linked to Aeschylus' *Suppliant Women* took place.[6] For both Barrett and Purcărte, the use of place is (envisaged as) distinct from site-specific practice, where not only is a performance generated for a specific site, but the site indelibly shapes the work in such a way that much of the production's meaning would fundamentally shift if it was remounted in another location.[7]

In her writing about Punchdrunk's 2013–2014 *The Drowned Man*, Rose Biggin details how the production was site-sympathetic rather than site-specific, noting that although the show was dependent on its host building for its physical layout, the world created inside was entirely self-sufficient and could theoretically be moved without significant changes

---

[4] Saville (2022).
[5] Machon and Punchdrunk (2019: 251).
[6] Machon and Punchdrunk (2019: 30).
[7] On the difficulty of defining site-specific theatre, see Pearson (2010: 7–17).

to its content.⁸ *The Burnt City*, like *The Drowned Man*, was site-sympathetic. The layout of the two distinct buildings, which Punchdrunk was granted permission to connect through a purpose-built link structure, shaped their choice of Trojan War source texts, with the provision of two buildings allowing the company to return to their thwarted, cross-building Trojan War concept from their 2010 *The Fates and the Furies*. *The Fates and the Furies* was envisaged for two empty buildings from the old Central Saint Martins college in Southampton Row, Holborn, with Barrett summarising the idea's genesis as arising from contemplating 'Having two buildings – what stories fit? What stories can you tell through that prism?'.⁹ Just as the structural offering of two buildings shaped the company's choice of narrative, the warehouse environment, which is of 'a mythic scale' according to Barrett and Doyle, informed the set design and choreography with, for example, elevated and aerial action tailored to the height of the industrial setting.¹⁰ In her review of *The Burnt City*, journalist Susannah Clapp commented upon the synergy between place and performance which was facilitated through its site-sympathetic nature, noting that the 'vast industrial buildings seem capable of conjuring a sense of infinite area. Where better to think about war, the waging of it and its devastating effects'.¹¹ Yet although *The Burnt City* could, having been created in sympathy with the architecture of its original venue, theoretically be remounted in another location, I am unconvinced that it is as portable and self-sufficient as *The Drowned Man*. The multi-building structure, for example, created an ecology of two distinct worlds that would need to be rethought for a multi-floor warehouse akin to the building used for the company's *The Drowned Man*. Similarly, the choreographic language of the production would need to be reconfigured if placed in a non-industrial setting without high ceilings. And not only did the architecture shape the production's meaning but, as evidenced in my approach from Woolwich DLR station to the performance, the geographic location did, too; shifting the performance's location away from the historic Arsenal would dilute the resonances gained by placing

---

[8] Biggin (2017: 184).
[9] Barrett, quoted in James (2022).
[10] See James (2022) and Waite (2022).
[11] Clapp (2022).

the Trojan War narrative within a landscape ghosted by a military presence. *The Burnt City*, in a relative rarity for a Punchdrunk work, was thus to a degree a form of site-specific as well as site-sympathetic theatre.

There is a tradition of drawing upon Marvin Carlson's model of theatrical ghosting in scholarship on site-specific and site-sympathetic theatre, which posits that a spectator's horizon of expectation ghosts their experience of a performance.[12] Mike Pearson, for example, adapted the metaphors of 'hosting' and 'ghosting' to argue that in his 2010 production of *The Persians*, everything at the outdoor Ministry-of-Defence-owned site in Bannau Brycheiniog (formerly known as the Brecon Beacons), Wales, worked together as a 'host' for the constructed scenography and performance that took place—the 'ghost'.[13] Pearson consequently argued that as a haunted space can only be comprehended by contemplating both the 'ghost' and the inhabited 'host', in *The Persians*, 'The site itself became an active component in the creation of performative meaning, rather than a neutral space of exposition or scenic backdrop for dramatic action'.[14] When writing about *The Drowned Man*, Biggin recalled Pearson's work and shifted it for Punchdrunk's masked theatre, arguing that the created fictional environment of *The Drowned Man* erased and replaced the geographic and architectural host, while the audience became coded, in place of the performance, as the ghost.[15] In *The Burnt City*, the company's intricately designed immersive world went some way to erasing the meanings associated with the host location, with new internal walls, and sometimes ceilings and flooring, constructed within the shell of the found space and all natural light removed. However, the listed status of *The Burnt City*'s two buildings and the connection between the buildings and their immediate environs meant that this erasure was incomplete. Like in *The Persians*, in *The Burnt*

---

[12] See Carlson (2003).

[13] See Pearson (2012: 70). Sophie Nield has problematised the metaphors of 'hosting' and 'ghosting', arguing that they have a 'troubling temporal hierarchisation' as 'the site precedes the performance, which is fleeting, evanescent, almost mystical. It is present for a short time and then it is gone, leaving the site deserted and abandoned, much as it was by its original inhabitants'. Nield proposes that we instead utilise Henri Lefebvre's 'horizon of meaning' to explore the relationship of performance to site. See Nield (2012: esp. 222–223).

[14] Pearson (2012: 70).

[15] Biggin (2017: 196).

City it was the place, rather than the space, that acted as host, as the site was not neutral but held the potential to be an active component in the creation of meaning.

The overall environment through which I walked when I crossed over Beresford Street in Woolwich has military associations going back to 1696, when ammunition began to be manufactured in a laboratory that had been relocated from Greenwich.[16] Gun-making commenced at the site in 1717, and it was formally designated the Royal Arsenal in 1805.[17] Although various places within the Arsenal were in active use by the Ministry of Defence from this point until the 1990s, the area reached its height of productivity during the First World War. During the First World War, the Arsenal played a decisive role manufacturing munitions and providing employment; Barbara Ludlow, for example, notes that more people worked in the Arsenal during the First World War than at any other point in time, including a large workforce (37%) of female 'munitionettes'.[18] The women's handling of explosives in a designated 'danger building' infamously turned their hair and skin yellow and gave them the nickname 'canaries'.[19]

The original purposes of the two warehouses that *The Burnt City* occupied were not as readily apparent to audiences as the overall Arsenal's history. The building designated by the Ministry of Defence as Building 17, also known as the Cartridge Factory and home to Greek Mycenae within the world of the show, was built in 1856 and was originally used to assemble paper cartridges. Although the corrugated iron roofing, original brick walls (albeit now painted black), and wooden roof beams remained visible within the performance, internally the space appeared to my untrained eye as a nondescript, industrial warehouse. The present form of Building 19, home to Troy and known as the Mounting Shed, was built in 1887 and was the site where guns were placed onto carriages. Minimal clues could be glimpsed internally within Building 19 regarding the space's military history. The few visible indicators of the historical connotations of the 'host' site included a cast-iron gantry under the roof

---

[16] Guillery (2012: 129).

[17] Guillery (2012: 129).

[18] Ludlow (1997: 54–55).

[19] See Ludlow (1997) and Gillow (1997). The Imperial War Museum's oral history of the munitions factory also contains first-person recollections from the so-called 'Canary Girls'. See Imperial War Museum (2022).

of the warehouse, which was used by travelling cranes to mount heavy guns, alongside railway lines which intersected the floor.[20] *The Burnt City* did not explicitly call attention to these features, or reference their original purposes; however, their presence was no doubt noted by some audience members, particularly as the gantry was utilised for two separate aerial sequences during the show (Polyxena's death, Scene Seven and her strop solo, Scene Nine).

Knowledge of the place that hosted *The Burnt City* had the potential to give added resonance to the content of Punchdrunk's production, which was not only intimately concerned with an exploration of warfare but specifically emphasised the female characters' lived experience of war. There were three primary ways that place shaped my reading of *The Burnt City*, via: (1) the geographic location of Woolwich, and specifically the suburb's division into two contrasting halves; (2) the historical associations of the Royal Arsenal, and specifically the military history it embodied; and (3) the architectural features of the host venue, which linked to the history of the Arsenal and influenced the production's design and choreography. These three layers could shape one's understanding of the performance separately, collectively, or not at all, in ways akin to my own spectatorial participation or otherwise. One might, for example, consider the architectural details of the host site during an aerial sequence without an awareness of the historic function of the building. The horizon of expectation with which I met *The Burnt City*, having walked from Woolwich DLR station, across Beresford Street and into the Arsenal, was likely distinct from that of first-time visitors to Woolwich from May 2022 onwards, who might arrive via the newly opened Elizabeth line directly into the Arsenal.

Engaging—or not—with any of the layers of meaning relating to place surrounding *The Burnt City* could thus shape one's reading of and experience in the performance. However, an awareness and understanding of place was an added extra to, rather than a precondition for, feeling enveloped in an alternate reality within *The Burnt City*. Instead, it was the multidimensionality of space within the production and the ability for the audience to progress through the different spatio-temporalities that was integral to audience immersion.

---

[20] Guillery (2012: 181) notes that the gantries were used for the testing of weapons up until the 1990s.

Space

I found myself in the Trojan Town Square midway through *The Burnt City*, listening to what I could now identify as the production's 'reset music', a sample of the song 'You Have the Power' from the film *Dark City* which marked the end of one loop—in this case the first—and the beginning of the next. I was facing the inner wall of the warehouse that represented Troy, which was titled through Art Deco neon signage 'Palladium'. A variety of posters stuck onto the wall of the Palladium advertised past performances, and banners over the top of the posters announced the venue's closing, all of which indicated the building's intended original function as a music hall. Immediately in front of me was a rectangular water butt, on which a suited male performer had recently pinned a daffodil. The water butt was plain grey and unadorned, and at the start of the reset music, it was entirely unlit until a travelling blue spotlight began to trace a line towards it, across the centre of the Town Square. Upon landing on the water butt the light's radius narrowed, zooming in until only the water butt was lit. Suddenly, gasping and spluttering, a woman emerged out of the water. She stood, dripping wet and wide-eyed, surveying the space, before slowly climbing out. She was barefoot, in black denim cut-off shorts and a black t-shirt on which GAIA was embroidered in yellow thread over the left breast. She was immediately distinct from all the other performers that I had so far encountered within *The Burnt City*. Standing in the water butt, she appeared to *see* the audience. Although performers made eye contact with audience members elsewhere in the show, where they gifted an individual spectator a beat of intimacy through eye contact or used the gaze to draw an individual out of the wider audience for a one-on-one, this character appeared to comprehend the audience as a collective. Her clothing was also at odds with the Weimar-inflected and Alexander McQueen-inspired costume aesthetic of the show; based on costume alone, and disregarding her wet and unmasked status, the performer could be mistaken for an audience member.

The female performer closed her eyes as she wiped the water away from her face and squeezed it out of her long, dark hair, before noticing the daffodil and bending down to pick it up. She wandered through the space, turning around in a disorientated fashion and continuing to take in the audience. As she made her way across the Town Square, she bent down to pick up another daffodil, then another, and another, until she found a final flower leaning against a door on the opposite side of the square. She knocked upon the door. It opened, and then she and I (and a throng of other spectators) entered. The room was wood panelled and read as expensive and mysterious. It was perfumed with a rich and slightly smoky fragrance and was carpeted with a thick pile rug. Sconces and candles illuminated small pockets of the space and its ornate furnishings. The woman, still dripping, edged cautiously towards the centre of the room, where the suited man now stood. With authority and assurance, he said 'welcome home'.

The geographic and architectural environment in which *The Burnt City* was situated imbued the performance with specific qualities and shaped both the company's choice of source texts, and the choreographic language through which Punchdrunk reinvented them. This external place was coupled with the dramaturgical and designed spaces of *The Burnt City* to create the alternate universe of the production in which audiences might be immersed. The multilayering of spaces was central to facilitating the potential for audiences to feel plunged into an alternate reality. Whereas, as Marie-Laure Ryan argues, one inhales place like an atmosphere, they orient themselves within space like they would on a map, observing the changing landscapes as they follow characters who are navigating its routes.[21] The moment described above hints at how spectators who followed Persephone and observed her narrative could become oriented in *The Burnt City* within the spatial realm of the ancient Greek mythic Underworld.

Persephone's narrative arc, like Hades', was unusual for a Punchdrunk character in that it lasted for two loops. Persephone's twenty-two scenes revolved around her attempt to understand the space in which she found herself and to locate her identity within it, having suffered amnesia due to re-entering the Underworld through the river Lethe, also known as the river of oblivion or forgetfulness. The hints towards Persephone's identity during the reset between Loop One and Two were so minute that only the most ardent of eagle-eyed classicists, or Punchdrunk superfans who had already gleaned that the performance was set in the Underworld from the show's press coverage, might immediately identify her. Persephone's costuming indicated that she had come not only from another place, but also from another time. The embroidery on her t-shirt provided a clue as

---

[21] Ryan (2003: 123).

to her origin, spelling the Greek word for (and the name for the primordial personification of) earth. For spectators who had previously cottoned on to the fact that the suited gentleman was Hades, and that the room Persephone entered was his house, Hades' 'welcome home' might have cemented the knowledge that Persephone was being welcomed back into the Underworld as part of her cyclic mythological journey. Other audience members discovered Persephone's identity (if they chose to follow her) alongside Persephone herself, with the final moment of revelation not occurring until a three-on-one (later to become a five-on-one) during Scene Eight and Nine of Loop Three. Although following Persephone's narrative and sharing in her process of rediscovery could be experienced somewhat in isolation from engaging with the rest of *The Burnt City*, it could also be experienced as the unlocking of a final spatiality, that of the Underworld. Layering multiple spaces upon each other was one of the ways that Punchdrunk facilitated audience immersion within *The Burnt City*.

The Underworld represented the deepest spatiality within *The Burnt City*. To access it, spectators had to progress through the shallower levels, including the sedimentary level created through the entryway to the performance. After entering One Cartridge Place and scanning my ticket when *The Burnt City* opened in April 2022, I immediately encountered a mock museum exhibition.[22] A central gallery space advertised, via a stand-alone banner, the exhibition 'The Burnt City: Visions of Troy', with the subtitle 'Treasures and Antiquities from the Chapman Collection'. With no further direction provided, I spent several minutes milling around the antechamber to the main performance space with a cluster of other audience members. A series of large display boards, accompanied by artefacts housed in glass display cabinets, were scattered throughout the space. Information banners recounted the story of the nineteenth-century archaeological search for Homer's Troy, alongside the narrative of the Trojan War; journalist Charlotte Higgins recognised that the make-believe museum would nod to the British Museum's 'Troy: Myth

---

[22] In this chapter, I analyse the cross-fade experience as it ran for the first months of the performance, from April 2022 until July 2022. After the summer of 2022, the cross-fade experience changed, and the framing device of a museum exhibition was removed. Instead, audiences gathered in the bar, before being called in separate groups (via a card calling system) to an antechamber, where they had an initial interaction with a performer (Hades), before progressing through the individual artefact rooms as in the first version of the experience.

and Reality' exhibition.[23] For spectators with knowledge of the history of Troy, it might have been apparent that the exhibition blended fact with fiction through the interpolation of the fictitious name of Arthur Chapman into the historical narrative regarding Heinrich Schliemann's excavations of Hisarlık in modern-day Turkey. Spectators without this knowledge who attempted to research Chapman's name after the fact would experience a similar, delayed blurring of fact and fiction as they sought to untangle the line between the historical and mythological basis of *The Burnt City*, and Punchdrunk's poetic licence; I know of the existence of such audience members as in my capacity as dramaturg I received emails asking for guidance on Chapman and his collection. The artefacts on display included a reproduction of the gold diadem unearthed during Schliemann's excavations and known as part of the 'Jewels of Helen', a mock Orphic tablet, an antiquarian book marked as the volume that sparked Schliemann's interest in Troy, and a red-figure mixing bowl depicting the gods Hades and Persephone. The nods to the Underworld captured in the iconographic representations of Hades and Persephone and in the Orphic tablet was furthered through another banner, titled 'Beyond Death: Visions of the Afterlife' and the inclusion of a photo of Dirk Bouts' c. 1470 oil painting 'The Fall of the Damned', which featured cascading naked bodies, accompanied by bats and monsters, tumbling down into hell.

After what felt like only a few minutes in the exhibition space, a performer called those present to an unobtrusive corner of the space for an audio tour of the rest of the exhibition. A black curtain was drawn aside, and we were shunted through to an even smaller room. Although my knowledge of the performance informed my understanding of the entrance, press week was my first experience of the museum entry as I had entered previews from backstage. I was immediately struck by the labyrinthine nature of the entryway and its enveloping darkness. Retracing my steps to find my way out of the museum felt impossible.

The first room featured a single, central glass display case in which resided what appeared to be a fragment of a mask. A barricade partitioned away a part of the room with a hole in the floor, through which I could glimpse rippling water. Meanwhile, a voiceover began to tell the story of the Trojan War. As the voice commented upon the centrality

---

[23] Higgins (2022).

of masks in antiquity, both for performers to bring characters to life in the ancient theatre, and for the deceased via the wearing of funeral masks, a steward handed me a Punchdrunk mask. While my fellow audience members and I fastened our masks behind our heads, the voiceover instructed us to follow the light through to the next gallery. A lightbox flashed, on which was written 'exhibition continues' above an until-now unnoticed door. Two subsequent rooms, each accessed through interconnecting doors, contained two individual pieces of faux c. fifth-century red-figure pottery. The vases depicted the sacrifice of Iphigenia and the murder of Agamemnon. A final display case held an object label describing a geometric mixing bowl depicting a deer sacred to Artemis; however, the display case was shattered. Instead of the artefact, a single lock of hair tied by a red thread lay in its place, as a ritual offering which recalled mourners' dedications at funerary monuments in antiquity.

The Burnt City's museum entrance worked to transition audiences from their everyday reality into the world of the performance. The company terms such a transition a cross-fade. In Punchdrunk's large-scale masked shows, the cross-fade facilitates the masking of the audience and includes the presence of individuals who straddle the two realities (here the museum exhibition staff who draw audiences into the audio tour).[24] Speaking about *The Burnt City* specifically, Barrett described the 'decompression zone' as facilitating 'the bleed between the hustle and bustle of the real world and then gradually slipping over 10–15 minutes into the fever dream of the show'.[25] The creation of a fictitious front for the performance as part of this cross-fade, which blurred the boundaries between the world of the show and that of wider reality, is a common Punchdrunk strategy. For the 2011 New York version of *Sleep No More*, for example, the company invented a history for their Manhattan warehouses, envisaged as a luxury hotel that was condemned just after the outbreak of the Second World War, six weeks before the hotel was due to open.[26] Similarly, for their 2013–2014 *The Drowned Man*, the company put forward the conceit that the Paddington warehouse they occupied was in fact the film studio Temple Studios, part of the Temple Pictures production company. The idea of One Cartridge Place as a gallery and

---

[24] Machon and Punchdrunk (2019: 69–70).
[25] Barrett, quoted in James (2022).
[26] Soloski (2022).

exhibition space, here opening with a viewing of the privately owned Chapman Collection, operated similarly to these other faux-histories. In the version that I experienced, the absence of the final object crucially ensured that the museum artifice not only worked to blur the boundaries between reality and *The Burnt City*, but that it did so by creating a feeling of disquiet and unease as I transitioned from the entrance into the performance space proper, via picking out a path through the shattered pieces of display case on the floor. When I described my first experience of the performance space during the 'Hide and Seek' rehearsal exercise in Chapter 3, I detailed how feeling the ground grow unsteady under my feet as I began walking, in the dark, upon sand, felt like an apt metaphor for the psychological experience of adjusting to the space. The sense of the museum experience going wrong as I came across the broken display case worked similarly to the feeling of the ground changing under my feet, transitioning me from one universe into another and infusing the journey with a sense of danger and alterity.

Spectators sent on the alternate route through the audio tour were funnelled into Troy, rather than Greece, and presented with iconographic representations of the narrative involving the Trojan characters, including the death of Polyxena and the blinding of Polymestor. The warping of the exhibit in the alternate trajectory included a fictitious commentary in the audio description in the second-to-last exhibit room detailing how Schliemann turned to researching and re-enacting mystery cult rituals in his later years, before a voiceover in the final room, claiming to recite Schliemann's writing, narrated 'For I have drunk of the *kykeon*, and I looked upon the face of Agamemnon. And through the great gate I entered at last that place I have dreamed of all my life. My burnt city', at which point a curtain opened, revealing the Trojan Town Square below the audience.

The significance of space to the creation of an immersive experience is well-documented. Biggin, for example, notes that the use and manipulation of space is crucial to fostering an immersive experience within Punchdrunk's practice. She suggests that in both *The Drowned Man* and *The Borough*, two contrasting Punchdrunk works for a large-scale masked audience and a solo spectator respectively, the relationship between the original host site and the ghost of the fictitious space intermixed to facilitate immersive experience.[27] What is less well-understood

---

[27] Biggin (2017: 202).

is the importance of multilayering spaces to facilitate the sensation of being immersed in an alternate reality, which is one of the key qualities required for an immersive experience. The museum exhibit that audiences encountered when they entered Punchdrunk's *Burnt City* acted as the first layer of the space's strata. This sedimentary layer encouraged audiences to behave in certain ways by, for example, wearing masks, spending time pouring over the small details of objects, proceeding quietly and cautiously in the dark, and adjusting to feeling confused and disoriented within a maze-like environment. It also acted as what Sarah Iles Johnston terms, via Mark Wolf, a distinct border partitioning the secondary storyworld from the primary world in any coherent and credible mythic universe.[28] The subtle weaving in of narrative within the exhibit, via the representation of scenes from the Trojan War on pottery, worked to introduce the world of the performance and the further layers of space one would shortly encounter. The cross-fade did not present a unified storyworld or, by itself, facilitate immersion, but rather worked akin to the rabbit hole that Alice falls down, as a portal to connect two different universes.

While the cross-fade represented the first layer of *The Burnt City*'s space strata, the spaces into which the audience were then funnelled, namely Building 17 (Greece) and Building 19 (Troy), represented the next two layers. The pathway through the museum exhibit concluded with a corridor that led me into a dimly lit, canvas-draped tent-like structure. A yellow glow from portable, antique lanterns and smart candles partially illuminated the new space. Clapp identified this area as the campaign headquarters of Agamemnon, reconstructed via a mix of classical references and early twentieth-century communication tools.[29] Draping canvases separated distinct office spaces and residences, as did sandbags below the tactile walls and the taught ropes responsible for erecting the structures. It was an immediate struggle to navigate through the canvas layers, with no obvious path through the space; the only apparent option was to squeeze through gaps and step over barriers. Maps and letters on stately looking desks hinted at the Trojan War backdrop and included a description of Calchas' interpretation from Aeschylus' *Agamemnon* of the portent of the two eagles devouring a pregnant hare

---

[28] Iles Johnston (2015: 286).
[29] Clapp (2022).

[104–159]. The canopy of canvases belied the vastness of the warehouse; once I made my way out of the warren, by identifying a boundary of chain-link fence which I followed until its end, I found myself in the cavernous No Man's Land, home to the restless troops of the Greek army in the opening scenes of each loop.

My familiarity with the performance space meant that unlike other audience members, I did not experience a delayed identification of the space's Greek identity but could immediately place my surroundings. For others (bar returning attendees), the process of discovery would be gradual, particularly because Warehouse 17 was not a literal representation of a recognisable locality, but rather reflected how Punchdrunk's masked shows are structured via a dream logic. The canvas-encased area featured very little performed action, but through a detailed design installation it managed, as evidenced by Clapp's review, to communicate the setting of the Greek military headquarters. However, whether the headquarters were intended to be those found in Aulis, where the Greek army gets becalmed on route to Troy, or (and?) to be the army base outside of the walls of Troy, where the army resides for the decade-long duration of the Trojan War, was opaque. The main warehouse space in contrast was almost entirely unadorned and was a space of epic proportions in which the warehouse's natural architecture was still visible; the only obvious additions were two imposing steel tank traps. The minimal design installation allowed No Man's Land to slide between representing different mythic locations during different moments of performance. For example, the space represented Aulis during the opening scenes, where Neoptolemus and Patroclus were waiting ahead of Iphigenia's sacrifice, to perhaps being Tauris when the reincarnated Iphigenia murdered Patroclus during Scene Nine, or even Mycenae when Clytemnestra welcomed Agamemnon home (also in Scene Nine). Elsewhere within Warehouse 17 were separate spaces that represented stable environments. For example, the upstairs mezzanine consistently represented the Mycenaean Royal Palace and was identifiable as Clytemnestra's home throughout the entirety of the production's loop (she spent nine of eleven scenes in the Palace), as well as the location of Agamemnon's murder. Meanwhile, the two rooms off to the side of the main warehouse space included a shrine to Artemis, in which Iphigenia dressed as a bear in the coming-of-age ritual modelled upon the Brauronia discussed in Chapter 3, and a barracks where Neoptolemus and Patroclus spent time ahead of Iphigenia's wedding.

Punchdrunk's mixing of different mythological localities within the same area of the set, alongside their references to geographically separate parts of mainland Greece mere steps from one another, created a slipperiness of location which was reinforced through design references to different temporalities. The costuming and set design, for example, included a prominent 1930s aesthetic communicated through, for example, the presence of Bakelite telephones in the army camp and a series of three gold Art Deco-style panels in the bathroom of the upstairs Mycenaean Palace. The central concrete plinth table in the Royal Palace had Brutalist overtones, while the wall paintings in the shrine to Artemis nodded to Pompeian frescos. Charlotte Higgins, drawing upon designer Livi Vaughan's words, identified the warehouse as '"stark and epic and big", with a classicising style that's overlaid … with the aesthetic of Fritz Lang's Metropolis—hints of 1920s Art Deco in a slightly sci-fi mode'.[30] Thom Waite similarly read the space as hybrid, seeing 'the frontline of the war' 'littered with dystopian checkpoints' and 'echoing sci-fi classics such as *Stalker*'.[31] The uncertainty surrounding the precise time and space in which audiences found themselves stopped the experience from being a reconstruction of a historical period which audiences could fact check. Instead, the design worked to communicate to audiences that they were within a space that mapped onto mythological ancient Greece but was nevertheless an original world unto itself which was governed by its own logic and design ecology. The rigour in the design of *The Burnt City* came not from creating a realistic representation of any one past, whether Bronze Age Mycenae or Weimar Berlin, but in creating a touch-real manifestation of the company's unique vision for their interpretation of the materials.

Even without my insider knowledge and disciplinary background, ample material existed within Warehouse 17 to communicate to the audience that they were in Greece. References, for example, in the artefact descriptions in the museum entrance to Greek characters and narrative points were picked up in the design of the army's headquarters, and signage and insignia at the military checkpoint at the boundary of No Man's Land explicitly named the location as Greece. For those with some background knowledge, obscure references such as to Calchas'

---

[30] Higgins (2022).
[31] Waite (2022).

prophecy, or via the presence of checkers—a game supposedly invented by the Greek soldier Palamedes during the Trojan War—might provide orientation within the narrative universe. *The Burnt City*'s version of Greece was unique, but unified, drawing upon and combining a fixed number of design referents. A plethora of design detail cannot guarantee an immersive experience, but it can encourage one to feel encased in an alternate reality. During my own attendance of *The Burnt City*, the design in Greece built upon the separation from reality fostered through the museum entrance experience and further encouraged me to suspend my disbelief as I went on to engage with performed action in the space.

The sense of two distinct civilisations, building upon the structural offering of the pair of Woolwich buildings, was key to the design ecology of *The Burnt City*. Doyle described to Anna James that Punchdrunk had 'tried to create a different feeling between Greece and Troy in aesthetic, the costume and the sound, but also in the characters and people you're going to meet and the stories you're going to encounter'.[32] The way that the central Town Square in Troy, previously mentioned as the location of Persephone's emergence from the water butt and the vista that audiences gaze upon when experiencing the Trojan strand of the museum opening, was immediately distinct from the central No Man's Land space in Greece reflected Doyle's vision of a bifurcated environment. As I walked through the double doors from the link structure into the Trojan Town Square, I was confronted not with a stark, open space with pockets of detailed design installation, but rather with what looked like a film set intended to represent a living, breathing city. I stood face-to-face with a bistro, complete with continental-style tables and chairs both inside and outside of its shopfront, dressed with tablecloths, menus, and flowers, named Ciacco's. Inside was a central counter, on which glasses and bottles of water rested, while a waitress stood behind the counter, doodling on a notepad. To the right of Ciacco's was the historic-looking Hades' House, unnamed and only on first glance recognisable as a private residence due to the closed wooden front door, either side of which were industrial, arched sash windows with heavy, velvet curtains and between which I spied a domestic interior. On the far wall was a department store, named Alighieri's and featuring mannequins in the two shopfront windows, while alongside the wall through which I

---

[32] Doyle, quoted in James (2022).

had just entered lay the water butt and neon signage naming the Palladium. The design fostered the sense of an urban city centre, with a slightly different geographic specificity to Greece due to the heavy use of neon across the shopfronts. The distinction was also present in the costuming. In Greece, the characters (aside from the military personnel) wore 1930s-inspired, expensive and sophisticated-looking costumes, with Clytemnestra, for example, in a floor-length, backless crushed velvet dress, and Aegisthus in high-waisted, satin trousers. In Troy, the costuming was far more contemporary, featuring metallics, leather, and beading, and hair and make-up including edgy undercuts and bright, vibrant eyeshadows.

The Town Square was the initial, central space through which audiences entered Troy. However, it was a small portion of what was a much more intricate space in comparison to Greece (Fig 5.1). Warehouse 19 featured a domestic tenement structure, a red-light district, Polymestor's base (not explicitly marked as Thrace but including his personal office and his own bar, the 'Klub'), alongside several other businesses such as Askalaphos' flower shop (Hesperides) and Zagreus' sake bar (The White Cyprus). Like Greece, the aesthetic of Troy was created through an original compilation of different design influences. The menus of The White Cyprus, the signage of select Trojan business, and the paper lanterns hanging in the alleyways all featured the Bronze Age Linear B script. However, the letters on the paper lanterns were rendered in the style of Japanese Kanji, in a nod to the Yoshiwara nightclub district in Fritz Lang's *Metropolis*. The aesthetic also communicated a very different economic outlook. In the Town Square alone, for example, it was evident that the sense of wealth that could be found in Greece had vanished. Whereas in the Mycenaean Royal Palace, Clytemnestra toasted her daughter's engagement with champagne and dined with Aegisthus on a multi-course banquet, in Troy, Ciacco's menu featured only rationed, powdered options. Not only had the Palladium closed down, but on my left as I entered the Town Square lay a pile of red velvet Art Deco-style theatre seats, appearing to have been stripped out of the ransacked venue. Inside Alighieri's were piles of empty, dusty gift boxes, implying that the shop was a mere shell of what it once was. Although the city appeared vibrant and colourful, with designer Beatrice Minns describing the atmosphere as of 'decadence, of parties, of Weimar', looking closely at the scenography revealed evidence of a city under siege.³³ The dramaturgical and designed spaces of Warehouse 17 and 19 thus communicated not only two separate identities, but allowed audiences to engage with the Trojan War narrative from two different embodied realities. The ability not only to see the story from the perspective of the different sides involved in the conflict, but to experience how the narrative reverberated through the two different localities was key to the enveloping nature of *The Burnt City* and the ability for an audience member to feel embedded within the production's narrative universe.

The museum entrance experience represented the sedimentary layer, the recreation of Greece and Troy the substantive strata, and the mythological Underworld the deepest, base layer of *The Burnt City*. The design of *The Burnt City* contained numerous hints regarding the presence of the Underworld spatiality, such as a flickering neon sign reading 'Hello There'

Fig. 5.1 Pin Chieh Chen as Kampe in Punchdrunk's *The Burnt City*, pictured in a corridor within Troy. Image credit: Julian Abrams. Courtesy of Punchdrunk

---

³³ Minns, quoted in Higgins (2022).

which glitched to read 'Hell here'. My earlier overview of the cross-fade experience mentioned bypassing a water source running underneath the floor of the first room in the museum exhibition; looking back on the experience after the performance, one might hazard that they had, at this point, crossed over the river Styx to enter the Underworld. Furthermore, in the Trojan Town Square, the bistro and the department store referenced the reception of the Underworld in Dante's *Divine Comedy*, with Ciacco's named after Dante's glutton and Alighieri's after Dante himself. The White Cypress bar was named after a geographic marker of the Underworld found in an Orphic gold tablet; the sakes available in the bar, as labelled on the menu and in the tap room behind the bar, were named after rivers providing access to, or found within, the Underworld, including Styx, Lethe, Acheron, Cocytus, and Phlegethon. The flowers for sale in Askalaphos' shop were all fake, due to the absence of natural light in *The Burnt City*'s Underworld (although outside of *The Burnt City*, plants do grow in the mythic Underworld, for example in the Asphodel Meadows). Within the tenement living quarters, each room was designed to reference an inhabitant of Tartarus. For example, a room filled with dangerous engagements with electricity nodded to Salmoneus, who created an imitation of Zeus' thunderbolt, while a living quarter featuring 49 pair of flip-flops, pants, toothbrushes, and hosiery, alongside bathtubs and leaky buckets, referenced the 49 Danaids who murdered their husbands on their wedding night. Personal effects in the Tenements, including books, letters, and postcards added further hints as to the absent residents' identities, including a postcard from Pelops to his father Tantalus in Tantalus' apartment, and a wash day rota in the Danaids' quarters.

The Underworld stratum was not a meticulously researched representation of any one Underworld but rather was Punchdrunk's unique assemblage of broadly understood cues, such as to the name Alighieri, with subtle references that might only be fully appreciated should the audience member go away and do their own research into, for example, Tartarus' inhabitants. A critical reading of the design compilation (and even the resident characters who occupy Troy, such as Askalaphos and Macaria) might see the mixture of sources as randomised, or even a form of Barthesian mythology, trafficking in a sign system but hollowing out the signifiers to create a fresh signification. Although I recognise such potential objections, to my mind the significance of the design ecology was that it came together as more than the sum of its parts, with the multiplicity of references working together to ensure that the greatest possible portion of audience recognised the alternate reality within which they were being enveloped.

The sense of an Underworld layer in *The Burnt City* was primarily established, however, not through the production's design but through its dramaturgy, and particularly through the narrative arc of Hades and Persephone (Fig. 5.2). A series of family trees in the foyer of One Cartridge Place revealed the cast of characters to audience members upon their arrival and communicated the presence of Hades and Persephone to those who stopped to study the material. Following Hades' and Persephones' journeys through the production unlocked the Underworld dimension. Particular moments of revelation included Hades' one-on-one, which fell between Loop Two and Three and revealed Hades as the architect of the purgatorial looping structure, and Persephone's three-on-one, which fell across Scenes Seven to Nine in Loop Three and saw her unlock her identity as queen of the Underworld and grant her three audience members safe passage through her kingdom. The exclusivity of these moments of revelation raises a question over the accessibility of the final Underworld spatiality. Despite the presence of references to the Underworld in the production's design, it is feasible that those who concentrated upon the narrative arc of the characters from *Agamemnon* and *Hecuba* might have remained ignorant of the Underworld dimension. The fact that only a privileged few could access Persephone's and Hades' revelatory scenes links to Adam Alston's suggestion that immersive theatre fosters a type of 'entrepreneurial participation' which shares the neoliberal values of entrepreneurialism, and the valorisation of risk, agency, and responsibility.[34] There is an inequality of opportunity to participate in one-on-one scenes, and one's chances are increased by having the means to finance repeated visits to the production, or by being educated in Punchdrunk's performance style. However, there will always be a portion of audience members who experience one-on-one scenes purely fortuitously. In a one-on-one workshop during rehearsals with Barrett, for example, he encouraged performers to choose not just the keenest or most confident spectator, but perhaps those more shyly invested in a character's storyline as well. I have first-hand experience of

---

[34] Alston (2013: 128).

such selection, being chosen for a one-on-one in Punchdrunk's 2013–2014 *The Drowned Man* when stood on tip toes, attempting to witness a scene involving the Doctor but being barricaded away from the action by the heavy throng of spectators in front of me. Whether considered as reflections of a neoliberal ethos or not, the small portion of audience who experienced the one- or three-on-one scenes with Hades and Persephone reflects just how deeply embedded the Underworld spatiality was within *The Burnt City*.

To realise that *The Burnt City* told the story not only of the fall of Troy but involved a purgatorial replaying of the Trojan War within the Underworld required the spectator to engage closely and actively with the world of the performance. Even if one did not experience the one- or three-on-one scenes, attending to the small details on costume, such as the embroidered GAIA on Persephone when she emerged from the water butt, observing the interactions of each character, such as Hades' presence during death scenes throughout the performance, and exploring

Fig. 5.2 Sam Booth as Hades in Punchdrunk's *The Burnt City*, pictured in The White Cyprus sake bar in Troy. Image credit: Julian Abrams. Courtesy of Punchdrunk

the scenography, such as the letter from Hades to Persephone's mother Demeter which lay in Hades' desk drawers, revealed the Underworld location. The performance's structure also reinforced the Underworld setting. Hades and Persephone did not loop, but rather told their story over twenty-two scenes (both were absent from the main performance space for much, if not all, of the first loop) and were notable for remaining in character during the finale. When the other performers descended the staircase, leaving behind their Greek and Trojan identities and abstractly echoing Dirk Bouts' *Fall of the Damned*, Hades and Persephone appeared on the mezzanine balcony under a spotlight, surveying their realm. Audience members who made the connection between the Underworld references and the wider dramaturgy of *The Burnt City* effectively, to return to Biggin's (and Pearson's) analogy, understood the Trojan War setting to be the ghost inhabiting the host of the Underworld, just as *The Burnt City* production could be thought of as the ghost inhabiting the host of the two munitions factories. Indeed, Hades' dialogue occasionally nodded to the layering of space within *The Burnt City*. For example, during the sacrifice of Polyxena in Scene Five, Loop Two, he turned to the audience in Hades' House and noted 'You understand it's not the real thing. It's a reflection. A re-presentation. With a beginning, and an ending. The real thing has no beginning. Is without end. It can never stop', metatheatrically alluding to the artificiality of performance but also offering the audience a clue as to how the looping narrative was an artificial device even within performance. The multilayered storyworld consequently progressively moved audiences away from reality, from initially seeing Punchdrunk's production as the ghost inhabiting the Woolwich host, through to seeing the fall of Troy as the ghost inhabiting the Underworld host. The layering acted akin to dream layering in *Inception*, offering greater possibilities for immersion as the spectator progressed through the dramaturgical layers. Experiencing the multiple spatialities of *The Burnt City* increasingly displaced the audience from their present reality in favour of embedding them deeper within the mythic reality of the show. The structure reflected the first quality of immersivity and was one of the primary mechanisms through which *The Burnt City* facilitated an immersive experience. Whether an audience member was immersed, however, depended upon their relation to the production's sense of place and space, and the presence of the remaining three qualities of an immersive experience. As such, I now turn to audience experience.

Experience

The interplay between place, space, and experience in *The Burnt City* helped propel Punchdrunk's reception of Greek tragedy into the realm of immersivity. Biggin emphasises that if we do not consider experience, and explore the presence of a 'graded, fleeting, intense and necessarily temporary state' of immersion, then we cannot pinpoint immersion within immersive theatre as the theatrical form is, for Biggin, defined as a genre which allows for—but does not guarantee—said experience.[35] Here, I further Biggin's interest in experience and give it added specificity, by suggesting that by analysing the coexistence of place, space, and experience, we can pinpoint how *The Burnt City* encouraged spectators to feel enveloped within alternate realities. I do so by putting my own encoded relationship to place and space in *The Burnt City* in dialogue with how Punchdrunk envisage audience experience, and how other scholars have theorised spectatorial experience within Punchdrunk's work as well. I suggest that the potential immersivity of *The Burnt City* was particularly acute due to the integration of antiquity within the production, as there was synergy between the audience's role within the performance and the content on which the performance was based. Examining place, space, and experience within *The Burnt City* therefore not only reveals how the production fostered immersion, but also shows the benefits of drawing upon antiquity within immersive experiences more generally.

Immersing an audience member in an alternate reality without shutting off their senses, as occurs when wearing a virtual reality headset or when listening to a binaural recording in complete blackout, is challenging and not without controversy. This is despite the fact that literary forms of immersivity are readily recognised and relatively uncontroversial, even though they take place via embodied cognition rather than through sensory deprivation. Marie-Laure Ryan's work is noteworthy for its influence in this area, drawing upon virtual reality and literary theory to develop a phenomenology of reading that recognises literary immersion.[36] Classicists have also argued for the presence of immersive literary techniques not just in contemporary texts, but in ancient epics, historiography, and rhetoric too, rooting literary immersion in the rhetorical devices of *ekphrasis*, where a scene is rendered in such pictorial detail that

---

[35] Biggin (2017: 1).
[36] Ryan (2015).

the reader or listener may feel as if plunged into, or immersed in, the moment described, as well as in *enargeia*, or the quality of vividness.[37] The controversy surrounding immersion in a theatrical context involving participatory performance is in part due to the overt casting of the audience member, in some productions, as part of the fictitious universe. Sophie Nield, for example, records a moment of crisis when being directly addressed by a performer in a Goat and Monkey production at Southwark Playhouse, questioning 'who on earth is this monk supposed to think I am?'.[38] Punchdrunk's approach to audience participation in their large-scale masked shows does not tend to give the spectator an individualised identity. Instead, from the company's perspective, the audience are understood to inhabit the broader, collective identity of shades.

During an audience management workshop in the rehearsal period, rehearsal director Emily Terndrup detailed how within Punchdrunk's creative practice, the audience of a masked show is explicitly encoded as shades. She instructed the cast, for example, that they should 'think of the audience as shades, or as lost souls' who they cannot really see or engage with but who inhabit the space as spectres, before clarifying the exceptions to the audience's invisibility, noting that 'you can see them in a one-on-one, if you've been killed, are a god, or have eaten the lotus flower [i.e. are drugged], but just because you can doesn't mean you should. Use this ability sparingly'.[39] Biggin's work also attests to a similar understanding, describing 'the masked audience members as ghosts or voyeurs, following the relationships between characters'.[40] That the audience represents a collective of shades is a loose metaphor rather than an exact description. However, comparing the audience's function to, for example, the Underworld inhabitants invoked in the *nekyia* scene in Book XI of *The Odyssey* shows the kinship between Homeric shades and Punchdrunk's audience

---

[37] See, for example, Walker (1993) for *enargeia* in historiography, and Huitink (2019: 188) for immersion in Homeric epic. These concepts are explored in greater depth in Chapter 6.

[38] Nield (2008: 531).

[39] The idea that Punchdrunk characters can see the audience if they are in an extreme mental state, dead, or magical is well attested in the company's writing. See, for example, Machon and Punchdrunk (2019: 209), where the company notes how these qualities affect a performer's moments of lucidity and presence. The section of the company's teacher resource pack on one-on-one experiences also contains relevant information; see Punchdrunk (2019: np).

[40] Biggin (2017: 31).

and the aptness of the metaphor. In *The Odyssey*, the ghosts called upon can only interact with Odysseus after partaking in a ritual experience (drinking the blood of an offering). The ritual allows the shades to enter a liminal zone where they can talk to the living, just like Punchdrunk's audience can talk to a performer when their mask is removed for a one-on-one. Despite being able to converse, however, Homer's ghosts cannot physically affect the events in the realm of the living, as is represented acutely when Odysseus attempts to hug his mother three times, only for her ghostly ephemerality to evade his embrace.

Punchdrunk offer some indications to their audience as to their ghostly identity. The audience is rendered as mute observers who are limited in their ability to intervene in a production's narrative and interact with its characters, meaning they have the same limited powers of affect as Odysseus' mother. In scholarship on the audience experience in Punchdrunk's earlier masked productions, much of the commentary is dedicated to debates over the relative activity versus passivity of Punchdrunk's audience, particularly via reading the company's audience as a representation of Rancière's stultified rather than emancipated spectator.[41] Even if audience members do not explicitly recognise their role as shades, such scholarship reveals that some spectators have historically found the shade-like limitations on active engagement frustrating, particularly in light of Punchdrunk's rhetoric surrounding audience empowerment. The coexistence of the audience's experience as Underworld inhabitants within the framing of an Underworld spatiality in *The Burnt City* can be thought of as attempting to circumnavigate these frustrations by encoding the audience's presence as a by-product of one of the production's spaces.

Alongside the broad indications in all Punchdrunk masked shows regarding the audience's collective identity, in *The Burnt City* there were explicit references as well. Spectators who followed Persephone's loop, for example, gained insight into their positionality as spectres of the dead. These insights were not exclusive to those spectators who experienced Persephone's three-on-one and were granted safe passage through her kingdom; in Loop Three, Scene Two, for example, Persephone had a palm reading scene with the resident character Laocoön, in which it was implied that according to Persephone's lifeline, she would never

---

[41] See Rancière (2009). Examples of scholarship on Punchdrunk that maps on to Rancière's approach include Maples (2016: esp. p. 120), Luckhurst (2017: esp. p. 13), and Worthen (2012: esp. pp. 94–95).

die. Persephone's reaction to the news, and to the swarms of spectators witnessing the scene, helped communicate the audience's identity as inhabitants of the Underworld. The critical response to *The Burnt City* demonstrates that this identity was successfully communicated to at least a portion of the audience: Anna James, for example, noted that 'it would seem we are all playing in the Underworld'; the *G Scene* review suggested 'We are ghosts in this narrative machine'; and Tabitha Chopping argued that each spectator became a 'lost soul, trapped behind a funeral mask … confined to a liminal, purgatorial space'.[42] Creating synergy between the audience's generic experience within all Punchdrunk masked shows and the specific spaces of *The Burnt City* incorporated the audience's limited ability to influence a production into their characterisation.

Although in *The Burnt City* rehearsal room, the audience was only conceived of as shades, elsewhere Barrett has suggested that his audience functions as 'sort of like a modern-day Greek chorus'. The obvious parallels between the tragic chorus and the Punchdrunk audience include the masking of both collectives, and the sense of both being bystanders, able to watch action but unable to intervene. There are also, according to Barrett and as discussed in Chapter 2, equivalents between the Punchdrunk audience and the specific tragic chorus of Aeschylus' *Eumenides*, with Punchdrunk's audience functioning as a pursuing collective who must seek out performers just as the Furies search for Orestes. Within the dramaturgy of *The Burnt City*, despite only the narrative of Aeschylus' *Agamemnon* and Euripides' *Hecuba* being staged, there was a conceit that when characters died, they were reincarnated as furies, as was the case with Polyxena and Polydorus. Yet Barrett's comment—made well before *The Burnt City*'s creation—is intended to be taken as a general guide as to his audience's overall position, rather than a literal framing, and within *The Burnt City* I doubt audience members felt themselves to be equivalent to Polyxena and Polydorus. However, although audience members may not have felt themselves to be furies, the concept does provide a useful metaphor for teasing out audience behaviours in immersive performance.

Research into the audience contract and theatre etiquette has gained momentum over the past decade, particularly through the work of Kirsty Sedgman. These audience studies have highlighted the challenges of navigating new theatrical forms where the more traditional rules of

---

[42] See James (2022a), G Scene (2022), and Chopping (2022) respectively.

modern spectatorship do not apply. Punchdrunk themselves have made the headlines on this subject, with a notorious *Buzzfeed* article highlighting the unruly behaviours that Punchdrunk performers experienced from audiences in the *Sleep No More* New York production, which stretched from drunkenness right through to sexual assault.[43] Punchdrunk's safeguarding of their performers now includes working with intimacy coordinators, issuing pre-performance guidance for audiences on expected behaviour, and strict procedures for performers, stewards, and stage managers for managing audiences mid-performance if and when they take liberties and jeopardise performer safety. Nevertheless, there remains a grey zone surrounding the fury-like behaviour of audiences who flock to characters and who, even if not tormenting the performers, may be feasibly tormenting their fellow audience members through their rapacious behaviour. Dipping a toe into fan discourse on Punchdrunk's work can make it seem like there is no way to experience shows like *The Burnt City* correctly. On the one hand, there is a sense that experiencing a character's full loop—and particularly their one-on-ones—is a desirable performance of one's fandom, while on the other hand references to 'dick mask' behaviour on Punchdrunk fandom pages hint towards an unspecified tipping point between invested spectatorship and ungenerous behaviour. I raise the question of whether being cast as a fury is inevitably a good thing when I consider some of the ethical questions surrounding immersive experience through the lens of ancient ideas such as *mimesis* in Chapter 6.

Although Punchdrunk have not spoken about their recent audiences in terms of furies or the Greek chorus, we can again find evidence within reviews of some spectators perceiving their role as equivalent to a chorus. Chopping, for example, noted that in *The Burnt City* she was transformed 'into a silent and haunting chorus', while D. J. Hopkins described how in *Sleep No More*, the mask 'made a profound contribution: the audience became both part of the scenography and a chorus among the characters'.[44] Such reviews rely upon a generic understanding of Greek chorality, but even though this role may not be theorised, it nevertheless shows how the audience's role in *The Burnt City* was given added purchase by want of the production being a classical reception, as it cast

---

[43] Jamieson (2018).
[44] Chopping (2022) and Hopkins (2012).

the audience as a formal device drawn from the production's source material. Enveloping the audience's role within *The Burnt City* as a by-product of the tragic or Underworld spatialities helped enfold the audience within the imaginative universe of the production, creating a unified frame that heightened the potential ways in which one could feel immersed in the production's alternate reality. The reviews quoted above reveal that such a unified frame does not rely upon expert knowledge about antiquity; even basic knowledge about the idea of ghostly spectres or the idea of a masked collective as a tragic chorus helped encourage spectators to take on a different embodied identity in *The Burnt City*.

Punchdrunk envisage their audience as shades or a chorus, it does not inevitably follow that all audiences understand their experience as such, and I end my investigation into the coexistence of place, space, and experience in *The Burnt City* by considering one final way of theorising the audience's role in Punchdrunk performances, as likened to that of ancient ritual participants. It is possible to read all spectatorial experiences within Punchdrunk masked performances through the lens of ritualised theatrical participation as rooted in the City Dionysia, where *The Burnt City*'s source tragedies were first performed.[45] At the multi-day Dionysia, the boundaries between participant and observer were, like in Punchdrunk's theatre, blurred. Although the fourth wall was rendered firmly intact during the actual staging of the theatrical texts, attending the theatre was nevertheless a participatory activity which included processing, eating, drinking, singing, and taking part in ritual enactments. Given that the chorus in ancient Greece was a civic *choreia*, it is feasible that a portion of the attending audience each year were performers from past iterations of the Dionysia, who watched the action through the lens of their embodied memories of performing. Cognitive research reveals that having first-hand experience of participating in physical activities means that one has a kinaesthetic response when witnessing future related activites, with greater expertise equating to stronger sensations of felt participation; someone who has trained in ballet, for example, will feel kinaesthetic empathy when watching ballet performances and translate the visual impression of the performance into a body-based response, by reading the visual

---

[45] My thanks to Stephe Harrop for the provocation to think of Punchdrunk's audiences through this particular approach.

through their embodied memory of the techniques on display.[46] In the Dionysia, too, watching may have felt like doing. The sacrificial procession that commenced the Dionysia, the *pompē*, can be thought of as akin to Punchdrunk's cross-fade, buffering spectators into the liminal zone of the City Dionysia through a ritualised experience. Although audiences did not physically follow performers around a performance space in ancient Greece, it is possible that audiences, given an annual performance schedule at the Dionysia encompassing three tetralogies and five comedies, did not watch the full submission each year but would actively exercise discretion regarding what they witnessed and when. Furthermore, although the performances were not site-sympathetic in the way that Punchdrunk's work is constructed as a response to site, the environment in which ancient drama was performed was still crucial to the audience's experience.

The open-air performance environment of the Theatre of Dionysus informed the imagery, dramaturgy, and resonances contained in Greek drama. Some productions even had an element of site-specificity. Aeschylus' *The Persians*, for example, revolved around the recent naval battle at Salamis during the Persian Wars; the island of Salamis is visible from the Acropolis, meaning that audience members may have looked out onto the scene of the battle during their approach to and exit from the theatre. Even plays depicting purely mythological events, such as *Agamemnon* and *Hecuba*, gained resonance through their performance environment. The architectural place, for example, shaped the dramaturgy of *Agamemnon*, with the device of the *ekkyklema* (wheeled platform) and the construction of the theatre with a *skene* behind an *orchestra* facilitating Clytemnestra's triumphant entrance above the slaughtered corpses of Agamemnon and Cassandra. The geographic place in which these tragedies were performed was, furthermore, an important political and religious site and was immediately by the coast, which could feasibly enrich the audience's reading of the Trojan War tragedies, given the focus in *Hecuba*, for example, on the forced migration and enslavement of refugees who were setting sail from Troy. Attendees at the City Dionysia were therefore festive celebrants participating in an overarching ritual event where the interrelation between place, space, and experience informed their engagement with each performance. Although the Dionysia is not immersive in my

---

[46] For other examples of how cognitive research has showcased the distinctive ways that professional dancers experience witnessing performance, see Olsen (2017).

sense of the term and is distinct from Punchdrunk's work in that it also had an important function in promoting civic identity, the ancient dramatic performances nevertheless hold parallels with, or are even an analogue too, Punchdrunk's masked performances. These resonances exist between the audiences at the Dionysia and the audience of all Punchdrunk's masked performances, but once again gain added significance in *The Burnt City* due to the production's status as a classical reception. Thinking through the audience experience in *The Burnt City* as akin to the celebrants' experience at the City Dionysia shows another way that Punchdrunk's production can be thought to fold audiences conceptually into the alternate reality of the performance and thus increase the possibility for immersion.

In addition to reading all spectatorial experience in Punchdrunk's masked shows through the lens of ancient ritual experience, Bastien Goursaud and Déborah Prudhon, as well as, separately, David Bullen, have touched upon how Punchdrunk cast the two audience-participants in their 2017 *Kabeiroi* as initiands into the Kabeiroi mystery cult.[47] Their arguments have bearing on how we might read audience participation in *The Burnt City* as well. The casting of the audience as initiands was in the context of *Kabeiroi* a literal casting, with the audience-participants positioned as the production's protagonists and undergoing a ritual initiation complete with pouring libations and experiencing a transition from a space of darkness into one of blinding brightness modelled on the more famous Eleusinian mysteries.[48] Bullen's focus is on the ethical issues surrounding the repackaging of what were or are sacred parts of lives and communities into immersive theatrical encounters; although in *Kabeiroi* the audience are actual initiands, Bullen's interest is in how immersive productions configure access to the sacred and taboo more broadly. Bullen raises significant points regarding the commodification of religious rituals for immersive experience and invites one to consider whether the efficacy of experiences that rely upon such practices might be underpinned by bad faith.

My earlier overview of *The Burnt City*'s cross-fade revealed that during the museum entrance experience that led into Troy, the audience

---

[47] See Goursaud and Prudhon (2018) and Bullen (forthcoming).
[48] For a description of the *Kabeiroi* finale, see Cole (2021: 523).

encountered references to ancient Greek mystery religion. In the second-to-last room, for example, the museum exhibit featured two terracotta drinking vessels, with a caption describing them as 'depicting Demeter and Persephone, goddesses in whose honour the Eleusinian mystery cults performed their rites'. The accompanying voiceover described how in his later years Schliemann turned 'his attention to researching and re-enacting the practices of mystery cults, whose worshippers drank hallucinogenic concoctions from vessels such as these, and took part in rituals to transcend the world of appearances and commune with the gods'. There is a broad connection between the fact that the Eleusinian mysteries, despite the opacity surrounding the exact rites, prepared initiands for the afterlife and the fact that in *The Burnt City* the audience inhabited the Underworld. Just as the Mycenaean entrance warped the conceit of the museum artifice, infusing it with drama through the stolen artefact and the broken display case, so too did the Trojan experience destabilise the boundaries between the cross-fade and the performance. In the Trojan half, the destabilisation was achieved through the implication that as the audience could now look upon 'the face of Agamemnon' and 'commune with the gods', so too must they have drunk the *kykeon* and be engaging with mystery religion.

There are two primary ways to interrogate Punchdrunk's references to mystery religion within *The Burnt City* through the ethical framework that Bullen proposes in his analysis of *Kabeiroi*. The first is through the company's invocation of a historic religious ritual that was of immense significance to its initiates in antiquity, as is evidenced by the prosecution of those individuals, such as Alcibiades, found to have profaned the mysteries. As Punchdrunk did not actually stage an initiation ritual for their audiences in *The Burnt City*, the ethical questions Bullen raises in relation to *Kabeiroi* are somewhat lessened. *The Burnt City* entrance experience included references to ritual and cult, which were part of the ecology of the universe of Punchdrunk's primary source texts and can be thought of as legitimate source material within Punchdrunk's broad engagement with ancient Greek culture. The second is through the implied result of becoming an initiate through the Trojan entrance of *The Burnt City*, where there was a specific blurring between Schliemann's engagement with mystery religion and his drinking of the *kykeon* to look upon his 'burnt city', and the audience's ability to look upon it, too. Barrett mentioned in his interview with James that *The Burnt City* is like a fever dream; the Trojan entrance gives this comment specificity, inviting audiences to conceive of Punchdrunk's Troy as Schliemann's dream. Schliemann's self-mythologising and notoriety makes him a fascinating figure, but he is also mired in controversy due to, for example, his unscientific excavation methodologies, which blurred together the layers of distinct civilisations and created enormous challenges for subsequent archaeologists, and the historical inaccuracies he perpetuated in service of his claims to have 'found' Troy, which included ethically problematic claims that the Trojans were an Aryan race.[49] Punchdrunk's invitation for audiences to view their iteration of Troy as Schliemann's fantasy, particularly coupled with the Weimar Berlin aesthetic, could, through Bullen's argument, be construed as an offering made in bad faith, in that it highlights a problematic moment of classical reception and plays into a history of Western-centric interpretations of classical antiquity which go right through to modern uses of ancient Greece in the service of white supremacy. Even the non-Western iconography within Troy was funnelled through the lens of the Yoshiwara nightclub district in Lang's *Metropolis*, although I note that Punchdrunk worked with a Japanese dramaturg on this representation rather than rely on Lang's intertext.

Reading *The Burnt City* through the lens of Bullen's comments on ritual, the sacred, and immersive offerings in bad faith highlights points of tension surrounding the type of experience that audiences were offered within Punchdrunk's production but deviates from my focus on the type of roles that audiences were invited to inhabit within *The Burnt City* and how these were encoded in relation to the dramaturgy of *The Burnt City*. The references to Greek religion within the cross-fade meant that there was a shared cultural origin between the implied role of the audience, as ritual initiands within the sedimentary spatial layer of the performance, and the narrative world in the two substantive strata of Greece and Troy. Once again, the synergy between place, space, and experience helped facilitate the transportation of the audience into an alternate reality and thus encouraged immersion. While the Trojan cross-fade device may have been powerful in terms of facilitating experience, I have here highlighted how this potentially came at a cost in terms of associating this component of the production with a politically uncomfortable strand of classical reception.

* * *

[49] Baker (2019: 161).

Within *The Burnt City*, the layers of meaning relating to place and space, and the audience's encoded experience in relation to both, helped foster immersion by imbuing the performance with one of the four key qualities of immersivity, namely the displacement of the audience from their present reality. There are no guarantees in any experience that someone will feel enveloped in an alternate reality, but nevertheless, as Biggin argues, theatre makers can do their best to facilitate the experience, which then relies on what Carina E. I. Westling terms a willing 'self capture' from the audience.[50] In this chapter, I have demonstrated how the relationship between *The Burnt City* and its Woolwich home helped locate the subject matter of the performance within a wider reality, and meant that echoes of the performance's content could be felt as audience members approached and left the performance. More significantly, however, I have showcased how the multilayering of dramaturgical and designed spaces in *The Burnt City* helped embed audience members in narratives that became increasingly removed from the outside world, much as dream layering in the film *Inception* increasingly removes the dreamer from reality. If an audience member understood themselves to be actively cast within these spaces, either in Punchdrunk's terms as a shade or a chorus member, or via other theorisations, such as in terms of a festive participant or ritual initiand, then the potential for feeling embedded in Punchdrunk's alternate reality became even greater. Although Punchdrunk's spectator can always be compared to an Underworld shade, a member of a tragic chorus, an initiand, or a festive celebrant, it is only in *The Burnt City* where all four identities were encoded in relation to the dramaturgy of the production. *The Burnt City* demonstrates that when Punchdrunk's trademark performance style is combined with a classical reception, then the opportunities to experience immersion gain added purchase as there is a greater overarching logic at play.

If an audience member did not experience the coexistence of place, space, and experience in such a way that it plunged them deeper and deeper into the world of *The Burnt City*, it did not necessarily matter. On the one hand, one could spend an entire performance in just Building 17 or 19 and still, theoretically, feel immersed in the narrative. Similarly, one could engage purely with the Trojan War narrative and remain oblivious to the Underworld spatiality without the production's affect

---

[50] Biggin (2017: 47). On immersion as self-capture, see Westling (2020), with the concept first introduced on p. 2.

necessarily being diminished. Unpacking how these spaces and those audience experiences engaged with the other three qualities of immersivity would unlock how immersion was achieved in such instances. On the other hand, one could visit both warehouses, and be cognisant of the different spatial layers embedded in the performance, and still experience the work from a critical distance, as displacing one from their present reality can support, but not guarantee, a temporary immersive experience. Rather than suggest that there is a relationship of direct causation between the layering of place and space in *The Burnt City* and the experience of being immersed, what I have suggested in this chapter is that there is a non-exclusive correlation between the two. Having shed light on one way that *The Burnt City* functioned in performance and invited its audience to experience immersion, I now turn to consider how the production might reshape our understanding of the history of immersivity, by augmenting and redefining immersivity in antiquity.

Works Cited

Alston, Adam. 2013. Audience Participation and Neoliberal Value: Risk, agency and responsibility in immersive theatre. *Performance Research* 18: 2: 128–138. https://doi.org/10.1080/13528165.2013.807177.

Baker, Abigail. 2019. *Troy on Display: Scepticism and Wonder at Schliemann's First Exhibition*. London: Bloomsbury.

Biggin, Rose. 2017. *Immersive Theatre and Audience Experience: Space, Game and Story in the Work of Punchdrunk*. Cham: Palgrave Macmillan.

Bullen, David. Forthcoming. Experiencing the Sacred in the Theatre of Pentheus: Bad Faith Immersion from the Performance Group to Punchdrunk. In *Experiencing Immersion in Antiquity and Modernity: From Narrative to Virtual Reality*, ed. Emma Cole. London: Bloomsbury.

Carlson, Marvin. 2003. *The Haunted Stage: The Theatre as Memory Machine*. Ann Arbor: University of Michigan Press.

Chopping, Tabitha. 2022. The Burnt City of Infinite Possibilities. *Varsity*, July 22. https://www.varsity.co.uk/theatre/24047. Accessed 31 October 2022.

Clapp, Susannah. 2022. The Week in Theatre. *The Observer*, April 24. https://www.theguardian.com/stage/2022/apr/24/punchdrunk-the-burnt-city-london-review-siege-of-troy-scandaltown-lyric-hammersmith-mike-bartlett-rachael-stirling. Accessed 31 October 2022.

Cole, Emma. 2021. Fragments, Immersivity, and Reception: Punchdrunk on Aeschylus' *Kabeiroi*. *International Journal of the Classical Tradition* 28: 510–525. https://doi.org/10.1007/s12138-020-00578-9.

G Scene. 2022. Review: The Burnt City—Punchdrunk. *G Scene*, June 18. https://www.gscene.com/arts/reviews/review-the-burnt-city-punchdrunk/. Accessed 31 October 2022.

Gillow, Bernadette. 1997. From Domestic to Danger Building: Women Workers in the Royal Arsenal. In *Aspects of the Arsenal: The Royal Arsenal, Woolwich*, eds. Beverley Burford and Julian Watson, 82–90. London: Greenwich Borough Museum.

Goursaud, Bastien and Déborah Prudhon. 2018. *Kabeiroi* by Punchdrunk. *(Re)constitutions/(Re)inventions/(Re)mediations in 20th Century English Literature* 54. https://journals.openedition.org/ebc/4408. Accessed 14 December 2022.

Guillery, Peter, ed. 2012. *Survey of London: Woolwich*. Volume 48. New Haven and London: Yale University Press.

Higgins, Charlotte. 2022. "Adrenaline-Fuelled": Punchdrunk Return with the Horrifically Timely Siege of Troy. *The Guardian*, March 21. https://www.theguardian.com/stage/2022/mar/21/adrenaline-fuelled-punchdrunk-horrifically-timely-siege-troy. Accessed 31 October 2022.

Hopkins, D. J. 2012. *Sleep No More* (review). *Theatre Journal* 64: 2: 269–271. https://doi.org/10.1353/tj.2012.0045.

Huitink, Luuk. 2019. *Enargeia*, Enactivism and the Ancient Readerly Imagination. In *Distributed Cognition in Classical Antiquity*, eds. Miranda Anderson and Douglas Cairns, 173–193. Edinburgh: Edinburgh University Press.

Iles Johnston, Sarah. 2015. The Greek Mythic Story World. *Arethusa* 48: 283–311.

Imperial War Museum. 2022. Nine Women Reveal the Dangers of Working in a Munitions Factory. *Imperial War Museum*. https://www.iwm.org.uk/history/9-women-reveal-the-dangers-of-working-in-a-first-world-war-munitions-factory. Accessed 1 November 2022.

James, Anna. 2022. Punchdrunk's Felix Barrett and Maxine Doyle: "This Place is On a Scale that is Truly Mythic". *The Stage*, April 7. https://www.thestage.co.uk/long-reads/punchdrunks-felix-barrett-and-maxine-doyle-this-place-is-on-a-scale-that-is-truly-mythic-the-burnt-city. Accessed 31 October 2022.

——— 2022a. The Burnt City Review. *The Stage*, April 22. https://www.thestage.co.uk/long-reviews/long-reviews/punchdrunk-the-burnt-city-review-at-woolwich-works. Accessed 31 October 2022.

Jamieson, Amber. 2018. Performers and Staffers at 'Sleep No More' Say Audience Members Have Sexually Assaulted Them. *BuzzFeed.News*, February 6. https://www.buzzfeednews.com/article/amberjamieson/sleep-no-more. Accessed 11 April 2023.

Luckhurst, Mary. 2017. Punchdrunk, the Immersive and Gothic Tourism. *About Performance* 14-15: 7–18.

Ludlow, Barbara. 1997. "She Can Sew a Flannel Cartridge" in the Royal Arenal, Woolwich. In *Aspects of the Arsenal: The Royal Arsenal, Woolwich*, eds. Beverley Burford and Julian Watson, 42–56. London: Greenwich Borough Museum.

Machon, Josephine and Punchdrunk. 2019. *The Punchdrunk Encyclopaedia*. London and New York: Routledge.

Maples, Holly. 2016. The Erotic Voyeur: Sensorial Spectatorship in Punchdrunk's The Drowned Man. *Journal of Contemporary Drama in English* 4: 1: 119–133. https://doi.org/10.1515/jcde-2016-0010.

Nield, Sophie. 2008. The Rise of the Character Named Spectator. *Contemporary Theatre Review* 18: 4: 531–535. https://doi.org/10.1080/10486800802492855.

——— 2012. Sitting the People: Power, Protest, and Public Space. In *Performing Site-Specific Theatre: Politics, Place, Practice*, eds. Anna Birch and Joanne Tompkins, 219–232. Basingstoke and New York: Palgrave Macmillan.

Olsen, Sarah. 2017. Kinesthetic Choreia: Empathy, Memory, and Dance in Ancient Greece. *Classical Philology* 112: 153–174. https://doi.org/10.1086/691550.

Pearson, Mike. 2010. *Site-Specific Performance*. Basingstoke and New York: Palgrave Macmillan.

——— 2012. Haunted House: Staging *The Persians* with the British Army. In *Performing Site-Specific Theatre: Politics, Place, Practice*, eds. Anna Birch and Joanne Tompkins, 69–83. Basingstoke and New York: Palgrave Macmillan.

Pearson, Mike and Michael Shanks. 2001. *Theatre/Archaeology*. Oxon and New York: Routledge.

Punchdrunk. 2019. *Teacher Resource Pack*. https://www.punchdrunk.org.uk/content/uploads/2019/10/Punchdrunk-Teacher-Resource-Pack-v7.pdf. Accessed 31 October 2022.

Rancière, Jacques. 2009. *The Emancipated Spectator*. Trans. Gregory Elliot. London and New York: Verso.

Ryan, Marie-Laure. 2003. *Narrative as Virtual Reality: Immersion and Interactivity in Literature and Electronic Media*. Baltimore and London: Johns Hopkins University Press.

——— 2015. *Narrative as Virtual Reality 2: Revisiting Immersion and Interactivity in Literature and Electronic Media*. Baltimore and London: Johns Hopkins University Press.

Saville, Alice. 2022. Punchdrunk Is Back! Behind the Scenes at New Show The Burnt City. *The Evening Standard*, March 22. https://www.standard.co.uk/culture/theatre/punchdrunk-the-burnt-city-behind-the-scenes-woolwich-b989141.html. Accessed 31 October 2022.

Soloski, Alexis. 2022. "Sleep No More" Awakens After a Long Hibernation. *The New York Times*, February 9. https://www.nytimes.com/2022/02/09/theater/sleep-no-more-reopens.html. Accessed 1 November 2022.

Waite, Thom. 2022. Inside Punchdrunk's Radical Immersive Theatre Show, The Burnt City. *Dazed Digital*, March 21. https://www.dazeddigital.com/life-culture/article/55727/1/inside-punchdrunks-monumental-immersive-theatre-show-the-burnt-city. Accessed 31 October 2022.

Walker, Andrew D. 1993. Enargeia and the Spectator in Greek Historiography. *Transactions of the American Philological Association (1974–2014)* 123: 353–377. https://doi.org/10.2307/284335.

Westling, Carina E. I. 2020. *Immersion and Participation in Punchdrunk's Theatrical Worlds*. London and New York: Methuen Drama.

Worthen, W. B. 2012. "The Written Troubles of the Brain": Sleep No More and the Space of Character. *Theatre Journal* 64: 1: 79–97. https://doi.org/10.1017/CBO9781107295544.003.

CHAPTER 6

The Burnt City's Legacy: Immersivity, Mimesis, and Enargeia

In Chapter 5, I explored one of the mechanisms through which Punchdrunk facilitated an immersive experience for their audience, by layering a sense of place and space within *The Burnt City* and inviting audiences to move progressively away from their everyday reality to become increasingly embedded within the psyche of the production. I suggested that Punchdrunk's strategy gained added purchase in *The Burnt City* because of the synergy between how we might understand audience experience in Punchdrunk's masked shows, and the antiquity-inspired content of *The Burnt City*. In this chapter, I continue my focus upon *The Burnt City* in performance, as a counterpart to my focus in the first half of this book on how *The Burnt City* was made. However, instead of looking at how the classical content reinforced the possible immersivity of *The Burnt City*, here I analyse how *The Burnt City* can help us to understand immersivity in antiquity. As the final substantive chapter of my book, this chapter is far removed from the intimacy of the rehearsal study with which I started Chapter 3. Instead, this chapter offers a more distanced, classics-informed analysis of immersivity over time. Despite the difference in approach, the purpose of the chapter is in keeping with the aim of my overall study, to explore how we experience immersion in *The Burnt City* and beyond, with the beyond in this instance stretching back to antiquity.

The concept of immersion goes back to antiquity, where critics theorised literature's ability to create the sensation that a reader or listener was

© The Author(s), under exclusive license to Springer Nature
Switzerland AG 2024
E. Cole, *Punchdrunk on the Classics*,
https://doi.org/10.1007/978-3-031-43067-1_6

present at the event being described. Instances of narratives facilitating immersion are found as far back as the eighth century BCE Homeric epics.[1] There are substantial differences in the technology and the techniques used to create immersion across time. Yet despite these differences, critics both ancient and modern reveal a similar understanding of the concept, whereby the immersant experiences the imaginative or embodied sensation of being transported from their present reality into a different time and place. Ancient critics, for example, used the term *ekstasis* to describe this process, meaning 'the displacement or transportation of the listener, who is so astonished that he [sic] leaves his normal state', while modern critics such as Lyn Gardner define today's immersive theatrical experiences as allowing an audience to 'feel as if they have dropped down a rabbit hole into another world'.[2] The kinship between the effects of immersion in antiquity and modernity invites a comparative dialogue between the two examples, to tease out unexpected insights from both periods and to further our understanding of the phenomenon.

To place immersivity in antiquity and modernity in conversation, I turn to two concepts from antiquity that we can link with immersion, namely the idea of *mimesis*, or representation, as theorised by philosophers such as Aristotle and Plato, and the literary quality of *enargeia*, or vividness, as understood by ancient critics and rhetoricians. I suggest that putting *The Burnt City* side-by-side with such concepts alters our understanding of the historical context in which Punchdrunk's work is situated and illuminates subtleties within both Punchdrunk's practice and ancient understandings of mimesis and enargeia which might otherwise go unnoticed. In particular, I highlight the significance of mimesis to the form of immersion facilitated through interactions between Punchdrunk performers and individual audience members, such as during one-on-one experiences, and the significance of theatricality to an understanding of enargeia. I show that despite *The Burnt City*, mimesis, and enargeia facilitating immersion through different approaches, there are common effects across the different forms of immersivity in modernity and antiquity. As such, my chapter works to invite one to reconceptualise ancient ideas, and to consider the significance of theatricality and embodied performance outside of the theatre and in relation to textuality as well.

---

[1] Allan et al. (2017: 35–36).
[2] Allan et al. (2017: 35) and Gardner (2014).

As in Chapter 5, I am defining an immersive experience as one that holds four qualities. To reiterate, an experience is immersive when it: (1) displaces one from their present reality; (2) engulfs one's senses; (3) encourages one to feel differently; and (4) encourages one to think differently. It is, as Rose Biggin argues, not necessarily an either/or state; rather, an immersive experience is, whether in ancient literature or modern-day performance, a graded, fleeting, intense and necessarily temporary state defined by an awareness of its temporal and spatial boundaries.[3] An aesthetic encounter can be discussed through the lens of immersivity if it encourages the reader, listener, or spectator to have, at times, an immersive experience. Below, I explore the contemporary context within which *The Burnt City* is situated, before turning to mimesis and enargeia, respectively.

IMMERSIVITY

The Burnt City is part of a lucrative immersive experience sector, estimated to be worth over £30 billion to the UK economy by 2025.[4] When *The Burnt City* opened in London in 2022, upwards of one thousand audience members per night could be found spread across Punchdrunk's production, alongside *The Great Gatsby*, *Peaky Blinders*, and *The War of the Worlds*. Anna James further noted that *DesignMyNight* categorised, in November 2022, over two thousand London experiences as 'immersive', meaning that if we look outside of theatre attendees, then the number of people experiencing immersion daily in London in 2022 becomes much greater.[5] As discussed in my introduction, Punchdrunk have an uncomfortable relationship with the immersive label, with Punchdrunk's Artistic Director and *The Burnt City* co-director Felix Barrett noting in November 2022 that 'we've never called ourselves immersive, but I acknowledge that we are part of the immersive movement. For my part, we come from a [site] sympathetic side in the middle of theatre, film and live art by ideology. But that's semantics, I suppose'.[6] Co-director and choreographer Maxine Doyle has contextualised the reason for the

---

[3] Biggin (2017: 1).
[4] HM Government (2018).
[5] James (2022).
[6] Barrett, quoted in Gayet (2022).

company hesitating to align their work with the sector, noting that 'We work so hard, we're inspired by craft and really good content, so I think often immersive theatre falls short on content [...] Actually, we're really really rigorous that it has to stand up to scrutiny'.[7] Despite the company's desire to ensure *The Burnt City* is understood as much more than fancy-dress or a night out, and instead 'could exist on stage at the National, we just choose to put it in a building', their website proudly proclaims a slew of quotations that describe *The Burnt City* as immersive.[8] Scholarship, too, uniformly reads the company's work through the lens of immersivity. Within *The Burnt City*, the company are unquestionably attempting to submerge spectators within the world of the performance through the complexity of the narrative universe and through a focused attention to detail. Punchdrunk's partial reluctance to associate their work with the immersive label is related to the subsection of the arts sector in which they are placed and the competition with which they are associated, rather than due to an ideological rejection of any association with the concept of immersivity.

Despite the popularity of immersive experiences within today's cultural industries, the immersive sector is still considered to be in its relative infancy. Josephine Machon, for example, traces the immersive theatre label as entering common parlance within academic and artistic circles around 2004, and theatre criticism around 2007.[9] Outside of the theatre, during the 1990s the term 'immersive' was also linked to virtual reality technologies and to literature. Ken Pimentel and Kevin Teixeira, for example, defined the then-emerging virtual reality technologies as a human–computer interface that was both sensory-immersing and interactive.[10] Meanwhile, Marie-Laure Ryan made the case for the terms immersive and interactive to be 'regarded as the cornerstones of a general theory of representation and communication', and argued for the transference of the two concepts from the technological to the literary domain 'to develop them into the cornerstones of a phenomenology of

---

[7] Doyle, quoted in Bloodworth (2022).

[8] Barrett, quoted in Bloodworth (2022). Punchdrunk's website quotes reviews describing Punchdrunk as 'hands down the best immersive theatre company in the world', 'pioneers of the "immersive theatre" phenomenon', 'immersive theatre on an epic scale', and 'pioneers of ultra-immersive drama'. See Punchdrunk (2022).

[9] Machon (2013: 65–66).

[10] Pimentel and Teixeira (1993: 15).

reading, or, more broadly, of experiencing art'.[11] Ryan's work is indicative of the fact that outside of theatre studies, there is a historicisation of immersion that goes back far earlier than the current infatuation with immersion in today's cultural industries. The history of immersivity moderates the rhetoric of innovation surrounding contemporary artistic practice, including Barrett's own comments regarding Punchdrunk's rule-breaking approach to theatre (his 2016 talk for the Future of StoryTelling was titled, although perhaps by The Future of StoryTelling rather than Barrett, 'burn the seats'). Nevertheless, within theatre studies, those scholars who historicise immersivity prior to 2004 tend to look back only to museum studies from the 1980s, where curators and designers increasingly positioned one inside an 'experience' rather than as a visitor to an exhibition, and to developments in computing terminology and online gaming from a similar period, which increasingly allowed players to create avatars and engage in world-building strategies.[12] Part of the objective of this chapter is to integrate classical scholarship on the poetics of immersion, going right back to some of our earliest examples of ancient Greek textuality, into theatre studies scholarship on immersive theatre, and to show the productive dialogue to be had between both disciplines surrounding immersivity.

The immersive theatre label, as is the case with many labels coined within academia to describe different theatrical forms, such as postdramatic or in-yer-face theatre, is a useful heuristic tool which draws attention to a cluster of theatrical productions that share qualities, but which risks obscuring their differences.[13] Forms of immersive theatre differ widely. Some productions take place for seated spectators in the dark and aim to immerse audiences through binaural technology, which creates the perception of a spatially realistic aural soundscape with the listener at its centre. Others, like Punchdrunk's *Burnt City*, create immersion through an open world experience, meaning that each spectator determines their own agenda and builds an experience that is not necessarily linear or structured. Across the spectrum of immersive theatre, the immersant is sometimes a bystander, and other times a protagonist whose choices shape

---

[11] Ryan (1994: np; 2015: 2). On immersion and virtual reality environments post-Pimentel and Teixeira, see Biggin (2017: 21–23).

[12] See Nield (2008: 531).

[13] On the potential for the in-yer-face and postdramatic labels to obscure the differences between works, see Cole (2019: 39–40).

a narrative and its meaning. In all instances, there is a prioritisation of the phenomenological over the semiotic and a shifting of the relationship between art, artist, and audience to something particularly dialogic and participatory, in that the audience member is always positioned as central to the experience. Crucially, productions aim to facilitate the possibility that spectators might experience the sensation of engaging with the performance as akin to Alice, falling down the rabbit hole. Audiences should, ideally, be engulfed in an alternate reality, which is to be experienced as a living, breathing entity.

Despite the difference between, for example, a binaural immersive experience and participating in a Punchdrunk masked show, or between immersion in the theatre and in virtual reality, or in an evocative piece of literature, or a relevant computer game, each example is constructed to facilitate those four aforementioned features of immersivity. My definition of an immersive experience is fluid, meaning that different components come to the fore in different experiences. Nevertheless, all immersive experiences attempt to displace one from their present reality, and do so by engulfing, or manipulating one or more of the senses. There is an engagement with the phenomenological, in that the immersive experience encourages one to be physically and emotionally engaged and to make meaning through their role as a participating presence within—even if just as a first-person witness to—the experience. Finally, there is an engagement with the immersant's cognitive faculties, in that the experience encourages one to think differently (and perhaps less objectively) about the content with which they are engaging than they would if it was being communicated in a non-immersive form. Barrett himself addresses the fusing of the phenomenological and cognitive aims of immersion within his practice directly when he argues that Punchdrunk's work is 'about engaging the other side of our brains, the adrenaline-fuelled, fight-or-flight heightened state … you're making choices in that sensorily heightened state'.[14] As mentioned in Chapter 5, the aims of encouraging one to feel and to think differently are interrelated and co-dependent. However, I address them separately due to the tendency within some modes of analysis to address literary immersion as if textual storyworlds are immaterial and disembodied, to ensure that, for example,

---

[14] Barrett, quoted in James (2020).

embodied performance techniques in literary examples of immersion are not subsumed or overlooked.

Before I put *The Burnt City* in dialogue with mimesis and enargeia, it is worthwhile touching upon the potential immersivity of Greek tragedy in antiquity to contextualise and historicise Punchdrunk's form of immersive theatre further. The potential immersivity of Greek tragedy is not exclusive to the tragic genre of dramatic performance, or to Greece's geographical location. Immersivity is not unique to texts and performances from the ancient classical world. However, I put Greek tragedy (and, in what follows, oratory, epic, and historiography) into dialogue with Punchdrunk's practice to demonstrate how Punchdrunk's work can be historicised within a trajectory that goes back to classical antiquity, and also because putting Punchdrunk's work into dialogue with these particular forms of immersivity sheds new light upon the ancient concepts as well.

Within classics, there is a history of scholars reading ancient literature via a poetics of immersion; recently, this has been extended to the genre of Greek tragedy. In Chapter 5 I argued that the experience of a festive celebrant attending the City Dionysia shares some commonalities with the experience of attending a Punchdrunk masked show, in that even in the Dionysia the boundaries between participation and observation were blurred, and spectators entered the liminal zone of the religious festival via the cross-fade equivalent of the *pompē*. Furthermore, Ryan proposes that if we follow (her reading of) Aristotle's interpretation of tragedy, then we can define the entire genre of Greek tragedy as immersive.[15] Ryan suggests that Aristotle's idea of catharsis indicates that Greek tragedy was an immersive genre, as spectators must have been immersed in the fate of the characters for the performance to be a deeply transforming, spiritual event. Ryan seems to suggest that the concept of catharsis indicates that spectators are more than merely invested in the characters of tragedy; they must be immersed. Although Greek tragedy may facilitate moments of immersion, I am reluctant to adopt Ryan's argument wholesale. Firstly, there is no scholarly consensus regarding what Aristotle meant by catharsis, with competing definitions including a purification, a purgation, and a moral education. Ryan's adoption of purification as a

[15] Ryan (2015: 217).

translation for catharsis belies the complexity of the term. Secondly, Aristotle's theorisation of catharsis did not occur until the 330s BCE, over a century after the death of Aeschylus and around seven decades after the deaths of Sophocles and Euripides. It is consequently hard to determine the extent to which Aristotle developed his theory based upon an engagement with staged performance, as opposed to reading play texts. The idea of catharsis is too unstable to be linked definitively with the experience of being immersed in the ancient theatre.

We can find more mileage in exploring the immersivity of Greek tragedy by using Biggin's definition of an immersive experience as graded, temporary, or fleeting. Rather than the genre being immersive, I suggest that select moments, such as within messenger speeches and choral odes, of the Dionysia individually pushed towards facilitating immersion. The potential immersivity of messenger speeches is not exclusive to the genre of Greek tragedy but is arguably a basic function of all theatrical speeches that narrate offstage action. However, this function is nuanced in Greek tragedy given that the content of messenger speeches is drawn from and modulates pre-existing mythological stories, and frequently augments the narrated action with references to sounds, touch, smell, and vision to invite audiences to have a sensory and kinaesthetic response. Sarah Olsen, for example, highlights how the messenger speech describing Neoptolemus' death in *Andromache* evokes the known landscape and architecture of Delphi, references choral song-dance, and associates Neoptolemus with pyrrhic dance to cue the original audience to visualise places and activities they have seen themselves.[16] Euripides thus capitalises upon the audience's first-person experiences and invites them to employ their own cultural knowledge to imagine the final moments of Neoptolemus' life.[17] Olsen's example shows how one particular messenger speech embodies, in particular, the second quality of an immersive experience, by enveloping the senses. On a more general level, Felix Budelmann and Evert van Emde Boas suggest that messenger speeches in Greek tragedy stimulate immersion by drawing our attention not to two spatialities, namely the narrative world of the performance and the physical environment in which the performance is taking place, but to three: the offstage world of the messenger's narrative; the messenger and his listeners onstage; and

---

[16] Olsen (2021).
[17] Olsen (2021: 167).

the performance qua performance.[18] In other words, messenger speeches transport the audience to an alternate reality, such as to Mount Cithaeron where Pentheus is torn apart by maenads in Euripides' *Bacchae*, which exists as a spatial reality on top of the setting of Thebes, where the messenger describes the scene, and the Theatre of Dionysus in Athens, where *Bacchae* was staged in c. 405 BCE.

Budelmann and van Emde Boas' argument shows that the layering of fictive and real space in Greek tragedy worked akin to the layering of spatialities within *The Burnt City*. The contours of this type of immersion involve a progressive displacement from one's present reality; Budelmann and van Emde Boas suggest that this process follows an 'immersive curve' which increasingly involves the audience swapping vision for imagination.[19] In attending to messenger speeches, one brings together their vision of the onstage action with their imaginative reconstruction of the offstage scene, which in Olsen's example is combined with Euripides inviting a sensory and kinaesthetic response from his audience by drawing upon their embodied memories of place, space, and experience. Punchdrunk's *Inception*-like strategy of layering distinct dreamscapes, one on top of the other, to facilitate immersion thus literalises a creative process of progressively enfolding audiences into multilayered alternate realities that goes back to fifth-century tragedy. Rather than suggest that Greek tragedy is unique, my point is that it reveals the presence of possible immersive experiences for audiences of dramatic performances going right back to the fifth century.

Choral odes worked in a similar way to messenger speeches, particularly when they employed the device of choral projection. Choral projections also drew the audience's attention to an offstage world. In these choral odes a chorus located its dance in a different temporal and spatial zone to the action of the other characters, effectively pausing the plot of the tragedy and transporting the audience to a different location to provide background narrative or a comparative example.[20] The projections combined the ability for a narrative to transport an audience to a different spatiality, seen in the device of the messenger speech, with an intermedial, danced narrative that invited the audience not only to

---

[18] Budelmann and van Emde Boas (2019).

[19] Budelmann and van Emde Boas (2019: 78).

[20] On choral projections, see Henrichs (1996) and Nikolaidou-Arabatzi (2015: 27–28).

see the alternate world in their imagination but also to witness it. Laura Gianvittorio-Ungar draws attention to a specific choral ode from the *parodos* of Aeschylus' *Seven Against Thebes*, and reads this scene in light of ancient testimony regarding the ability of one of Aeschylus' dancers, Telestes, to 'make manifest' the events of the plot through dance.[21] Gianvittorio-Ungar argues that Telestes may have performed a solo martial dance in the chorus' war report to make manifest the military manoeuvres described by the chorus, with his weapon dance bringing offstage events onstage and making them visible as they happen.[22] She argues that such choreography would heighten the experiential and immersive qualities of the war narrative by engaging the senses of the spectators and evoking real-life experiences.[23]

I mentioned in Chapter 5 that a percentage of the audience at the City Dionysia would have prior experience and thus an embodied memory of performing in the civic *choreia*. Weapon dances were performed throughout the entirety of the Greek-speaking world, meaning that when choral choreography on the tragic stage involved martial routines, an even greater portion of the audience would feel kinaesthetic empathy with the performed action. Julia M. Ritter suggests that immersive productions today feature an elicitive dramaturgy, characterised by dancers making deliberate efforts to employ choreographic strategies that go beyond evoking emotions and elicit physical and verbal responses from a spectator.[24] The possible employment of a recognisable weapon dance within *Seven Against Thebes*, and the felt response it may have invited, corresponds to how Ritter sees dance and immersivity working together today. The contours of audience immersion within choral projections brings the sensory and phenomenological dimension of an immersive experience to the fore, as such scenes encouraged the audience to feel an embodied connection to the action being staged. Not only could spectators be displaced from their present reality like in messenger speeches, but through odes such as the parodos of *Seven Against Thebes* they were also invited to experience kinaesthetic empathy, or to feel the bodily sensations that accompany being a participant in the action, as well. The level

[21] Gianvittorio-Ungar (2019).
[22] Gianvittorio-Ungar (2019: 243).
[23] Gianvittorio-Ungar (2019: 244).
[24] Ritter (2020: 109).

to which audiences might experience the sensation of being a participant in Greek tragedy, by watching choral choreography, is distinct from the sensations one experiences when they physically step into Punchdrunk's labyrinthine sets, but the comparison nevertheless again shows the significance of embodiment to immersive experiences going back to classical antiquity.

In both messenger speeches and choral odes, we see ancient tragedians employing devices that start to push audiences towards having, for fleeting moments, an immersive experience. Both structures of performance might facilitate a displacement of the audience from their present reality, engulf the senses, and foster phenomenological and cognitive engagement. Already we can see that despite the rhetoric of innovation that surrounds today's immersive sector, other forms of immersivity can be identified across several twentieth-century industries and even in the original fifth-century performances of the source texts on which *The Burnt City* is based. My subsequent sections continue to put *The Burnt City* in dialogue with ancient literature to explore the kinship between forms of immersion in antiquity and modernity.

Mimesis

Mimesis, usually translated as representation or imitation, is a concept that is closely tied to immersion. The idea of mimesis is perhaps most famous due to its centrality in Aristotle's *Poetics*, where Aristotle claims that theatre should be mimetic not to persons but to action and life [1450a14–19]. The pedestalisation of Aristotle's treatise in the neoclassical era meant critics prized the concept of mimesis and placed special value upon classical receptions, such as the tragedies of Racine, which were often more Aristotelian than the ancient tragedies themselves. In the twentieth-century theatrical practice of Brecht and Artaud the idea of mimesis was, rhetorically at least, pushed aside, with Artaud for example seeking to move away from the imitative aim of art.[25] More recently, however, the idea of mimesis has once again come into the spotlight,

---

[25] See Tomlin (2016: 55). Diamond notes that Brecht's anti-Aristotelianism is now well-understood to disguise key connections with Aristotle, and that in some ways Brecht insisted on more mimesis, rather than less, via the idea of mimesis not as representation but as a mode of reading that transforms an object into a *gestus* or a dialectical image. See Diamond (1997: ii, viii–ix).

with scholars such as Hans-Thies Lehmann offering a reinterpretation of the concept which positions mimetic theatre as theatre that corresponds, to some degree, to reality rather than imitates it. In postdramatic productions that feature an irruption of the real, for example, the undecidability regarding whether performers are acting or are really experiencing the pain or fatigue they are communicating becomes a co-player in the performance.[26] Mimesis is thus a shifting target, which always refers to a gap between representation and reality but characterises this gap in different ways at different times. Mimesis links to immersion, particularly in Plato's understanding of the concept, in that it can create instances whereby an audience might find themselves unable to distinguish between appearance and reality. Such examples bring to the fore the quality of an immersive experience that encourages people to think differently.

Mimesis might initially appear to stand in opposition to Punchdrunk's masked theatre. Although the set designs are touch-real, defined by the company as being 'as close to "real" as possible; offering authenticity in the sensual reality of rooms and contiguous spaces' to establish 'experiential accuracy', the main spaces of *The Burnt City* were overtly theatrical and not mimetic to action and life.[27] Instead, qualities of alterity and atemporality pervaded the production. Once spectators were through the cross-fade, the device of the mask, the looping structure, the vocabulary of Doyle's (and the performing company's) choreography, the soundscape and lighting design, and the Weimar-inflected set and costume aesthetic all worked to transport the audience into an artificial reality, rather than to blur the boundaries between performance and reality. However, moments of eye contact between performers and audience members, and one-on-one experiences involving the audience member being de-masked and directly addressed, can be theorised in relation to mimesis. Although only a percentage of Punchdrunk's audience experience such moments, the dual presence of both an overtly theatrical artifice and the intimacy of seemingly realistic moments of connection lies at the heart of the ecology of Punchdrunk's masked universe.

Although the idea of mimesis might be most famous thanks to Aristotle, it is in the work of Plato that we find the term linked to immersion

---

[26] Lehmann (2006: 100).
[27] Machon and Punchdrunk (2019: 277).

and a more overt interrogation of the dual nature of mimesis as encompassing both imitation and reflection. Plato's consideration of mimesis in his *Republic* is notoriously inconsistent, with Stephen Halliwell arguing that it 'is a classic case of a concept that receives fluctuating and constantly revised treatment' and Elizabeth Belfiore more specifically summarising that many believe Plato uses the term to mean 'impersonation' in Book Three and 'representation' in Book Ten.[28] At the heart of the differences across the *Republic* is an apparent acceptance of certain limited forms of mimetic poetry in Book Three, but an outright refusal of all mimetic art in Book Ten. Despite these differences, the sense that mimetic art represents a form of immersion is maintained throughout the different books. For Plato, this made mimetic art forms problematic; in Jean-Marie Schaeffer and Ioana Vulter's words, Plato 'concluded that immersion, being inaccessible to analytical thought, was dangerous and epistemically void'.[29] In Book Three, for example, Plato cautions against a poet eliding their voice and creating the appearance of an unmediated narrative unfolding in real time [3.393c–d]. Such a strategy can encourage closer identification between the listener and a character, which Stephen Halliwell terms a 'heightened degree of absorption'.[30] It can also potentially have a corrupting influence upon the soul of a listener when a character is depicted as engaging in immoral behaviour. In Book Ten, Plato builds upon this discussion and branches out from poets to include other artists such as painters. Here, he notes that all forms of mimesis are potentially dangerous due to their twice-removed relationship to reality. Painters and tragedians, for Plato, are imitators not of reality but of the representations of reality that others manufacture. These artists do not capture the truth of their subject and have little knowledge of its reality [10.600e–601]; viewers of the visual and theatrical arts are consequently presented with a virtual reality.

The idea that mimetic art can absorb a viewer or listener so completely that they are unable to distinguish how far removed it is from real behaviour, or that it could encourage such close affiliation with a character as to influence one's habits and shape their soul, indicates that Plato understood mimesis in a way that is similar to how an irruption of the real

---

[28] Halliwell (2002: 38) and Belfiore (1984: 121).
[29] Schaeffer and Vultur (2005: 238).
[30] Halliwell (2002: 53).

makes the ambiguity between real and performed action part of a performance. The level of absorption Plato suggests mimesis encompasses also equates to how some artists today understand immersion. Mimetic art puts its audience face-to-face with an alternate reality, encourages sensory absorption, and, by blurring the lines between illusion and reality and influencing one's psyche, changes the way one thinks and feels. Irrespective of whether one is attempting to create a mimetic art form in antiquity, or an immersive theatre output in modernity, the artists at the helm are always attempting to conjure a hyper-realistic, alternate reality.

Although the presence of mimesis in the main performance space of *The Burnt City* may be questionable, Punchdrunk identify those same qualities that Plato cautions against as the central purpose of their practice. The idea, for example, that mimesis is inaccessible to analytic thought is in part reflected in Barrett's aforementioned comments about Punchdrunk's approach, where he suggests that Punchdrunk's work stands in opposition to rational, objective cognitive processing and is instead about engaging the other side of our brains, meaning the adrenaline-fuelled, fight-or-flight heightened state.[31] Barrett's quote captures Plato's fear of art being inaccessible to analytic thought. Furthermore, Barrett's goal in his large-scale immersive shows is to make audiences forget the wider reality that exists prior to the cross-fade. Although one may remain aware of the artifice of performance, doing so does not contradict Barrett achieving his goal of 'trying to build a parallel universe. For a few hours inside the walls, you forget that it's London and slip into this other place'.[32] *The Burnt City* in its entirety may not interrogate the boundary between representation and reality, but mimesis remains a useful analogue through which to read Punchdrunk's overall production given the similar effects at play as idealised by Barrett and cautioned against by Plato.

Any questions about whether *The Burnt City* overall can be read as an imitation or reflection of reality dissipate when we examine those moments of performance where the theatrical artifice recedes into the background and a more immediate engagement between performer and audience is present. There are two specific components of Punchdrunk's masked work that can be thought to interrogate the gap between representation and reality, namely what Barrett referred to in *The Burnt City*

---

[31] Barrett, quoted in James (2020).
[32] Barrett, quoted in Hoggard (2013).

rehearsals as 'the weight of the gift of eye contact in transient moments', and one-on-one experiences. An extreme contrast exists between the scale and the theatricality of the overall performance, and the immediacy and seemingly 'real' connection between performer and audience which arose during these two moments. The contrast heightened such moments' mimetic power (and, for Plato, their danger). Both instances were engineered as seemingly serendipitous moments within the overall experience of *The Burnt City*, where audiences might question whether a performer's behaviour was scripted and in character or was a genuine beat of intimacy between performer and spectator. Such undecidability is not unique to Punchdrunk's form of theatre and is present in all instances of an irruption of the real in contemporary performance; my proposal here is that the ancient ideas of mimesis can help us to unravel what is unfolding in such moments of Punchdrunk's work, and that these points are of relevance to wider studies of performance as well.

Fleeting moments of eye contact (and/or touch) in Punchdrunk's masked performances are distinct from one-on-one experiences, in that one-on-ones are micro-scenes with a beginning, middle, and end which follow a particular formula irrespective of a scene's content. Nevertheless, both the small-scale moments and the one-on-one scenes were built into the infrastructure of *The Burnt City*, and the aim of both was to create the impression that the individual spectator might think that they were alone in having each experience. Barrett described in rehearsals that hearing about these anecdotes was his personal marker of success, saying that when people 'tell me as though they were the only person to experience it. It's absolutely rewarding when it's done what we hoped it would do, when its transcended theatrical experience and become a moment, an anecdote that rolls into their life'. Despite the difference in scale and content between the two moments of performance, both gained their currency by creating the impression that they were unique moments of genuine connection; in other words, they gained their power due to embodying a mimetic form of immersivity.

On first glance it might appear that an unknowing audience member was required for Barrett's aspirations regarding the power of performance to be realised. Someone new to the structure of Punchdrunk's work may have felt that they experienced something unique and revolutionary during a one-on-one experience, without understanding that such scenes were repeated multiple times per performance and were just as tightly choreographed as everything else in the show. Biggin's analysis of the fan mail Punchdrunk received following their productions *Faust* (2006–7) and *The Masque of the Red Death* (2007–8) highlights, by drawing upon the audience members' own words, how that first one-on-one experience can lead to spectators feeling as if they have formed relationships with performers and completed an interaction with them rather than witnessed a series of performed events.[33] Given the dates of Biggin's case studies, one can assume that the effusive praise contained in the fan mail was in part linked to the fact that the writers may have been unaware of Punchdrunk's practices prior to attending a performance. Nevertheless, the fetishisation of one-on-ones within Punchdrunk's community of superfans reveals that despite knowing that the quality of intimacy crafted in these encounters is part of the artifice of performance, the scenes do not necessarily lose their poignancy. Julia Ritter's analysis of the 'incidental and intentional ethnography' contained in the social media accounts of Punchdrunk superfans, some of whom had attended *Sleep No More* New York over one hundred times and self-described as 'Sleep No Whores', attests to how one-on-ones remain affective despite an audience member knowing what to expect (and potentially having even experienced that exact one-on-one before).[34] For returning audience members, experiencing one-on-ones may create the illusion of facilitating a genuine, if not unique, connection between performer and audience, but there are likely more factors at play in accounting for their prized status, including 'levelling up' and experiencing the deeper layers of a character's narrative, as well as 'completing' different tracks of the production. Such motivations link to Adam Alston's ideas of entrepreneurial participation which I touched upon in Chapter 5. It does not matter whether the moments of eye contact or one-on-one experiences successfully blurred the boundaries between illusion and reality for any given audience member. Rather, what is significant is that there was the potential for a Platonic form of mimesis to arise in these moments, which collapsed the distinction between the alternate realities of the show and the spectator's own reality.

Applying a Spectator-Participation-as-Research approach to two moments from *The Burnt City* demonstrates the kinship between the concept of mimesis and the beats of intimacy embodied in moments of eye contact and in one-on-one experiences. During one of the preview

---

[33] Biggin (2015: 306–307).
[34] Ritter (2017).

performances of *The Burnt City*, I experienced a moment of eye contact between myself and Apollo, then played by Morgan Bobrow-Williams. I had been following one of the Greek soldiers as they journeyed to Troy after the sacrifice of Iphigenia in No Man's Land. Apollo and Zagreus had, in this iteration of the performance, opened the double doors connecting the link structure to Troy to allow the four soldiers (Agamemnon, Neoptolemus, Patroclus, and the Watchman) through to Troy, alongside the sizeable audience following those characters. Caught at the back of the crowd, I suddenly found myself alone in the doorway with Apollo, who paused and held my gaze for several beats before disappearing down a corridor. The juxtaposition between going from part of a seemingly invisible masked throng of spectres to holding Apollo's gaze stopped me in my tracks. The beat of intimacy came as a surprise, despite my knowing that immortal characters in *The Burnt City* such as Apollo and Artemis can choose to see the audience whenever they wish. It jolted me out my previous mode of spectatorship and reconfigured my relation to Apollo within the world of the performance by making me, as Emma Cole rather than as a masked spectator, a ghost, or a pursuing fury, feel seen, and thus ever so slightly blurring the boundaries between illusion and reality (Fig. 6.1).

Six months later, when attending another performance of *The Burnt City* in September 2022, I found myself once again frozen on the spot as Polydorus, here played by Jordan Ajadi, paused, locked eyes with me, and held my gaze. The moment came at the end of Polydorus' loop, after he had been sacrificed to Kronos by Polymestor and reincarnated into a fury. His re-emergence into the show, in just grey slacks and Palladium boots, involved an intense dance solo in the Trojan tenement courtyard, following which he and Polyxena completed an agile parkour-inspired scene in the neon backstreets of Troy. A group of spectators followed Polyxena and Polydorus down the narrow alleyways. Most continued with Polyxena, who was heading towards the blinding of Polymestor, but I stuck with Polydorus, eventually finding myself back in the courtyard, holding his gaze. He extended his hand to me, not breaking eye contact. I took his hand, and he led me into a small cupboard under the stairs, where he closed the door, gently exerted a downward pressure on my forearms to encourage me to sit, and then removed my mask.

Polydorus' one-on-one took place in a claustrophobic cupboard and broke the artifice of Punchdrunk's performance through numerous strategies. Firstly, as was the case in all one-on-one scenes, the spectator's mask

Fig. 6.1 Morgan Bobrow-Williams as Apollo in Punchdrunk's *The Burnt City*. Image credit: Julian Abrams. Courtesy of Punchdrunk

was removed. The removal of the mask equated to the removal of a security blanket and was a moment of transformation involving the performer striping away the faceless character that the spectator inhabited for the duration of the performance to leave their actual identity on display. The removal of the mask invalidated the option of voyeuristically observing the work and invited audience members to co-create the experience. Indeed, during the rehearsal period Barrett stressed the need to choose an audience member for one-on-one scenes wisely, noting that the scenes 'only work if the audience are with you and want the insight into your character'. Carina E. I. Westling notes that a willingness to 'self capture' is essential for the process of immersion; in one-on-one experiences, which Barrett suggested are 'Punchdrunk distilled', such willingness is especially necessary.[35]

Alongside disrupting the masked/unmasked division between audience and performer and visually rendering the audience member temporarily

[35] Westling (2020: 2).

on the same plane as the cast, one-on-one scenes also use dialogue in place of the dance-based language that dominates the wider performance. In Polydorus' one-on-one, the scene utilised a fable from within the second stasimon of Aeschylus' *Agamemnon*, which takes place just prior to Agamemnon's long-awaited entrance to the stage. The fable tells the story of a lion cub, reared and doted upon by a family only to massacre their flock (and perhaps the family themselves) when it reaches adulthood [717–735]. In the Ted Hughes translation, which Polydorus delivered, the *peripeteia*, or reversal, is vividly captured and removes any ambiguity surrounding whether the massacre is of the family themselves, or simply takes place within the family home; Hughes writes that 'the day of the lion dawned / Over the farmer's whole family - / The screams and roars went up, and under the doors / Blood came hurrying from the work of the lion. The high priest of death, at the altar of corpses' [1083–1087]. Polydorus's one-on-one thus not only shifted the language of communication between performer and audience from a dance-based language to a verbal one, but did so while the narrative was invoking tragic pathos, with both the form and content combining to raise the scene's emotional stakes.

Within Aeschylus' tragedy, most read the lion cub's mistaken identity as standing in for Helen, welcomed into Troy only to provide the Greeks with a reason to lay siege to and ultimately obliterate the civilisation. However, some see the cub as standing in for the firebrand Paris, or representative of the cycle of intergenerational revenge within the House of Atreus.[36] Punchdrunk's decision to position the monologue as part of Polydorus' loop invited the audience to read the lion as standing in for Polymestor, who was trusted to look after Polydorus only for his real nature to be revealed after he sacrificed Polydorus and took possession of Hecuba's treasure. The communication of this insight via dialogue felt confessional due to the claustrophobic environment in which the one-on-one took place. A bespoke soundtrack underscored the monologue, increasing in volume and turning menacing in tone during the second half of the scene. At the conclusion of the dialogue, throughout which Polydorus had remained sitting opposite me, knees almost touching, holding my hands, and continuing intense eye contact, he reached down to pick something up. He turned one of my palms face up and began weaving a

---

[36] See Raeburn and Thomas (2011) and Nagy (2013) for an overview of these debates.

red thread between my fingers, before positioning what I later realised was a brass-coloured horse charm hanging from the thread in the centre of my palm and enclosing my fingers around it, explaining that although he had been unlucky, this object would keep me safe. With a gentle squeeze of my hand and a final look of reassurance, he reached up to retrieve my mask, put it back on, opened the door, and welcomed me back into the main performance space.

Punchdrunk write in their encyclopaedia that it is common for audience members to be given a token or trinket during a one-on-one encounter, both as a memento and as 'a marker of moving on or into another stage within the world'.[37] Heavily worded comments about not removing items from the set could be found in the paratextual information given to audiences before the performance, as well as during the cross-fade experience, and acted as a theft deterrent. Any gifts given during one-on-one experiences thus became another marker of the distinction between the production and its audience overall, and between individual performers and spectators during one-on-one experiences. The removal of the audience member's mask, the close physical proximity of performer to audience, the confessional-style delivery of dialogue, the intense eye contact, and the giving of a gift that I could take with me out of the show worked together in Polydorus' one-on-one to create a supercharged version of the sense of intimacy and individualisation that I experienced during my moment of eye contact with Apollo. We might usefully think of one-on-one scenes not just in Barrett's terms, as 'Punchdrunk distilled', but also as instances where the type of immersion that Punchdrunk facilitate can be put into dialogue with Plato's ideas of mimesis. Such scenes can create the impression that the performer is engaging with an individualised audience member, rather than an anonymous member of the broader collective, and through touch and eye contact can foster the sensation that the encounter involves a 'real', rather than performed, emotional connection. The contrast between the scenes and the overt theatricalisation of the wider performance is partially responsible for the sense that one-on-one experiences collapse the distinction between performance and reality. Other examples of contemporary performance might dive deeper and more exclusively into the questionability surrounding Lehmann's irruption of the real, and thus Plato's fear

---

[37] Machon and Punchdrunk (2019: 244).

of mimetic art being so lifelike that it convinces its audience that it is in fact reality and can shape their soul accordingly. However, the moments of *The Burnt City* that interrogated the boundaries between representation and reality still encouraged audience immersion. Such moments attempted to displace spectators from their usual mode of operation within the performance and changed their relationship to the characters in the show.

Reading Punchdrunk's *The Burnt City* through the idea of mimesis accomplishes two things. Firstly, it associates Punchdrunk's work with a poetics of immersion going back to antiquity. Secondly, it opens a conversation about the ethics of immersion during these powerful, personalised moments. Plato's comments, if not about immersion corrupting the soul, then more broadly about the dangers of being unable to distinguish how far removed an aesthetic experience is from real behaviour, are worth keeping in mind when we analyse scenes which involve an aesthetics of seduction. Is being fooled into thinking that such an experience is for one alone, and characterised by a genuine connection between performer and audience, inevitably a good thing? For me, it increased the value I put on my attendance at those performances, with the one-on-one scenes making the overall experience of *The Burnt City* feel more special, intimate, and powerful, but it is feasible that others may feel short-changed if they learn that a seemingly genuine moment of connection was simply part of a professional performer's skillset. In Chapter 5 I noted that one could question whether the audience's potential embodiment of a rapacious, pursuing fury was necessarily positive; putting *The Burnt City* into dialogue with mimesis reminds us that we should remain cognisant of the ethics of immersive theatre and opens up opportunities for further analysis along such lines.

Linking Plato's thought with Punchdrunk's practice might encourage us to moderate effervescent praise of the most mimetic forms of immersive experience, but it is not the case that Punchdrunk's work, or even the twentieth-century immersive experiences touched upon earlier in my chapter, represent a volte-face from a classical disavowal of immersive experiences. Rather, the company's belief in the power of immersivity goes back to antiquity as well. As such, I now turn to the synergy between one way that immersion was avowed in antiquity, and Punchdrunk's practice.

Enargeia

Although Plato's consideration of mimesis as a form of immersion focuses on the dangers that mimesis represents to humanity, later critics recognised and championed the power of narrative to overwhelm the senses and praised effective instances of the phenomenon, often through the notions of ekphrasis and enargeia. Both terms are used extensively in first-century BCE rhetorical handbooks and are difficult to untangle, with the opacity surrounding the terms made more complicated by the fact that ekphrasis has different meanings in antiquity and modernity.[38] At the simplest level, ekphrasis refers to a practice, such as a rhetorical exercise, or to a textual feature, such as a narrative digression or a type of description, where a scene is rendered in such pictorial detail that the reader or listener may feel as if plunged into, or immersed in, the moment described. Froma Zeitlin summarises appropriate subjects for ekphrasis in antiquity as including battles, landscapes, festivals, seasons, people, animals, and objects, while Ruth Webb notes that an ekphrasis has almost unlimited scope, in that it 'can be of any length, of any subject matter, composed in verse or prose, using any verbal technique'.[39] The modern understanding of ekphrasis refers specifically to the extended description of a visual object, and is often theorised with reference to antiquity, with examples ranging from descriptions of heroic objects such as the shield of Achilles in *Iliad* 18 [478–608], through to everyday objects such as the description of the carved wooden bowl in Theocritus' *Idyll* 1 [27–54]. The use of the term today is much narrower in scope but is nevertheless encompassed by the ancient definition, with the defining feature of both object-based descriptions in texts and broader descriptions of scenes or events in language being, per the ancient rhetoricians, that it brings its subject before the eyes or makes listeners into spectators.

---

[38] Zeitlin summarises that it 'would not be hyperbole to suggest that no other rhetorical term [than ekphrasis] has aroused such interest in recent years among classicists and non-classicists alike, involving aesthetic considerations, theories of vision, modes of viewing, mental impressions, and the complex relationships between word and image'. See Zeitlin (2013: 17). For a summary of the differences between ekphrasis in antiquity and modernity, see Webb (2009: 1–2). Although the terms are not extensively theorised until the first century CE, they can be found much earlier. The adjective *enarges* (visible, manifest), for example, is found as early as Homer; see Allan et al. (2017: 35).

[39] Zeitlin (2013: 18) and Webb (2009: 8).

Enargeia, in turn, was understood in antiquity as a quality that could be found within an ekphrasis. Most simply translated as 'vividness', the concept refers to how vividly an image can be evoked for a listener or reader and is defined by Dionysius of Halicarnassus in his commentary on Lysias as the power of 'bringing the things that are said before the senses of the audience' to enable the audience to feel as if they 'can see the actions which are being described going on and that he is meeting face-to-face the characters in the orator's story' [Lysias 7].[40] Enargeia represents the component of an ekphrasis that could affect a reader or a listener emotionally; for Quintilian it had a time-warping function which could make someone feel transported either to the past, or to a hypothetical future [*Institutio Oratoria* 9.2.40–1], and according to Webb it was a tool of persuasion which, when combined with corresponding arguments, could change the mental disposition of a listener and encourage them to believe a speaker's story as the truth.[41] Quintilian sees it as a great virtue of rhetorical style, which by evoking events in a way that goes further than the eyes is more likely to convince a listener of an argument and lead to the 'total domination' of a court judge [*Institutio Oratoria* 8.3.62ff].[42] In the homicide defence speech *Lysias* 1, for example, a much greater portion of the speech is devoted to a vivid description of Euphiletos' marriage than to the charge at hand.[43] Euphiletos attempts to convince the jurors that he acted within the law through an emotional appeal via a vivid representation of his domestic life, complete with rich characterisation and directly quoted speech, rather than through details of the crime and why he is innocent of the charge according to the law.[44] The example demonstrates the clear links between enargeia and the idea of immersivity more generally, with the *Lysias* example showcasing how enargeia transports a listener to an alternate reality, dominates the senses, and encourages them to feel differently, as involved or participating in the narrative even if just as a first-person witness, and to think differently, by persuading them to acquit Euphiletos. That the device may

---

[40] Trans. Usher (1974). On the Dionysius of Halicarnassus passage, see Zanker (1981: 297).

[41] Webb (2009: 128–129).

[42] Huitink (2019a: 170).

[43] See Peter O'Connell's analysis of this ratio in O'Connell (2017: 239).

[44] On this strategy within modern law, see O'Connell (2017: 232–233).

trick the listener into believing a false reality, rather than the truth, showcases its connection to mimesis, too; encountering enargeia is as much an aesthetic experience as it is a literary feature. Its affective potential to change one's mental disposition is integral. Whereas ekphrasis refers to a type of language which encourages imagined projections, enargeia denotes how, or the degree to which, a reader or listener might feel immersed within a projection, and consequently it is enargeia that is most illuminating when put into dialogue with Punchdrunk's practice.[45]

I am not the first to link the historical use of enargeia with a poetics of immersion, with narratologists in particular detailing the specific linguistic strategies through which certain historical texts might immerse a reader or listener. Using insights gleaned from modern literary theory, Luuk Huitink has detailed the specific linguistic strategies found in passages noted for their rich degree of enargeia, which he sees as including the narration of bodily movement, the verbalising of perceptual-enactive explorations of the world in direct speech, and 'experiential iconicity' in which the structure of language mirrors not the represented action itself, but the perception of it.[46] Along with Jonas Grethlein and Aldo Tagliabue, he notes that while enargeia often refers to the experience of visual imagery, ancient critics imply that such imagery also comes complete with sounds and haptic sensations, and stresses that enargeia reveals that for the ancients '"imagining" can feel like "doing" and that it can lead to a strong (and especially emotional) identification with protagonists in the storyworld'.[47] Irrespective of how multi-sensorial enargeia might be, it is clear that for ancient critics it is predicated upon the imagination; one experiences enargeia either by evoking an image in their mind's eye, or/and by experiencing an embodied connection with the imagined situation, which may include proprioceptive awareness and kinaesthetic response.[48]

---

[45] Allan et al. (2017), see enargeia as a predecessor of the modern notion of immersion and position it as of key importance within the history of the poetics of immersion.

[46] Huitink (2019a: section 4). O'Connell adds to this list deictic pronouns and adverbs, the so-called historical present, and most importantly detailed descriptions. See O'Connell (2017: 226). Although speaking about immersion in ancient literature more generally, rather than enargeia specifically, Allan's catalogue of immersive textual features is also relevant, and includes the use of proximal spatial and temporal deictics and first- and second-person pronouns. Allan (2019: 18–19).

[47] Grethlein et al. (2019: 2–3) and Huitink (2019b: 190).

[48] While enargeia refers to the reader evoking or imagining the narrated events, ancient critics were also familiar with the opposite phenomenon, namely the sensation of a listener

Whereas narratologists focus on how a text creates enargeia, cognitivist approaches to enargeia focus (at least in part) on the effect of enargeia on the respondent. Luuk Huitink divides the cognitivist approaches into two 'generations' of theory, with the first, termed the pictorialist, focused on responses to literature occurring through internal visual representations seen via the mind's eye, and the second, termed the enactivist, focused on understanding vision 'in terms of an ongoing, attentive interaction between an embodied observer and the environment, mediated by the observer's mastery of the laws of sensoriomotor contingencies'.[49] Huitink's preferred mode, the enactivist, emphasises the performativity involved in enargeia, in that the connection between the real and the imagined lies, he argues, 'in the embodied, enactive structure of experience: to imagine something, that is, is to simulate an embodied exploration of what one imagines'.[50] In this reading, the level of pictorial detail contained in the narrative is considered inessential and is instead trumped by the 'bodily-perceptual "feel"' of a text. Irrespective of the school of thought that one follows, what is clear is that enargeia is a concept considered immersive not only in antiquity but is thought to be an effective strategy for a modern readership as well.

The enactivist approach to enargeia is indicative of a growing tendency to connect enargeia to performance environments. Too often, however, such approaches are limited to exploring the performativity involved on the part of a reader or listener imagining an enargeic passage coming to life. Even when analysts turn to exploring enargeia in performance, there is a temptation to focus on the literary technique as embodied in dialogue, rather than positioning the feature explicitly within a corporeal and embodied art form. For the remainder of this chapter, I work to provide an antidote to this focus, to read enargeia as part of the same spectrum of immersivity as Punchdrunk's *The Burnt City*, to reinforce the significance of embodied performance to so-called immersive literary techniques such as enargeia.

There is a difference in directionality when it comes to the ancient understanding of immersion embodied in the term enargeia, and the

---

being transported to the narrated events. Longinus saw this dislocating strategy as characteristic of the sublime [*On the Sublime* 1.4]; on the relevance of the sublime to immersion, see Allan et al. (2017: 37).

[49] See Huitink (2019a, esp. p. 176).

[50] Huitink (2019a: 178).

possible modern experience of immersion in *The Burnt City*. In the former, the imagined world enters the contemporary moment, while in the latter, we step into the other world. The difference corresponds to a distinction between enargeia as absence, and Punchdrunk's immersivity as presence. Enargeia achieves immersion by encouraging one to imagine events as if they were in front of them, while Punchdrunk's work enacts a totalising manifestation of the events. Yet the effect of both experiences is, if not the same, in synergy, in that one is invited to be displaced from their present reality, to have their senses engulfed, and to feel and to think differently. Furthermore, a sense of theatricality is key to both experiences, if we think of theatricality following Nik Wakefield's rewriting of Michael Fried, as the moment of confrontation between a spectator and performed action, and as something that can be both interdependent and interrelated with absorption.[51] To showcase this kinship, I touch upon two passages of ancient literature from outside of Greek tragedy, both of which ancient critics and modern scholars have classified as immersive due to containing the feature of enargeia. My choice of non-dramatic examples is deliberate, to demonstrate that while on the one hand, comparing *The Burnt City* with ancient literary immersion contextualises Punchdrunk's work within a history of immersivity, on the other hand the process also illuminates the theatricality inherent in immersive literary episodes from antiquity as well.

The examples that critics draw upon when theorising enargeia go back as far as the Homeric epics and encompass a wide variety of textual forms including historiography, rhetoric, and visual art which contains a 'narrative sting'.[52] My first example is the description of the chariot race in Patroclus' funeral games from Book 23 of Homer's *Iliad*. Book 23 takes place after Achilles has killed Hector outside the walls of Troy. Although the fall of Troy is not narrated in the *Iliad*, Hector's death signals that it is imminent, yet his delayed burial, due to his corpse being in the possession of the Greek army and due to Patroclus' funeral games, effectively pauses this wider narrative.

Patroclus' funeral games take up the majority of Book 23 (640 verses), with the chariot race representing more than half of this space [262–652]. There are several features within the passage that can be analysed in terms

---

[51] Wakefield (2019).

[52] I borrow the term 'narrative sting' from Grethlein et al. (2019: 8).

of immersion, but it was the first ten lines of the race itself that an anonymous ancient scholiast described as enargeic, noting that the description is projected 'so vividly that the listeners are no less captivated than the spectators'.[53] The so-called enargeic passage commences:

> All of them raised their whips above their horses and struck them with the reins and shouted "Go"! Swiftly the horses raced across the plain and soon the ships were far behind. The dust flew up and gathered underneath their chests like clouds or like a whirlwind, and their manes trailed in the gusts of air. The chariots bounced, and sometimes rested on the fertile earth, and sometimes hurtled up into the air. The heart of every man was thumping fast, and all of them were hoping they would win. All of them urged their horses ever onward. They flew and raised the dust across the plain. [*Iliad* 23, 362–372, trans. Wilson 2023]

A narratological analysis of the passage would stress the presence of linguistic strategies to create a multi-sensorial narration of bodily movement, and the fixed temporal sequence of events, which combine to help the listener 'see' the episode and include the dust rising against the horses' chests, their manes flowing in the wind, the chariots skimming close to the earth and then flying in mid-air, the feeling of hearts beating, and the sound of a cacophony of shouts. Nicholas Richardson's commentary notes that the description vividly gives a picture of the scene and effectively portrays the emotions of the competitors.[54] Time on the one hand stands still, the moment before the whips strike the horses to commence the race, and on the other hand speeds up, with its elasticity helping the reader or listener to visualise the scene by providing contrasting pieces of information to allow for a multidimensional sense of the experience. The multi-sensorial narration of bodily movement and the pacing of the scene work together to provide a reader or listener with slices of experience that they can weave together in their mind's eye to project the whole.

The description of the commencement of the chariot race represents a moment where readers and/or listeners of the *Iliad* may experience a fleeting, graded, or temporary sense of immersion, via an alternate reality seemingly appearing before their eyes. Yet other moments of the wider chariot race also vividly zoom into the event in such a way as to make one

---

[53] Translation adapted from Huitink (2019b: 188).
[54] Richardson (1993: 214).

feel as if they are witnessing it. Just as Euphiletos' defence speech enabled the jurors to feel as if they were bearing witness to his version of the day of the crime, through arresting descriptions of several moments across the course of the day rather than just one enargeic passage, so too does the broader chariot race sequence in Homer work to bring the overall race before one's eyes. For example, as the race builds momentum a dispute arises between Antilochus and Menelaus, who come second and third in the race respectively, after Antilochus overtakes Menelaus by veering off the track and forcing Menelaus to slow his horses to avoid a collision. The moment builds dramatic tension, and includes three instances of directly quoted speech, from Antilochus to his horses as he approaches the opportune moment for overtaking Menelaus [403–416], and Menelaus to Antilochus both before the narrowly avoided collision, and afterwards in rebuke [426–428, 439–441]. Before the conclusion of the race, the narrator switches perspective, veering away from that of the charioteers to that of the Argive audience, watching the chariots approach from a distance and seeking to determine who is in the lead. Through directly quoted speech again, Idomeneus and Ajax debate, with the tensions on the racetrack echoed within the ranks of spectators. As observers of the race, they work as an embedded audience and highlight the theatricality of the episode. On the one hand, the device distances the reader or listener from the action by positioning one as watching the original audience watching the race, rather than watching the race itself, while on the other hand it aids in our absorption of the scene by giving us a fixed vantage point from which to imagine it, delaying our knowledge of the outcome of the race, and then allowing us to experience the moment of victory together with the embedded spectators.

Although this enargeic passage fosters immersion through different means to *The Burnt City*, the effect of experiencing the scene is, if not the same, then in kinship. Both the chariot race sequence and *The Burnt City* share the same four features of immersivity. Both enable one to experience an alternate reality, with the former doing so by inviting one to imagine it in their minds eye, and the latter by inviting one to step into a mythic universe. Both experiences dominate the senses, building dramatic tension to provoke emotional suspense and reaction. They each use a multiperspectival approach to allow one to think of a scene in different ways. The temporary facilitation of immersion through the enargeic passage in the *Iliad* works akin to how we might define immersion in *The Burnt City*, which is not a switch between two states but, as Biggin defines, as a graded, fleeting, intense and necessarily temporary state defined by an awareness of its temporal and spatial boundaries. Not every moment of an immersive theatre production will immerse spectators, but rather individual moments of theatricality will (attempt to) stimulate a graded experience of immersion.

Putting the *Iliad* passage in conversation with Punchdrunk's practice highlights particular features of immersion within both Homer's text and Punchdrunk's masked performances that might fly under the radar if considered in isolation. On the one hand, for example, the chariot race sequence is usually (including until now in this chapter) considered in terms of its linguistic qualities. However, if we situate the passage within a history of immersivity stretching forward up until *The Burnt City*, then we are reminded that while the words may vividly describe the narrative, it is highly likely that this vividness was exacerbated, due to the *Iliad*'s origin as oral poetry, by the embodied materiality of performance. The act of a rhapsode narrating the passage, varying his or her voice to convey different characters and to build dramatic tension, would further the psychological suspension of disbelief necessary for envisaging the scene. On the other hand, positioning Punchdrunk's work within a chronology that stretches back to Homer's *Iliad* and includes the enargeic chariot race highlights how two characteristic features of Punchdrunk's masked performances have a historical association with immersion. These features are the fragmentation of information, given that Punchdrunk's loop structure atomises narrative throughout space, and the invitation to view a narrative from a combination of different perspectives.

So far in this book I have touched upon the totalising dimension of Punchdrunk's masked form of immersive theatre, examining the consistency surrounding their layering of different spatialities, the depth of their touch-real set designs, the complexity of their mythopoiesis, and the rigour of their interrogation of *Agamemnon* and *Hecuba*. Considering the chariot race episode as possessing the quality of enargeia reveals that immersivity does not require exhaustive detail, as the specific strategies that the individual riders employ within the chariot race are notoriously ambiguous. In particular, the location of the dispute that arises between the charioteers Antilochus and Menelaus is unspecified, and critics to this day continue to debate as to whether it took place at the turning post, or on the return track. Furthermore, the strategy that Antilochus employs to overtake Menelaus is also unclear.[55] An episode clearly does not need to be logical and exhaustively detailed for a reader or listener to feel as if the scene is projected before their eyes and to experience the dramatic tension of a (runner up) victory won by mere inches, by a man with slower horses but either more guile, or more charioteering prowess. When Punchdrunk's work is read through such a lens, it becomes apparent that although a spectator may experience *The Burnt City* as a totalising and unified world, this is not necessary for the facilitation of immersion. The *Iliad* example reminds us that even if one experiences inconsistencies and confusion as can happen when encountering fragmented information and a multiplicity of perspectives (Duška Radosavljević, for example, notes that 'Truth be told, it is not always entirely clear what it is the audience is watching'), then that is not necessarily anathema to experiencing immersion.[56] The multiple, simultaneous stories taking place at once in *The Burnt City*, and the ability for the audience to experience the same scene from alternate perspectives by following different characters in the different loops, reflects the differing perspectives that Homer grants us access to within the chariot race, whether that be of the omniscient narrator, the embedded spectators, or the individualised, racing charioteers. To accept that the chariot race sequence in *Iliad* 23 is both enargeic and inconsistent thus offers a useful lens for reconciling records of spectatorship in Punchdrunk's masked work that see the work as either immersive or as episodic.

For my second example, I zoom forward a few centuries and shift genre, from epic to historiography, to land on Thucydides' fifth-century narration of the Peloponnesian War. Unlike Homer's *Iliad*, which was composed for oral performance, Thucydides likely wrote his history to be read. However, he authored his history within the context of a primarily oral society, meaning that, as Liz Webb points out, Thucydides' first audience may have also listened to recitations of passages.[57] We can thus still think about how the embodied performance of a hypothetical

---

[55] See Gagarin (1983).

[56] Radosavljević (2022). Indeed, in Cole (2021) I argue that the fragmentary nature of the underpinning source text in Punchdrunk's *Kabeiroi* facilitated a depth of immersion, positing that the sense of lack contained within the fragmentary form provided a productive impetus for the audience to create the unified imaginary world necessary for a 'deep' form of immersion.

[57] Webb (Forthcoming).

oral communication of Thucydides' *History* may have shaped the effect of enargeic passages within the text. Even outside of this hypothetical scenario, there is still merit in putting Thucydides into dialogue with modern immersive theatre, as the conversation continues to highlight recurring features across the history of immersivity.

Like Homer's *Iliad*, Thucydides' *History* has been analysed as containing the quality of enargeia since antiquity. Plutarch, for example, claims that 'Thucydides is always striving for enargeia in his writing, since it is his desire to make the reader a spectator, as it were, and to produce vividly in the minds of those who peruse his narrative the emotions of amazement and consternation which were experienced by those who beheld them' [*On the Fame of the Athenians* 347a].[58] Plutarch cites as an example *par excellence* Thucydides' narration of the doomed Sicilian expedition [7.71], and in particular his decision to narrate the Athenians' defeat at Syracuse from the perspective of the spectators watching from the shore. He argues that Thucydides' description is 'characterised by pictorial vividness in its arrangement and its power of description' [*On the Fame of the Athenians* 347c].[59] The power of the passage lies in the combination of its placement within the wider narrative, at a dramatic moment within the overall Peloponnesian War; the outcome of the wider conflict hangs in the balance during this individual naval battle between the Athenians and the Syracusans. Furthermore, Thucydides not only narrates the battle from the perspective of the embedded spectators, but notably from the perspective of both armies, giving a multiplicity of viewpoints upon the action. Even within the different allegiances, he explicitly draws attention to the fact that not all the spectators are looking in the same direction at once, further bifurcating the reactions of those present. Andrew Walker argues that the passage contains a poetics of realism with the implicit goal of an aesthetics of illusion where the author produces 'representations so like the originals that they become indistinguishable from reality'.[60] The reader is invited to imagine an event in such vividness that they seemingly experience it from a variety of specific, constructed perspectives; in other words, they become so immersed in a narrative that they feel as if they are, in some ways, living it.

---

[58] Translation adapted from Babbitt (1936).
[59] Translation adapted from Babbitt (1936).
[60] Walker (1993: 358).

Thucydides' description of the naval battle not only qualifies as an example of enargeia for ancient and modern critics, but also reinforces how enargeia can be read as a form of immersivity. By making the readers into spectators, the passage manifests an alternate reality for the immersant, dominating their visual sense and even the aural sense through the invocation of lamentations, cheering, and cries throughout the excerpt. Both Thucydides' scene and Homer's race involve more specifically literary strategies than mimesis, but they work similarly to invite one to see an alternate reality.

Reading the scene as an immersive episode and in dialogue with the form of immersion found in *The Burnt City* highlights four common features across the two examples. Firstly, just as in the Homeric passage, a sense of multiperspectivalism is integral to the creation of immersion. The ability to create a totalising whole is fostered by empowering the reader, or audience, to knit together a selection of different perspectives upon the action. Secondly, when we put the episode in dialogue with modern immersive theatre, then the theatricality of Thucydides' employment of embedded spectators becomes pronounced, irrespective of whether the embodied materiality of the performance of the passage was ever a part of the text's history. Like the chariot race sequence, we witness this episode from the side-lines as performed action. Crucially, it is action that the embedded spectators have an invested interest in, meaning that the stakes surrounding the confrontation between the spectator and the performed action are heightened. Both Thucydides' narration and Punchdrunk's performance create affect through the dramatic tension developed via watching high stakes, highly theatrical material, where there is emotional investment between the spectating participants and the performing players. In both scenarios, such a sense of theatricality is independent of, but also coexistent with, absorption within an immersive experience. Thirdly, Thucydides' episode, as Walker argues, is constructed as a *mise-en-abyme*, or a scene within a scene. Like Idomenaus and Ajax, the spectators who watch the naval battle are part of a larger scene. The embedding of different scenes within a broader narrative is not a direct equivalent of the different stratum of spatialities in *The Burnt City*, but there is a connection in that both techniques create sub-strands within a broader narrative discourse, which work to allow an immersant to penetrate deeper into the psyche of an aesthetic experience. Finally, there is a blurring of the boundary between embedded spectator and participant in the Thucydidean excerpt, as ultimately the fleet reaches the shore and the spectators become participants, in turn helping their navy, guarding the wall, and/or attempting to ensure their own safety. Although the conflation between watching and participating is within the narrative rather than something that affects the reader or listener, whereas within Punchdrunk it concerns the spectator themselves, it is nevertheless clear that a blurring of boundaries feeds into both experiences.

Conceptually, the type of immersion invited through vivid descriptions in antiquity and the embodied materiality of modern participatory performance is related, in that both require an imaginative leap of faith for an immersant to experience a reality outside of their own. A literary description requires the reader's cooperation in imagining, and becoming immersed in, a narrative, and similarly a theatrical experience requires a suspension of disbelief for a spectator to feel part of, and become immersed within, a performance. However, the kinship between immersion, ancient and modern, is not just limited to the type of buy-in required from the immersant. It also includes what we might deem to be the function of the immersive experience, and the benefits—or dangers—that arise through the experience, which include gaining additional perspectives upon a story, and experiencing narrative from the inside-out.

* * *

As the final substantive chapter of *Punchdrunk on the Classics*, this chapter has zoomed out from the more focused performance analysis of Chapter 5 to consider the bigger-picture significance of *The Burnt City* within the historicisation of immersivity. To do so, I have considered how Punchdrunk's work has traditionally been examined within the history of immersion and have then put two ancient concepts linked with immersion, namely mimesis and enargeia, into dialogue with *The Burnt City*. The structure of my chapter has revealed that Punchdrunk's work is related to history of immersion stretching right back to our earliest examples of ancient Greek textuality, and what's more, that there are consistent features within the immersive experiences fostered through both ancient literary examples and Punchdrunk's creative practice.

It has not been my intention to write an encompassing survey about mimesis as immersion, or about enargeia as immersion. Such a task would be too large for a subsection of a single chapter and is out of step with the focus of this book. Rather, my intention here has been to highlight the commonalities between mimesis and Punchdrunk's practice, and between enargeia and Punchdrunk's practice, to demonstrate how all are part of the history of immersion and can foster fleeting immersive experiences. Reconceptualising the history of immersion as encompassing enargeia in Homeric epic right through to participatory performance in the twenty-first century shifts how we read both the ancient and modern forms of immersion and illuminates all too frequently overlooked components. It highlights, for example, the significance of embodied performance to even literary examples of immersivity in antiquity, as well as common transhistorical practices including offering audiences slices of information from a multiplicity of perspectives which they can weave together to create an alternate reality in which to immerse themselves.

Initiating a dialogue between immersivity in antiquity and modernity changes the way we might go on to read mimesis and enargeia in other classical examples. It also changes the chronology in which we situate productions such as *The Burnt City*, and the type of dialogue that the production enables us to enter into with antiquity. In Chapter 2, I explored the significance of classical literature from antiquity to Punchdrunk's entire œuvre. Punchdrunk are unique within the immersive theatre sector in the duration of their artistic practice and thus the regularity with which they have been able to return to antiquity when generating work. Nevertheless, a survey of contemporaneous ensembles and companies within the United Kingdom reveals that antiquity is a popular launch pad for the creation of immersive experiences across the board with, for example, ZU-UK turning to Medea for their overnight *Hotel Medea* (2009–12), dreamthinkspeak [sic] turning to the myth of Eurydice and Orpheus for their 2003–8 *Don't Look Back*, and Shunt turning to the myth of Theseus and the minotaur for their 2012 *The Architects*. In late 2023 in the UK alone, Sleepwalk Immersive staged an immersive re-imagining of Euripides' *Bacchae*, Get Out of My Space produced an immersive *Antigone*, and Punchdrunk performer and Rehearsal Director Vinicius Salles directed *Immaculate*, an immersive theatre performance inspired by Ovid's writing about the myth of Echo. It is perhaps unlikely that either Punchdrunk's creative team or the artists behind the broader immersive art forms in today's experience economy are familiar with the ancient fascination with and theorisation of notions of immersivity, and I am not suggesting that we find so many conscious borrowings from antiquity in immersive theatre today because of any awareness of this history. However, the relevance of ideas of mimesis and enargeia to modern immersive experiences, and the fact that ancient literary critics, philosophers, and rhetoricians understood their contemporary texts to hold these qualities in abundance means that they are ripe for realisation in today's cultural industries. Furthermore, today's artists are familiar with, draw upon, and compete against other paradigms of an immersive antiquity, from digital reconstructions through to 3D cinema, opera, and computer games. It is consequently perhaps no surprise that the ancient world and its texts are frequently used as a touchstone for the creation of modern immersive experiences. It is the combination of the in-built potential for immersion in ancient Greek literature, and the texts' ability to function as what I have elsewhere termed a form of narrative shorthand or semantic scaffold, whereby the ancient texts exist as a framework in an otherwise disorienting piece of theatre, that makes the literature so compelling to practitioners, and useful for audiences, within immersive experiences.[61] The conversation commenced in this chapter thus helps us to rethink experiencing immersion in antiquity, and to reconceptualise current preoccupations with immersive antiquities in today's cultural industries.

WORKS CITED

Allan, Rutger J. 2019. Narrative Immersion. In *Experience, Narrative, and Criticism in Ancient Greece: Under the Spell of Stories*, eds. Jonas Grethlein, Luuk Huitink, and Aldo Tagliabue, 15–35. Oxford: Oxford University Press.

Allan, Rutger J., Irene J. F. de Jong, and Casper C. de Jonge. 2017. From Enargeia to Immersion: The Ancient Roots of a Modern Concept. *Style* 51: 1: 34–51. https://doi.org/10.5325/style.51.1.0034.

Babbitt, Frank Cole. Ed. 1936. *Plutarch. Moralia, Volume IV*. Cambridge, Massachusetts, and London: Harvard University Press.

Belfiore, Elizabeth. 1984. A Theory of Imitation in Plato's *Republic*. *TAPRA* 114: 121–146. https://doi.org/10.2307/284143.

Biggin, Rose. 2015. Reading Fan Mail: Communicating Immersive Experience in Punchdrunk's *Faust* and *The Masque of the Red Death*. *Participations: Journal of Audience & Reception Studies* 12: 1: 301–317.

———. 2017. *Immersive Theatre and Audience Experience: Space, Game and Story in the Work of Punchdrunk*. Cham: Palgrave Macmillan.

---

[61] On ancient literature as a semantic scaffold in experimental performance see Cole (2019, esp. p. 3).

Bloodworth, Adam. 2022. Immersive Theatre Giants Punchdrunk: "We Want Audiences to Feel a Sense of Danger". *City AM*, April 12. https://www.cityam.com/1864248-2-immersive-theatre-giants-punchdrunk-the-burnt-city-woolwich-arsenal/. Accessed 29 November 2022.

Budelmann, Felix, and Evert van Emde Boas. 2019. Attending to Tragic Messenger Speeches. In *Experience, Narrative, and Criticism in Ancient Greece: Under the Spell of Stories*, eds. Jonas Grethlein, Luuk Huitink, and Aldo Tagliabue, 59–80. Oxford: Oxford University Press.

Cole, Emma. 2019. *Postdramatic Tragedies*. Oxford: Oxford University Press.

———. 2021. Fragments, Immersivity, and Reception: Punchdrunk on Aeschylus' *Kabeiroi*. *International Journal of the Classical Tradition* 28: 510–525. https://doi.org/10.1007/s12138-020-00578-9.

Diamond, Elin. 1997. *Unmaking Mimesis: Essays on Feminism and Theatre*. London and New York: Routledge.

Gagarin, Michael. 1983. Antilochus' Strategy: The Chariot Race in *Iliad* 23. *Classical Philology* 78: 1: 35–39.

Gardner, Lyn. 2014. Immersive Theatre: Living Up to Its Name, or Just an Overused Gimmick?. *The Guardian*, September 19. https://www.theguardian.com/stage/theatreblog/2014/sep/19/immersive-theatre-overused-marketing-gimmick. Accessed 9 December 2022.

Gayet, Mattieu. 2022. "A Modern Contemporary Audience Needs to Have Agency and Empowerment"—Felix Barrett, Maxine Doyle (Punchdrunk). *XR Must*, November 8. http://www.xrmust.com/xrmagazine/felix-barrett-maxine-doyle-punchdrunk/. Accessed 29 November 2022.

Gianvittorio-Ungar, Laura. 2019. Dancing the War Report in Aeschylus' *Seven Against Thebes*. In *Experience, Narrative, and Criticism in Ancient Greece: Under the Spell of Stories*, eds. Jonas Grethlein, Luuk Huitink, and Aldo Tagliabue, 235–251. Oxford: Oxford University Press.

Grethlein, Jonas, Luuk Huitink, and Aldo Tagliabue. 2019. Introduction: Narrative and Aesthetic Experience in Ancient Greece. In *Experience, Narrative, and Criticism in Ancient Greece: Under the Spell of Stories*, eds. Jonas Grethlein, Luuk Huitink, and Aldo Tagliabue, 1–12. Oxford: Oxford University Press.

Halliwell, Stephen. 2002. *The Aesthetics of Mimesis: Ancient Texts and Modern Problems*. Princeton: Princeton University Press.

Henrichs, Albert. 1996. Dancing in Athens, Dancing on Delos: Some Patterns of Choral Projection in Euripides. *Philologus* 140: 48–62. https://doi.org/10.1524/phil.1996.140.1.48.

HM Government. 2018. *Press Release: Creative Industries Sector Deal Launched*. https://www.gov.uk/government/news/creative-industries-sector-deal-launched. Accessed 28 March 2023.

Hoggard, Liz. 2013. Felix Barrett: The Visionary Who Reinvented Theatre. *The Observer*, July 14. https://www.theguardian.com/theobserver/2013/jul/14/felix-barrett-punchdrunk-theatre-stage. Accessed 25 July 2023.

Homer. 2023. *The Iliad*. Trans. Emily Wilson. New York and London: W. W. Norton & Company.

Huitink, Luuk. 2019. *Enargeia*, Enactivism and the Ancient Readerly Imagination. In *Distributed Cognition in Classical Antiquity*, eds. Miranda Anderson and Douglas Cairns, 169–189. Edinburgh: Edinburgh University Press.

———. 2019a. Enargeia and Bodily Mimesis. In *Experience, Narrative, and Criticism in Ancient Greece: Under the Spell of Stories*, eds. Jonas Grethlein, Luuk Huitink, and Aldo Tagliabue, 188–209. Oxford: Oxford University Press.

James, Anna. 2020. Felix Barrett: "I Want to Create Work That Leaves You Spinning". *The Stage*, September 30. https://www.thestage.co.uk/big-interviews/felix-barrett. Accessed 5 December 2022.

———. 2022. Putting Down Roots: How Immersive Theatre is Evolving. *The Stage*, November 10. https://www.thestage.co.uk/long-reads/putting-down-roots-how-immersive-theatre-is-evolving. Accessed 5 December 2022.

Lehmann, Hans-Thies. 2006. *Postdramatic Theatre*. Trans. Karen Jürs-Munby. London and New York: Routledge.

Machon, Josephine. 2013. *Immersive Theatres: Intimacy and Immediacy in Contemporary Performance*. Basingstoke: Palgrave Macmillan.

Machon, Josephine and Punchdrunk. 2019. *The Punchdrunk Encyclopaedia*. London and New York: Routledge.

Nagy, Gregory. 2013. *The Ancient Greek Hero in 24 Hours*. Cambridge, MA: Harvard University Press.

Nield, Sophie. 2008. The Rise of the Character named Spectator. *Contemporary Theatre Review* 18: 4: 531–544. https://doi.org/10.1080/10486800802492855.

Nikolaidou-Arabatzi, Smaro. 2015. Choral Projections and "Embolima" in Euripides' Tragedies. *Greece & Rome* 62: 1: 25–47. https://doi.org/10.2307/43297510.

O'Connell, Peter A. 2017. *Enargeia*, Persuasion, and the Vividness Effect in Athenian Forensic Oratory. *Advances in the History of Rhetoric* 20: 3: 225–251. https://doi.org/10.1080/15362426.2017.1384766.

Olsen, Sarah. 2021. Narrating Neoptolemus: Dance and Death in Euripides' *Andromache*. In *Choreonarratives: Dancing Stories in Greek and Roman Antiquity and beyond*, eds. Laura Gianvittorio-Ungar and Karin Schlapbach, 156–179. Leiden and Boston: Brill.

Pimentel, Ken and Kevin Teixeira. 1993. *Virtual Reality: Through the New Looking Glass*. Blue Ridge Summit, PA: Windcrest/McGraw-Hill/TAB Books.

Punchdrunk. 2022. *Punchdrunk*. https://www.punchdrunk.com/. Accessed 9 December 2022.

Radosavljević, Duška. 2022. "The Burnt City", One Cartridge Place. *The Theatre Times*, May 24. https://thetheatretimes.com/the-burnt-city-one-cartridge-place/. Accessed 9 December 2022.

Raeburn, David and Oliver Thomas, eds. 2011. *The Agamemnon of Aeschylus: A Commentary for Students*. Oxford: Oxford University Press.

Richardson, Nicholas. 1993. *The Iliad: A Commentary. Volume VII: Books 21–24*. Cambridge: Cambridge University Press.

Ritter, Julia M. 2017. Fandom and Punchdrunk's *Sleep No More*: Audience Ethnography of Immersive Dance. *TDR: The Drama Review* 61: 4: 59–77.

———. 2020. *Tandem Dances: Choreographing Immersive Performance*. Oxford: Oxford University Press.

Ryan, Marie-Laure. 1994. Immersion vs. Interactivity: Virtual Reality and Literary Theory. *Postmodern Culture* 5: 1. https://www.pomoculture.org/2013/09/24/immersion-vs-interactivity-virtual-reality-and-literary-theory/. Accessed 29 March 2023.

———. 2015. *Narrative as Virtual Reality 2: Revisiting Immersion and Interactivity in Literature and Electronic Media*. Baltimore: Johns Hopkins University Press.

Schaeffer, Jean-Marie and Ioana Vultur. 2005. Mimesis. In *Routledge Encyclopedia of Narrative Theory*, eds. David Herman, Manfred Jahn, and Marie-Laure Ryan, 309–310. London: Routledge.

Tomlin, Elizabeth. 2016. *Acts and Apparitions: Discourses on the Real in Performance Practice and Theory, 1990-2010*. Manchester: Manchester University Press.

Usher, Stephen. Ed. 1974. *Dionysius of Halicarnassus: Critical Essays, Volume I: Ancient Orators*. Cambridge, Massachusetts, and London: Harvard University Press.

Wakefield, Nik. 2019. Theatricality and Absorption: Politics of representation in Michael Fried, The Wooster Group and Robert Wilson. *Performance Research* 24: 4: 35-43. https://doi.org/10.1080/13528165.2019.1641321.

Walker, Andrew D. 1993. Enargeia and the Spectator in Greek Historiography. *Transactions of the American Philological Association* (1974-2014) 123: 353–377. https://doi.org/10.2307/284335.

Webb, Liz. Forthcoming. Immersion, Emotion and Sensory Hierarchy: Thucydides Beyond Enargeia? In *Experiencing Immersion in Antiquity and Modernity: From Narrative to Virtual Reality*, ed. Emma Cole. London: Bloomsbury.

Webb, Ruth. 2009. *Ekphrasis, Imagination and Persuasion in Ancient Rhetorical Theory and Practice*. Surrey: Ashgate.

Westling, Carina E. I. 2020. *Immersion and Participation in Punchdrunk's Theatrical Worlds*. London and New York: Methuen Drama.

Zanker, G. 1981. Enargeia in the Ancient Criticism of Poetry. *Rheinisches Museum für Philologie*, Neue Folge 124: 3: 297–311.

Zeitlin, Froma. 2013. Figure: Ekphrasis. *Greece & Rome* 60: 1: 17–31. https://doi.org/10.1017/S0017383512000241.

CHAPTER 7

Conclusion

The June 2023 announcement that Punchdrunk would close *The Burnt City* in the autumn of 2023 was bittersweet. In an interview with *The Stage* announcing the production's closure, the company stressed the show's achievements: Punchdrunk had employed over 600 people to work on *The Burnt City*; had already sold over 200,000 tickets; and its duration, at eighteen months, was the company's longest-running masked show in London.[1] Yet although *The Burnt City* was in many ways a triumph, aspirations hinted at in earlier interviews that would now go unrealised indicated that the closure was not inevitable. In a *City AM* review after the production's opening, for example, Steve Dinneen noted that there may be a chance to stay in the venue overnight later in the run, while in an interview to celebrate the production's one-year milestone, published just one month prior to the closure announcement, Maxine Doyle noted that the production had 'not settled into its final form [...] it's the joy of an ongoing show, especially a show where it's in our home—we have the possibility to keep developing it. I think it's got several more iterations yet'.[2] Extra square footage behind the souk at the back of Troy could have theoretically been unlocked, and the titling of the Spring Ascension post-show party as 'Divine Rites: Chapter One'

[1] Nettle (2023).
[2] Dinneen (2022) and Doyle, quoted in James (2023).

© The Author(s), under exclusive license to Springer Nature Switzerland AG 2024
E. Cole, *Punchdrunk on the Classics*,
https://doi.org/10.1007/978-3-031-43067-1_7

implied plans for a regular series of events, akin to the long-established fixtures at *Sleep No More* New York. The spectre of COVID-19 that had delayed the production and then haunted rehearsals, which were punctuated by regular, sometimes daily, testing among the cast and creative team, who often rehearsed in masks and whose schedules were often disrupted by periods of isolation, may have continued to affect attendance patterns, as no doubt did the cost-of-living crisis which was also plaguing the UK throughout the production's run. Although there may have been alternate versions of the production's lifespan, its closure in September 2023 did not diminish *The Burnt City*'s significance. The production cannot claim the mantle of London's longest-running immersive show, which goes to Immersive Everywhere's *The Great Gatsby* (which closed in January 2023 after a five-year run), but its size and scope still made it a defining cultural output of twenty-twenties British theatre. It was also quite possibly the most high profile and widely seen staged adaptation of Greek tragedy since at least the Second World War.

The Burnt City was significant in and of itself. To conclude my study of the production, however, I highlight three of the broader contributions of my book: to the practice of conducting rehearsal studies; to the use of the classics within immersive artforms; and to an understanding of Punchdrunk's practice. One of the original contributions of my book is the development of a new methodology for the study of rehearsals, for which I adapted the form of performance analysis known as Spectator-Participation-as-Research and combined it with an ethnographic analysis of rehearsals. My autoethnographic research methodology allowed me to put my positionality, as a member of *The Burnt City*'s creative team as well as an embedded researcher, at the forefront of my analysis and provided a methodological bridge to connect the rehearsal study conducted in Chapters 3 and 4 with the performance analysis and historical investigation into the poetics of immersion contained in Chapters 5 and 6. I posit that Spectator-Participation-as-Research has potential for application in other rehearsal studies where the researcher is also a member of the creative team, or where the approach to creating theatre involves parallel rehearsals and renders full access to the entire rehearsal process impossible for a lone ethnographer.

Not only does my methodology offer new routes into the study of rehearsals, but my subject matter highlights the need for further studies of the rehearsing of immersive and dance-based practice, too. It has been a central claim of my book that process informs product, and that understanding process illuminates debates about how a work can be experienced and theorised. Much of what I have highlighted within my rehearsal study appears to be in stark contrast to the documentation of studio-based and collaboratively created theatre in other rehearsal studies. From an outside perspective, there can appear to be tension between the director-led material in *The Burnt City*, including the rigidity of the loop plan and the pre-written *précis* for each scene given to performers ahead of the commencement of rehearsals, and how the performers were empowered to generate their own characterisations and choreography. Within the freelance dance world, however, developing a performance through a collaborative mentality while under the leadership of a choreographer is common. The apparent uniqueness of Punchdrunk's approach in relation to current scholarship highlights the need for further rehearsal studies of dance-based and immersive practice.

My claim that process informs product also begs the question, given the production's eighteen-month run, of how long this might be the case. In a November 2022 interview, Doyle commented that 'A show like *The Burnt City* evolves constantly. From the previous shows in Spring 2022, the biggest shift actually is the space. Felix totally redesigned the bar and the entrance completely. The content of the show actually is more nuanced, even if it's essentially the same thing'.[3] Not only did the entrance experience shift in July 2022 away from the Treasures and Antiquities from the Chapman Collection exhibition discussed in Chapter 5, but the set design continued to evolve as well, with, for example, a complete transformation of the Klub in Troy occurring in mid-2022 complete with an image of a Minotaur from a black-figure *kylix* on the floor. Performer costumes also changed during the summer to accommodate rising temperatures inside the industrial warehouses, while in the winter of 2022 additional one-on-ones, VIP and sponsored experiences, and even new scenes within the loop chart were added. Finally, in January 2023, twelve months after rehearsals had begun, many members of the original performing company moved on and a second cast of performers began. Performer Ali Goldsmith, who was a member of both the Contract One and Contract Two casts, explained that during the handover the original cast put forward five facts about their characters on a family

---

[3] Doyle, quoted in Gayet (2022).

tree, including points such as their character's status within the world, their personality traits, and a history of certain scenes in relation to one another. When performers such as Goldsmith taught the choreography to the new cast, they communicated the context of the character and their narrative, to inform the choreography as an undertone and particularly to 'give purpose for going between each scene'. Just as I argued that the initial development of *The Burnt City* equated to a form of contemporary mythopoiesis, so too did Goldsmith suggest that a long-running show such as *The Burnt City* continues to develop via a form of contemporary oral poetics, with the company's mythmaking and production's stories carried on to each new iteration of the cast by voice. Although the choreography might stay the same, each performer offered a new interpretation of the material, meaning that the show was, to quote Goldsmith, 'always in some sort of process'. The history of *The Burnt City*'s creation contained in this book is thus only the beginning.

One of the other overarching contributions of my book has been to highlight how the use of the classics within *The Burnt City* furthered the potential immersivity of the experience. In my prior publications, I have showcased the potential that Greek tragedy holds within experimental, postdramatic, and immersive forms of performance, whether that be extant Greek tragedies acting as a semantic scaffold in an otherwise disorienting experience, or productions based upon fragmentary Greek tragedies trading in the sense of lack found in the fragmentary form to prompt an audience to create a unified imaginary world.[4] Within the creation of *The Burnt City*, the plethora of sources linking to Trojan War mythology from classical antiquity offered the creative team an unparalleled resource from which to construct their own narrative universe. By supplementing *Agamemnon* and *Hecuba* with materials drawn from other dramatic texts, iconographic evidence, and ancient cult and ritual experiences, the artists were able to braid together a unique assemblage of sources, which they then supplemented with their own original material to create their own megatext. The layering of the mythological Underworld as a spatial stratum lying underneath the Trojan War narrative facilitated a depth of immersion by inviting audiences to, *Inception*-like, descend deeper and deeper into the psyche of *The Burnt City*. Not only did the inclusion of the Underworld layer, and the presence of Hades and

---

[4] See Cole (2019 and 2021).

Persephone, give a logic to the structure of Punchdrunk's masked work, but it also characterised the audience, who have always been conceived of by Punchdrunk as shades or as a chorus, in a way that made sense in relation to the performance for the very first time. As I mentioned in the conclusion to Chapter 5, Punchdrunk are not alone in creating immersive receptions of classical antiquity, but what my study has highlighted is just how much potential there is for more work to be done within the theatre industry in this vein. The ancient world was intrinsic to the creation of the secondary storyworld of *The Burnt City* and to the ability for the performance to displace audience members from their present reality; continuing to mine antiquity is not an inevitable formula for success, but it does have unparalleled potential and proven results.

The final macro-level contribution of *Punchdrunk on the Classics* has been to highlight the until-now overlooked significance of classical antiquity to Punchdrunk's practice. In Chapter 2, I stressed how central the classics were to the development of Punchdrunk's masked theatre, shaping the form of the audience's mask and Barrett's decision to stage his looping masked shows indoors and via a dance-based language. It is thus of no small significance that it appears that Punchdrunk's engagement with Greek tragedy in *The Burnt City* will bookend their large-scale masked practice. In the interview announcing *The Burnt City*'s closure, Barrett commented that 'We're fairly sure *The Burnt City* will be the last new mask show the company makes, and what comes next will be different and unlike anything we have done before'.[5] Reflecting on the history of Punchdrunk's practice reveals that the company have turned to the classics at decisive moments within their practice, during their experiments in their first year for *The House of Oedipus*, during their period of professionalisation for the thwarted *The Fates and the Furies*, for experiments with magic-touch devices (via Punchdrunk Enrichment) in *The Oracles* and geo-locative forms of performance in *Kabeiroi*, and now for their biggest ever, and final, new masked show in *The Burnt City*. Whether the classics will continue to provide such an important lynchpin in Punchdrunk's next phrase of work is yet to be seen, but if the company's first two-and-a-half decades of work is anything to go by, then it is more than a little likely. Irrespective of the role of antiquity in Punchdrunk's future, understanding its presence in Punchdrunk's past is

---

[5] Barrett, quoted in Nettle (2023).

integral to understanding the company's history and their approach to fostering immersion. In *The Burnt City* and beyond, antiquity has proven crucial to immersivity.

Works Cited

Cole, Emma. 2019. *Postdramatic Tragedies*. Oxford: Oxford University Press.
———. 2021. Fragments, Immersivity, and Reception: Punchdrunk on Aeschylus' *Kabeiroi*. *International Journal of the Classical Tradition* 28: 510–525. https://doi.org/10.1007/s12138-020-00578-9.
Dinneen, Steve. 2022. The Burnt City Review: Punchdrunk Return in Spectacular Fashion. *City AM*, April 22. https://www.cityam.com/the-burnt-city-review-punchdrunk-return-in-spectacular-fashion/. Accessed 7 July 2023.
Gayet, Mathieu. 2022. 'A Modern Contemporary Audience Needs to Have Agency and Empowerment'—Felix Barrett, Maxine Doyle (Punchdrunk). *XR Must*, November 8. https://www.xrmust.com/xrmagazine/felix-barrett-maxine-doyle-punchdrunk/. Accessed 25 January 2023.
James, Anna. 2023. The Burnt City one year on: Punchdrunk's dystopian take on the Trojan war continues to thrill. *The Stage*, May 8. https://www.thestage.co.uk/features/the-burnt-city-one-year-on-punchdrunks-dystopian-take-on-the-trojan-war-continues-to-thrill. Accessed 7 July 2023.
Nettle, Gemma. 2023. Punchdrunk calls time on masked work as it announces closure of The Burnt City. *The Stage*, June 22. https://www.thestage.co.uk/news/punchdrunk-calls-time-on-masked-work-as-it-announces-closure-of-the-burnt-city. Accessed 7 July 2023.

Index

A

Abstraction, 63, 103, 114, 126, 128, 136, 144
Achilles, 7, 64, 79, 109, 204, 208
Aegisthus, 6, 11, 76, 83, 102, 104, 119–128, 138, 162
Aeschylus, 40, 43, 130, 134, 147, 192, 201
   Agamemnon, 4–9, 11, 17, 58, 59, 63, 64, 67, 76, 77, 94, 95, 102, 105, 107, 109, 120, 121, 128, 133, 135, 138, 140, 158, 165, 171, 174, 201, 211, 226
   Kabeiroi, 42, 43, 45, 46, 175, 176, 227
Agamemnon, 4–8, 10, 11, 60, 62, 68, 75, 78–81, 83, 91, 101–107, 115, 117, 119–121, 123, 127, 131–136, 156–159, 199, 201
Alighieri, Dante, 10, 161, 162, 164
Almeida theatre, 9
Apollo, 11, 12, 70, 82, 83, 133, 199, 200, 202
Aristotle, 184, 189, 190, 193, 194
Artemis, 10, 11, 64–66, 78, 106, 133, 156, 159, 160, 199
Askalaphos, 10, 11, 85–88, 96, 108, 162, 164
Audience, 1–3, 6–16, 18, 23–26, 33, 35, 36, 38–45, 50, 59, 60, 66, 71, 74, 75, 77, 80, 82–90, 92, 94–96, 101, 103–105, 112, 115, 116, 119, 120, 139, 143–146, 149–179, 183–185, 187, 188, 190–194, 196–203, 205, 210, 212, 214, 216, 217, 227

B

Barrett, Felix, 2, 3, 9, 11, 23, 33–36, 39–41, 45, 46, 55, 58, 61–64, 67–69, 71, 73, 75, 78, 80, 81, 84–86, 90, 92, 93, 97, 101, 105–107, 110, 111, 114–116, 119, 121, 123, 126, 129, 139, 147, 148, 156, 165, 171, 176, 185–188, 196, 197, 200, 202, 227

© The Editor(s) (if applicable) and The Author(s), under exclusive license to Springer Nature Switzerland AG 2024
E. Cole, *Punchdrunk on the Classics*,
https://doi.org/10.1007/978-3-031-43067-1

INDEX

Biggin, Rose, 2, 3, 16, 25–27, 144, 147, 149, 157, 167–169, 178, 185, 190, 197, 198, 210
Blade Runner, 12, 95
Blue cast, 76, 81, 82, 110, 116, 124–126
Bouts, Dirk, 58, 89, 90, 95, 130, 155, 167
Brauronia, 64–66, 159
Building 17, 10, 62, 70, 150, 158, 178
Building 18, 62
Building 19, 10, 62, 150, 158

C

Calchas, 80, 158, 160
Cassandra, 6, 11, 63, 75, 82, 83, 91, 93, 105, 108, 120, 133, 135, 174
Chariot race, 208–212, 214
Chorus, 6, 36, 39–41, 43, 65, 107, 109, 120, 146, 171–173, 178, 191, 192, 227
Ciacco's, 10, 161, 162, 164
City Dionysia, 4, 42, 173–175, 189, 192
Clytemnestra, 4–6, 8–11, 63, 64, 66, 67, 75, 76, 80, 83, 85, 90, 92, 102, 104, 105, 119–127, 130–135, 138, 159, 162, 174
Coronavirus, 1, 22, 24, 55, 57
COVID-19. *See* Coronavirus
Cross-fade, 9, 12, 78, 89, 96, 145, 154, 156, 158, 164, 174–177, 189, 194, 196, 202

D

Deianeira, 77
Dionysia. *See* City Dionysia
Dionysius of Halicarnassus, 205

Do Androids Dream of Electric Sheep, 96
Dobbie, Stephen, 44, 81, 89, 95, 117, 126
Doyle, Maxine, 3, 16, 23, 41, 48–51, 59–71, 73–75, 78–82, 86, 89–94, 97, 101–103, 105, 107, 110–113, 118, 121, 123, 124, 126, 129–131, 133, 138, 139, 148, 161, 185, 186, 194, 223, 225
Duggan, Kath, 58, 61, 69, 90, 91, 123, 125–127, 129
Dystopic science fiction, 12, 60

E

Ekphrasis, 168, 204–206
Eleusinian mysteries, 175, 176
Emancipation, 14–16, 36
Enargeia, 18, 169, 184, 185, 189, 204–208, 211, 213–216
Euripides
  Bacchae, 5, 93, 191
  Hecuba, 4, 5, 7–9, 11, 17, 58, 67, 93–95, 102, 105–107, 109, 110, 113, 119, 128, 138, 140, 165, 171, 174, 211, 226
  Iphigenia among the Taurians, 11, 64, 66, 95, 131
  Iphigenia at Aulis, 5, 9, 11, 64, 95, 109
  Trojan Women, 5

F

Finale, 10, 34, 58, 60, 69, 89–94, 104, 108, 115, 117, 129–132, 136–138, 167, 175
Furies, 40, 93, 146, 171, 172

H

Hades, 2, 10, 11, 48, 58, 74, 90, 93, 96, 108, 139, 145, 153–155, 161, 165–167, 226
Hades' House, 10, 161, 167
Hecuba, 7, 8, 62, 85, 90, 92, 93, 102, 106, 108, 110, 114, 116–118, 131, 201
Hesperides, 10, 86, 87, 162
Hide and Seek, 71–74, 157
Homer, 170, 204, 214
Iliad, 79, 204, 208–212
Odyssey, 5, 116, 121, 169
Hughes, Ted
Agamemnon, 89, 105, 120, 129, 130, 132–134, 136
Oresteia, 105

I

Icke, Robert, 9
Initiation, 44, 175, 176
Iphigenia, 5, 6, 8, 9, 11, 64–67, 72, 75, 78–81, 102, 106, 109, 114, 117, 119, 122, 127, 128, 131, 156, 159, 199

K

Kampe, 11, 93, 96
Kanji, 162
Kronos, 11, 61, 199

L

Lang, Fritz, 10, 59, 60, 95, 160, 162, 177
Laocoön, 11, 12, 80, 170
Loop chart, 59, 60, 62, 66, 68, 107, 129, 225
Luba, 11, 12, 93, 96
Lysias, 205

M

Macaria, 11, 93, 108, 164
Martha Graham Dance Company, 16, 48–50
Deo, 16, 48, 50
Mask, 15, 35, 36, 38, 39, 44, 45, 50, 84, 88, 96, 155, 170–172, 194, 199, 200, 202, 227
ancient Greek dramatic mask, 39–41
Punchdrunk mask, 9, 35, 156
McKittrick Hotel, 156
Memling, Hans, 58, 89, 95
Messenger speeches, 190–193
Metropolis, 10, 160
Mimesis, 18, 172, 184, 185, 189, 193–198, 202–204, 206, 214–216
Mnouchkine, Ariane, 9, 64
Museum entrance, 78, 90, 156, 160, 161, 163, 175
Mycenae, 4, 10, 62, 70, 72, 89, 93, 105, 107, 119, 121, 127, 129, 131, 132, 145, 150, 159, 160

N

National Theatre Wales
The Persians, 149, 174
Neoptolemus, 11, 63, 75, 76, 78, 79, 81, 107, 109, 111, 114, 117, 119, 159, 190, 199
No Man's Land, 10, 70, 72, 78, 80, 92, 93, 121, 131, 133, 135, 159–161, 199

O

One Cartridge Place, 145, 146, 154, 156, 165
One-on-one, 12, 13, 24, 25, 84–88, 102, 115, 139, 152, 165, 166,

169, 170, 172, 184, 194, 197–203, 225
Oracle, the, 66, 122–124, 126, 135
Ovid, 87, 88, 95
Metamorphoses, 86, 87, 95, 106

P
Palladium, 10, 115, 117, 152, 162, 199
Patroclus, 11, 63, 78, 79, 91, 107, 131, 159, 199, 208
Pearson, Mike, 144, 147, 149, 167
Peep Cabaret, 11
Penthesilea, 108, 110
Persephone, 10–12, 16, 48–51, 76, 85–87, 96, 115, 153–155, 161, 165–167, 170, 171, 176, 227
Plato, 184, 194–197, 202–204
Polydorus, 7, 11, 93, 106, 171, 199, 201, 202
Polymestor, 7, 8, 11, 60, 62, 75, 76, 92–94, 102, 103, 106, 115, 157, 162, 199, 201
Polyxena, 7–9, 11, 79, 93, 102, 104, 106–111, 113–119, 138, 151, 157, 167, 171, 199
Punchdrunk
  Kabeiroi, 3, 16, 22, 23, 42–47, 50, 61, 143, 147, 175, 212
  Sleep No More New York, 56, 172, 198, 224
  Sleep No More Shanghai, 16, 56
  The Borough, 3, 42, 157
  The Drowned Man, 1, 3, 14, 16, 34, 40, 42, 60, 68, 74, 139, 147–149, 156, 157, 166
  The Fates and the Furies, 41, 60, 148, 227
  The House of Oedipus, 16, 34–37, 39–41, 44, 46, 47, 50, 227
  The Third Day, 3, 55, 64

Punchdrunk Enrichment, 3, 33, 37, 43, 46–48
The Oracles, 16, 42, 46–48, 51, 227
Purcărete, Silviu
  Les Danaïdes, 147

R
Rancière, Jacques, 13, 14, 170
Red cast, 80, 122, 129
Rehearsal directors, 69, 75, 90, 121, 123, 129, 136
Royal Palace, 6, 10, 72, 79, 91, 102, 121–123, 159, 160, 162
Ryan, Marie-Laure, 144, 153, 168, 186, 187, 189

S
Sacrifice, 6, 9, 11, 64, 65, 78–81, 102, 104, 106–119, 121, 131, 138, 156, 159, 167, 199
Schliemann, Heinrich, 62, 63, 155, 157, 176, 177
Shades, 146, 169–171, 173, 227
Site-specific theatre, 147
Site-sympathetic theatre, 149
Spectator-Participation-as-Research (SPaR), 19, 22, 24–27, 56, 104, 139, 145, 198, 224

T
Tartarus, 10, 11, 60, 61, 164
Temple Studios, 156
Thucydides, 212–214
Town Square, 76, 92, 93, 107, 114–117, 152, 157, 161, 162, 164
Translation, 4, 17, 89, 102–105, 113, 120, 128–134, 136–138, 190, 201, 209, 213

Troy, 2, 4–6, 9–11, 41, 60, 62, 63, 72–75, 78, 82, 87, 91, 92, 107, 108, 110, 111, 114, 118, 119, 127, 128, 130, 138, 145, 150, 152, 154, 155, 157–159, 161–164, 166, 167, 174, 175, 177, 199, 201, 208, 223, 225

U

Underworld, 10, 11, 48, 50, 59, 60, 70, 85–87, 89, 97, 108, 145, 153–155, 163–167, 169–171, 173, 176, 178, 226

W

Watchman, 6, 11, 76, 82, 108, 117, 119, 120, 199

Woolwich, 22, 55, 62, 101, 146, 150, 151, 161, 167, 178
   Royal Arsenal, 1, 10, 58, 145, 146, 150, 151

Y

Yoshiwara, 10, 162, 177

Z

Zagreus, 11, 12, 82, 108, 162, 199

Printed by Printforce, United Kingdom